Question&Answer

LAND LAW

Develop your legal skills

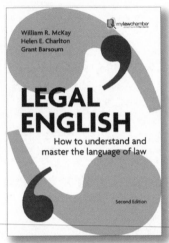

William R. McKay
Helen E. Charlton
Grant Barsoum

LEGAL ENGLISH

How to understand and master the language of law

Second Edition

9781408226100

Steve Foster

HOW TO WRITE BETTER LAW ESSAYS

Tools and techniques for success in exams and assignments

new edition

9781447905141

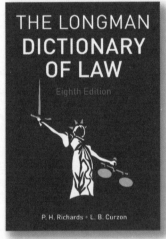

THE LONGMAN **DICTIONARY OF LAW**

Eighth Edition

P. H. Richards • L. B. Curzon

9781408261538

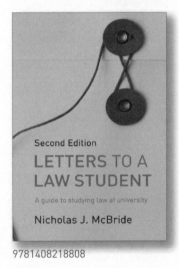

Second Edition

LETTERS TO A LAW STUDENT

A guide to studying law at university

Nicholas J. McBride

9781408218808

Written to help you develop the essential skills needed to succeed on your course and prepare for practice.

Available from all good bookshops or order online at:
www.pearsoned.co.uk/law

Question&Answer

LAND LAW

2nd edition

John Duddington
Former Head of the Law School,
Worcester College of Technology

Harlow, England • London • New York • Boston • San Francisco • Toronto • Sydney • Auckland • Singapore • Hong Kong
Tokyo • Seoul • Taipei • New Delhi • Cape Town • São Paulo • Mexico City • Madrid • Amsterdam • Munich • Paris • Milan

Pearson Education Limited
Edinburgh Gate
Harlow CM20 2JE
United Kingdom
Tel: +44 (0)1279 623623
Web: www.pearson.com/uk

First published 2012 (print)
Second edition published 2014 (print and electronic)

ISBN: 978-0-273-78355-8 (print)
        978-0-273-78357-2 (PDF)
        978-0-273-78356-5 (eText)

British Library Cataloguing-in-Publication Data
A catalogue record for the print edition is available from the British Library

10 9 8 7 6 5 4 3 2 1
17 16 15 14 13

Print edition typeset in 10/13pt Helvetica Neue LT Pro by 35
Print edition printed and bound in Malaysia, CTP-PJB

NOTE THAT ANY PAGE CROSS REFERENCES REFER TO THE PRINT EDITION

Contents

Supporting resources

Visit the **Law Express Question&Answer** series companion website at **www.pearsoned.co.uk/lawexpressqa** to find valuable learning material including:

- **Additional essay and problem questions** arranged by topic for each chapter give you more opportunity to practise and hone your exam skills.
- **Diagram plans** for all additional questions assist you in structuring and writing your answers.
- **You be the marker** questions allow you to see through the eyes of the examiner by marking essay and problem questions on every topic covered in the book.
- Download and print all **Attack the question** diagrams and **Diagram plans** from the book.

Also: The companion website provides the following features:

- Search tool to help locate specific items of content.
- Online help and support to assist with website usage and troubleshooting.

For more information please contact your local Pearson sales representative or visit **www.pearsoned.co.uk/lawexpressqa**

Acknowledgements

To my father, Walter Duddington, who first encouraged me to become a lawyer, and who would, I think, have enjoyed land law; to my wife Anne, for her constant support, loyalty and technical expertise over very many years and without which my books would never begin to be written; to my daughter Mary, for her seemingly faultless proofreading and sense of fun which keeps me going and to my son Christopher for just being himself.

I would also like to thank the staff of Pearson, especially Gabriella Playford, for her endless encouragement, cheerfulness and practical guidance, and all the reviewers who sent in such helpful comments on preliminary drafts of this book. I have considered them all and adopted most of them.

Nor must I forget happy afternoons spent at the ground of Worcestershire County Cricket Club where, during quiet passages of play, many of the ideas for the questions in this book first came to my mind.

Finally, readers should know that this book is based on sources available to me at 14 November 2012.

John Duddington

Publisher's acknowledgements

Our thanks go to all reviewers who contributed to the development of this text, including students who participated in research and focus groups which helped to shape the series format.

What you need to do for every question in Land Law

Books in the *Question and Answer series* focus on the *why* of a good answer alongside the *what*, thereby helping you to build your question answering skills and technique.

This guide should not be used as a substitute for learning the material thoroughly, your lecture notes or your textbook. It *will* help you to make the most out of what you have already learned when answering an exam or coursework question. Remember that the answers given here are not the only correct way of answering the question but serve to show you some good examples of how you could approach the question set.

Make sure that you regularly refer to your course syllabus, check which issues are covered (as well as to what extent they are covered) and whether they are usually examined with other topics. Remember that what is required in a good answer could change significantly with only a slight change in the wording of a question. Therefore, do not try to memorise the answers given here, instead use the answers and the other features to understand what goes into a good answer and why.

When you first look at a question in a land law exam, ask yourself three questions:

1 What type of right is claimed? Is it a proprietary right or a personal right, and if it is a proprietary right then is it legal or equitable?
2 Then check if the right claimed has been properly created.
3 Then check if title to the land is registered or unregistered.

Here is an example from a problem question. Suppose that you are faced with a question in the exam which told you that:

> X and Y agreed in writing that Y would have a ten-year lease of a flat. Title to X's land is registered.

Now look at this using the three steps above:

1 Identify the right. Here we are told that it is a lease, and a lease is a proprietary right.

2 How has it been created? We are told that X and Y 'agreed in writing'. This looks like an equitable lease.

3 Is title to the land registered or unregistered? It is registered.

This gives you the bare bones of an answer and you should always start from here but let us go further in search of those extra marks.

■ We are told that X and Y agreed on a lease. Check if, in fact, it is really a lease.

■ We are told that X and Y agreed in writing. This could be a deed and, if so, the lease would be legal. On the other hand, the writing might not satisfy all the requirements for a valid equitable lease. If so, what would be the position?

So, in problem questions in land law:

■ Get the basic points absolutely clear.

■ Then go on and ask *questions* about the facts given.

Where the question is an essay, remember that you are not being asked to just state all that you know on a point but are being asked to comment critically on a particular aspect of land law. The advice for problem questions applies here in that you need to be absolutely clear on the basic points but then you must go further. Look for areas which have caused controversy or have been the subject of recent cases or of Law Commission reports. Obvious examples are trusts of the home, easements and restrictive covenants and so you should come to your own view on controversial points in these areas before the exam.

Guided tour

What you need to do for every question in Land Law

What to do for every question – Identify the key things you should look for and do in any question and answer on the subject, ensuring you give every one of your answers a great chance from the start.

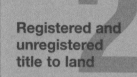

How this topic may come up in exams – Understand how to tackle any question on this topic by using the handy tips and advice relevant to both essay and problem questions. In-text symbols clearly identify each question type as they occur.

Essay question

Problem question

Attack the question – Use these diagrams as a step-by-step guide to help you confidently identify the main points covered in any question asked. Download these from the companion website to use as a useful revision aid.

Answer plans and Diagram plans – A clear and concise plan is the key to a good answer and these answer and diagram plans support the structuring of your answers, whatever your preferred learning style.

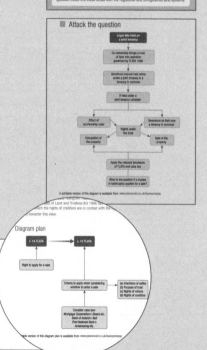

Answer plan

→ Set out the criteria in section 15 and explain how they are exercised on an application under section 14.

→ Briefly mention the previous law to evaluate if and how the law has changed.

→ Consider *Mortgage Corporation* v *Shaire* and in particular Neuberger J's views on the application of section 15.

→ Evaluate how subsequent courts have dealt with applications under section 15: consider each decision and contrast the approaches taken by each court.

→ Emphasise that the approach has to be flexible and so the statement in the question is not in fact a criticism of the law.

Answer with accompanying guidance – Make the most out of every question by using the guidance to recognise what makes a good answer and why. Answers are the length you could realistically hope to produce in an exam to show you how to gain marks quickly when under pressure.

Answer

Although it is stating the obvious to say that the Human Rights Act (HRA) 1998 is about 'human rights' this point does tell us a great deal about its impact in land law.[1] In Gray (2002) he remarks (at p. 211) that the 'intricate machinery of the Law of Property Act 1925 and its attendant satellite legislation contains little which could be confused with the positive protection or reinforcement of basic concepts of human rights, dignity and freedom'. This is, as he points out, because the 1925 property legislation was primarily concerned with upholding 'transaction based rights'. This is a completely different emphasis from that in the HRA.

One major area has been in the application of Article 8(1): respect for family life and the home.[2] One fundamental issue is whether Article 8(1) concerns property because on its wording it could be said primarily to protect privacy, a point to which we shall return. The right in Article 8(1) is qualified by Article 8(2)[3] which provides that no interference with these rights shall be justified except in the interests

[1] This opening paragraph is important as an average answer would just begin with an account of the cases which are dealt with later on in this answer. Here, however, we are setting the scene.

This is supported by ***Thomas v Clydesdale Bank Plc*** [2010] EWHC 2755[7] where, as here, the owners were absent due to the renovation of the house when the bank's interest arose. The court held that the degree of occupation had to take into account the fact that the house was not being used as a residence on the date of disposition.

[7] There have been a number of recent cases on overriding interests of occupiers, of which this is one. Make sure that you keep up to date with them.

In both ***Lloyds Bank Plc v Rosset*** and ***Thomas v Clydesdale Bank Plc*** the owners frequently visited the property; in ***Thomas*** they were there almost every other day and Ramsey J pointed out that 'the degree of occupation must take into account the fact that the house was not being used as a residence'.

Case names clearly highlighted – Easy-to-spot bold text makes those all important case names stand out from the rest of the answer, ensuring they are much easier to remember in revision and an exam.

✓ Make your answer stand out

■ Remember to deal first with whether Mel, and later Dot have a beneficial interest at all.
■ Look at *Jones* v *Kernott* and at what the Supreme Court decided as well as the judgments of Lords Kerr and Wilson, whose reasoning differed from the majority.
■ Mention in relation to Dot's claim the decision in *Re Sharpe* [1980] 1 WLR 219 which would reinforce her claim.
■ Read Gardner (2004) Quantum in *Gissing* v *Gissing* Constructive Trusts. LQR, 120: 541. This article deals with the decision in *Oxley* v *Hiscock* on quantification of the beneficial interests and is valuable as most articles on this area deal with acquisition of a beneficial interest.
■ Consider the argument in the above article that in these types of cases as Gardner puts it: 'the true driver of these trusts is and should be the ethic of the parties' relationship'. This would contrast with a search for the intentions of the parties.

Make your answer stand out – Really impress your examiners by going the extra mile and including these additional points and further reading to illustrate your deeper knowledge of the subject, fully maximising your marks.

! Don't be tempted to . . .

■ Confuse the right of the licensee to reasonable packing up time with a right to reasonable notice of termination of the actual licence.
■ Discuss *Hurst* v *Picture Theatres Ltd* [1915] 1 KB 1 CA which tried to use the idea of a licence coupled with a grant to extend the status of contractual licences. This is no longer good law.
■ Mix up common law remedies with equitable ones.
■ Divert your answer into a discussion of the facts and detailed reasoning in *Binions* v *Evans*.
■ Overlook the different rules which apply if title to the land is registered or unregistered and estoppel is claimed.
■ Miss out estoppel altogether or spend too long on it.

Don't be tempted to – Points out common mistakes ensuring you avoid losing easy marks by understanding where students most often trip up in exams.

Bibliography

Bibliography – Use this list of further reading to really delve in and explore areas in more depth, enabling you to excel in exams.

Andrews, G. (2002) Undue Influence – Where's the Disadvantage? *Conveyancer* 456.
Auchmurty, R.S. (2004) Not Just a Good Children's Story: A Tribute to Adverse Possession. *Conveyancer* 293.

Bandali, S.M. (1977) Injustice and Problems of Joint Tenancy. 41 *Conveyancer* (NS) 243.
Bogusz B. (2011) Defining the Scope of Actual Occupation under the LRA 2002: Some

Guided tour of the companion website

 Book resources are available to download. Print your own **Attack the question** and **Diagram plans** to pin to your wall or add to your own revision notes.

 Additional Essay and Problem questions with **Diagram plans** arranged by topic for each chapter give you more opportunity to practise and hone your exam skills. Print and email your answers.

 You be the marker gives you a chance to evaluate sample exam answers for different question types for each topic and understand how and why an examiner awards marks. Use the accompanying guidance to get the most out of every question and recognise what makes a good answer.

All of this and more can be found when you visit **www.pearsoned.co.uk/lawexpressqa**

Table of cases and statutes

Cases

TABLE OF CASES AND STATUTES

TABLE OF CASES AND STATUTES

▌Statutes

International Conventions

Rights over land – the impact of the Human Rights Act: finder's titles

How this topic may come up in exams

This is an area where there are fewer reasonably standard and predictable areas for exam questions than others and you will need to check your syllabus and past exam questions to see which topics are likely to arise. Examples are questions on fixtures and fittings and on the impact of Article 8 of the ECHR on land law. However, one topic which is essential for all land law exams is that of estates and interests in land. Even here you may find that this area is treated only as background material and that you will require this knowledge in questions on, for example, registered and unregistered land (see Chapter 2).

Attack the question

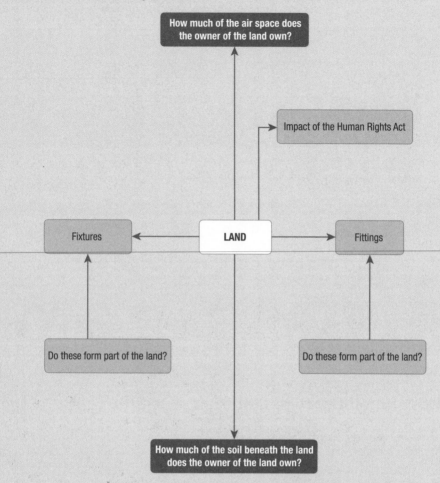

A printable version of this diagram is available from www.pearsoned.co.uk/lawexpressqa

 Question 1

Do you consider that the maxim 'he who owns the land owns everything reaching up to the very heavens and down to the very depths of the earth' is still an accurate statement of the law, especially in the light of the decision in *Bocardo SA* v *Star Energy UK Onshore Ltd* [2010] UKSC 35?

Answer plan

→ What the maxim means.

→ Explain the decision in Bocardo.

→ Three-dimensional quality of land.

→ Evaluate the maxim in relation to the rights of landowners.

→ Different owners have rights in different strata of the land.

→ Should we concentrate on the idea of 'stratified ownership'?

Diagram plan

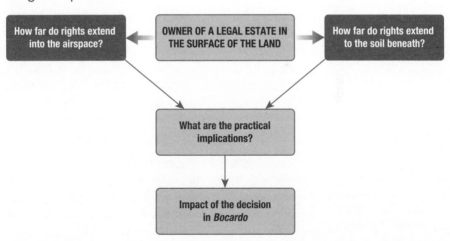

A printable version of this diagram plan is available from www.pearsoned.co.uk/lawexpressqa

Answer

This statement read literally means that whoever has a legal estate in land owns not only the surface of that land but also the airspace above the land to an unlimited extent and the land below also to an unlimited

[1] This must not be the end of your answer but you do need to start by explaining what the maxim means.

extent.[1] It is an ancient maxim dating from the 13th century or even earlier and was most recently considered in depth by the UK courts in *Bocardo SA v Star Energy UK Onshore Ltd* [2010] UKSC 35.

Star Energy had a licence to search for, bore for and get petroleum. Its predecessors had drilled three wells diagonally which entered the substrata below land owned by Bocarda at depths of up to 2,900 feet below ground level. In the words of Peter Smith J in the High Court, this did not 'interfere "one iota" with Bocardo's enjoyment of its land'.

[2] There were other issues in this case, such as assessment of compensation on a compulsory purchase of land. These are not relevant so make sure to concentrate on the point which you are asked!

Nevertheless Star Energy were held liable for trespass. One issue[2] was the extent to which rights of landowners extended beneath the surface. Lord Hope referred to arguments that the rights should only extend to 1,000 feet below, but he rejected any definite limit although he observed that 'There must obviously be some stopping point, as one reaches the point at which physical features such as pressure and temperature render the concept of the strata belonging to anybody so absurd as to be not worth arguing about'. In this case the wells were being worked and so they were 'far from being so deep as to reach the point of absurdity'.

One argument used by Star Energy was that possession, not ownership, was essential to a claim and here Bocardo was not in possession of the substrata 800 feet below the surface of its land. The concept of possession is important in cases where a squatter claims title on the basis of adverse possession but here Bocardo were the actual owners and, as Slade J said in *Powell v McFarlane* (1977) 38 P & CR 452: 'In the absence of evidence to the contrary, the owner of land with the paper title is deemed to be in possession of the land'.[3]

[3] This is a good example of how in land law certain concepts, in this case possession, are relevant in different areas. When you study land, make a note of any underlying themes like this. It will make your study easier and increase your marks. See Chapter 10 for more details of this area.

The law on rights to the airspace above the ground is different in some respects. Section 76(1) of the Civil Aviation Act 1982 provides that no action shall lie in respect of trespass or nuisance by reason only of the flight of an aircraft over any property at a height above the ground, which, having regard to wind, weather and all the circumstances of the case is reasonable. In *Lord Bernstein v Skyviews and General Ltd* [1978] QB 479 HC the defendants took an aerial photograph of the claimant's country house and offered to sell it to him. The claimant, however, rejected the offer and instead claimed damages for trespass and/or invasion of privacy for entering the air space above his property and taking the photograph without permission. It was held that an owner of land has rights in the airspace above his land only to such a height as is necessary for the ordinary use and enjoyment of his land and here the aircraft did not cause any interference with any use to which the claimant might wish to put his land. Thus, where the branches of a neighbour's tree overhang the land of an adjacent owner then that owner is entitled to cut them down (**Lemmon v Webb** [1895] AC 1 HL). On the other hand the limited nature of the right is shown by the fact that the adjacent owner does not own the fruit and commits the tort of conversion[4] if she takes it (**Mills v Brooker** [1919] 1 KB 555 HC). In **Kelsen v Imperial Tobacco Co** [1957] 2 QB 334 HC the claimant, who was the lessee of a one-storey tobacconist's shop, was granted an injunction requiring the defendants to remove an advertising sign from the wall above his shop which projected into the airspace above the shop by a distance of some eight inches.

It was argued in the **Bocardo** case[5] that, just as there are limitations on ownership of the airspace, so there should be on ownership of the strata beneath it. However, as Aikens LJ said in the Court of Appeal [2010] Ch 100, 'it is not helpful to try to make analogies between the rights of an owner of land with regard to the airspace above it and his rights with regard to the strata beneath the surface'. As Lord Hope pointed out, 'As a general rule anything that can be touched or worked must be taken to belong to someone.' Thus the strata beneath the land must have an owner, unlike the airspace above.

In fact, it is possible and very common for different owners to have rights in different strata of the land.[6] Indeed section 205(1)(xi) of the Law of Property Act (LPA) 1925 expressly recognises this possibility by providing that the term 'land' includes land held apart from the surface 'whether the division is horizontal, vertical or made in any other way'. For example, where there is a public highway maintained by a public authority, then under section 263 of the Highways Act 1980 that authority has a determinable fee simple interest in the highway and so much of the airspace above and the earth beneath as is needed to enable it to carry out its statutory duties.[7] However, apart from this, the earth beneath is owned by the adjoining landowners. Another example is where the owner of the freehold might grant a lease of the cellar underneath his land or even a cave.

The maxim does have a value as an attempt to illustrate the point that land is not one-dimensional but in a sense has a three-dimensional quality,[8] in that whoever has a legal estate in the land

---

[4] You could at this point explain what the tort of conversion means but only give a brief explanation otherwise you will go off the point.

[5] Note that we have brought the discussion back to the *Bocardo* case. Although you need to mention other points the question did mention this case specifically.

[6] This is where your answer will start to gain those extra marks to get you a good pass. You could have simply continued by giving yet more examples of how the maxim does or does not apply. However, you have made your point and you need to move on.

[7] This is a good example and is easy to remember as it deals with an everyday situation.

[8] Try to bring this idea of land having a three-dimensional quality into your answer. If you use this as an idea, it can bring the answer away from the rather sterile discussion of whether the maxim is strictly correct (which of course it is not) and instead give it a more philosophical slant.

[9] Note that we are tying in our answer to the quotation in the question.

[10] This is an excellent way to end. You have not summarised the law, something which is not necessary anyway, but have suggested another way in which the law can deal with this situation. In this way, you have moved the answer away from the purely descriptive and made it more evaluative.

does have certain rights in the airspace above and some rights in the land below. The question is really whether those rights are so limited as to make the general point illustrated by this maxim virtually worthless, despite Lord Hope's statement in *Bocardo* that the 'proposition commands general acceptance'.[9] There is a practical point here: if we are, for example, advising a client who has bought 155 High Street, Hanbury and she asks us exactly what she has bought, what answer shall we give?

It might be better to abandon this ancient maxim and instead concentrate on the concept of 'stratified ownership'[10] by recognising that in fact ownership of one piece of land can be held in different ways and by different people and so it is misleading to speak of the owner as having rights upwards and downwards from the land owned.

Make your answer stand out

■ Consider replacing some of the cases with a more philosophical discussion on the whole concept of what ownership of land means. You could argue that this maxim is simply a way of the common law avoiding any attempt to grapple with exactly what ownership means and instead taking refuge in an ancient and misleading maxim.

■ Begin by lifting the answer to a different plane by making the point that the discussion on this maxim is based on confusion between the physical aspects of land and abstract perceptions of land. Thus, the use of the maxim refers to an abstract perception of land but, as the answer demonstrates, the physical aspects of ownership of land conflict with it.

■ Integrate into the answer a short mention of how the landowner does not even have unrestricted rights over the surface of the land, e.g. the need to obtain planning consent for certain types of 'development'. You need not spend long on this but it does show how the landowner, far from having unrestricted rights above and below the land does not even have unrestricted rights on the surface.

■ Look at different ideas on how far ownership of the surface should extend to the strata beneath. See Howell (2002) Subterranean Land Law: Rights below the Surface of Land. *Northern Ireland Legal Quarterly*, 53: 268.

> **! Don't be tempted to . . .**
>
> - Just set out a list of cases without any attempt to relate them to the question.
> - Give too many examples which all illustrate the same point.
> - Fail to come to a conclusion which engages with the words of the question.

✎ Question 2

In *Harrow LBC* v *Qazi* [2004] 1 AC 983 Lord Steyn referred to 'the new landscape created by the Human Rights Act 1998'.

Critically consider this statement in the context of land law and especially of recent decisions of the Supreme Court.

Diagram plan

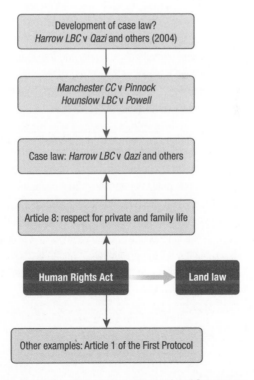

A printable version of this diagram plan is available from www.pearsoned.co.uk/lawexpressqa

Answer plan

→ Contrast the emphasis of land law on the process of transferring rights as contrasted with human rights.

→ Explain Article 8 of the ECHR.

→ Critically consider the decision in *Harrow LBC* v *Qazi.*

→ Consider other cases involving possession proceedings, especially recent Supreme Court ones.

→ Other examples of the impact of the HRA on land law.

→ Conclusion – referring back to the question.

Answer

Although it is stating the obvious to say that the Human Rights Act (HRA) 1998 is about 'human rights' this point does tell us a great deal about its impact in land law.[1] In Gray (2002) he remarks (at p. 211) that the 'intricate machinery of the Law of Property Act 1925 and its attendant satellite legislation contains little which could be confused with the positive protection or reinforcement of basic concepts of human rights, dignity and freedom'. This is, as he points out, because the 1925 property legislation was primarily concerned with upholding 'transaction based rights'. This is a completely different emphasis from that in the HRA.

[1] This opening paragraph is important as an average answer would just begin with an account of the cases which are dealt with later on in this answer. Here, however, we are setting the scene.

One major area has been in the application of Article 8(1): respect for family life and the home.[2] One fundamental issue is whether Article 8(1) concerns property because on its wording it could be said primarily to protect privacy, a point to which we shall return. The right in Article 8(1) is qualified by Article 8(2)[3] which provides that no interference with these rights shall be justified except in the interests of national security, public safety or the economic well-being of the country, for the prevention of health or morals, or for the protection of the rights and freedoms of others'. In effect this lays down a test of proportionality.

[2] You could describe here how the HRA works but if you did you would have less time for land law issues and this is not a Constitutional Law essay!

[3] When you mention Article 8(1) you have to mention Article 8(2).

This has been considered by the courts in the context of whether established procedures under domestic law should be subject to juridical scrutiny under the ECHR.[4] The courts initially limited the scope of Article 8(2) so that it had almost no effect at all. In *Harrow*

[4] An average answer would just set out the facts of *Harrow* v *Qazi* but this opening sentence adds to your marks by placing the case in its context in UK domestic law.

LBC **v** *Qazi* [2004] 1 AC 983 a local authority claimed possession of a council house from Qazi who was a former joint tenant with his wife. She had given a unilateral notice to quit the premises which had terminated Qazi's tenancy. The House held, by a majority, that the test of proportionality is irrelevant where the party claiming is, as here, already entitled to an automatic possession order against a former tenant. Lord Millett, for the majority, held that it was not for the courts to engage in 'social engineering in the housing field' and that the landlord's proprietary rights under domestic law must not be 'deflected' by some discretionary judgment based on the effect of eviction on the tenant's home life.[5]

[5] It is of crucial importance to stress the continuing debate among the judges on the application of the HRA in particular cases. A poor answer will simply say that 'the court held that' but for a good mark you need to mention at least in outline the main argument of the majority and that of the minority. This is one area where you really do need to read the cases.

The result was that the test of proportionality was not, as it were, a free-standing one. As Lord Hope put it in *Kay* v *Lambeth LBC*; *Leeds CC* v *Price* [2006] 2 AC 465 provided that the courts consider if 'the requirements of the laws and the procedural safeguards which it lays down for the protection of the occupier' have been satisfied then there is no room for any challenge under human rights law.

However, there were dissenting voices.[6] In *Harrow LBC* v *Qazi* [2004] Lord Steyn, who was in the minority, held that the approach of the majority 'emptied Article 8(1) of any or virtually any meaningful content' and held that the interpretation of Article 8(1) should not be 'coloured' by 'domestic notions of title, legal and equitable rights, and interests'. Thus, to the basic question: has the HRA changed the nature of property in land law? Lord Steyn would have certainly answered 'yes'. Similarly in *Kay* v *Lambeth LBC* Lord Bingham stressed the applicability of the conditions in Article 8(2) and said that individual defendants must be given the opportunity to contend that they have not been met, and the ECtHR in *McCann* v *United Kingdom* [2008] 2 FLR 899 endorsed this. However, Lord Nicholls said that there would be a 'colossal waste of time and money' if, in every case where possession proceedings were brought under a statutory framework, there could be a challenge under the HRA.[7]

[6] It is especially important to quote dissenting judgments in this question because, as we shall see, they have now been recognised in the most recent cases as representing the law. The dissenters are no longer dissenting!

[7] This is exactly the type of passage which the examiner is looking for. You have clearly contrasted the two arguments.

The ground has shifted significantly as a result of two decisions of the Supreme Court: *Manchester CC* v *Pinnock* [2010] UKSC 45 and *Hounslow LBC* v *Powell* [2011] UKSC 8.

In *Pinnock*, a local authority sought possession against a tenant on the ground that some of the children resident at the property had been guilty of serious anti-social behaviour. The Supreme Court, in the words of Lord Neuberger, held that, in order for domestic law to be compatible with Article 8, 'where a court is asked to make an order for possession of a person's home at the suit of a local authority, the court must have the power to assess the proportionality of making the order, and, in making that assessment, to resolve any relevant dispute of fact'. Thus the test of proportionality has now become a separate one which is not automatically satisfied purely because the requirements of domestic law have been met. Nevertheless the use of the proportionality test does not mean that tenants will find it easy to resist applications for possession orders. Lord Neuberger said that the proportionality of making an order for possession in favour of the local authority 'will be supported not merely by the fact that it would serve to vindicate the authority's ownership rights'. He also pointed out that a local authority has other duties, such as 'the fair allocation of its housing stock' which will often support an application for possession.

Has the HRA had a great impact in other areas?[8] In *Aston Cantlow and Wilmcote PCC with Billesley PCC v Wallbank* [2004] 1 AC 546 one issue[9] was whether liability to repair the chancel of a church imposed on purchasers of land was in breach of Article 1 of the First Protocol: 'No one shall be deprived of his possessions except in the public interests and subject to the conditions provided for by law and the general principles of international law.' However, Ferris J, in the High Court, with whom Lord Nicholls in the House of Lords agreed, said that he did not 'find it possible to distinguish it from the liability which would attach to the owner of land which is purchased subject to a mortgage, restrictive covenant or other incumbrance created by a predecessor in title'. This looks like Lord Millet's reasoning in *Qazi*.[10] There was also the preliminary point, which was decisive, that the PCC was not a public authority and so the HRA was inapplicable.

Lord Steyn's hope that the HRA would bring about a new landscape may now have been fulfilled in the area of applications for possession orders where a person faces the prospect of losing their home. Whether this new landscape will apply to other areas of land law is still in doubt.

[8] This will add to your marks. So many answers will only consider the impact of the HRA on possession proceedings but, although this is probably the most important area, the question asks about the impact of the HRA on 'land law'.

[9] The other issue is dealt with later but bring out the main HRA issue first.

[10] This is a really good point, showing the ability to apply the reasoning of one judge in one case to that of another judge in another case.

✓ **Make your answer stand out**

- Mention the point made by Gray (2002) Land Law and Human Rights, in Tee (ed.) *Land Law, Issues, Debates, Policy* at p. 222: the tension in land law between the perspectives of the 'property absolutist' and the 'property relativist'. Think about what these terms mean and how they could be applied to a question on the impact of the HRA on land law.

- You could build your discussion around the contrasting views expressed by Lord Steyn and Lord Millett in *Harrow* v *Qazi* and develop these in depth. In order to make room for this you might have to leave out some of the discussion of later cases but you should at least mention them otherwise the discussion will be unbalanced.

- Refer to an article which analyses the recent Supreme Court decisions. See, for example, Cowan and Hunter (2012) 'Yeah but, no but' – Pinnock and Powell in the Supreme Court. *MLR*, 75(1): 75–91.

- Mention other areas apart from possession actions, e.g. adverse possession as here, or prescription. See Chapter 8 for the latter.

! **Don't be tempted to . . .**

- Start your answer with the details of a case without first setting the scene by explaining the relevant parts of the HRA.
- Give very full details of a case and not relate it to the argument.
- Fail to explain the contrasting ideas and approaches of the judges.
- Concentrate on just *Harrow LBC* v *Qazi* and fail to mention later cases.
- Give the false impression that the law here is settled.

? Question 3

Meg bought a house, which has a large garden, from Jean.

(a) Would the following items, which were not specifically included in the contract, be included in the sale?
 (i) a greenhouse;
 (ii) rare shrubs planted in the garden;
 (iii) miniature trees in tubs on the patio;

(iv) a garden seat secured to the land;

(v) a statue of the Duke of Wellington.

(b) Just before the sale, the garden was opened to the public. Ted, a visitor, found a gold bracelet which has been dated to 1470 together with 12 gold coins from the reign of King Harold II. Ted also found a gold ring dated 1947. He told Jean about the find of the bracelet and the coins but he kept the gold ring. Ted's wife was concerned when he told her of what he had done and has now come forward and told Jean that Ted has the ring. Jean asks you for advice on who is entitled to these items.

Answer plan

→ Explain the distinction between fixtures and fittings and the two main tests used to decide into which category an article will fall.

→ Examine each situation in (a) and apply the tests and relevant cases.

→ Apply the law on finding of treasure to the cases of the gold bracelet and the coins.

→ Apply the law on who is entitled to property which is found to the case of the ring.

Diagram plan

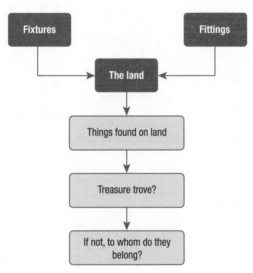

A printable version of this diagram plan is available from www.pearsoned.co.uk/lawexpressqa

Answer

(a) All of these items are either fixtures or fittings. If they are fixtures then, as the contract is silent on this point,[1] they would be transferred to Meg on the sale. If they are fittings, they will still belong to Jean. The distinction between fixtures and fittings is not clear cut[2] but the traditional method is to consider two issues:

(i) the method of annexation and the degree of annexation;

(ii) the purpose of annexation.

(*Holland* v *Hodgson* (1872) LR 7 CP 328 HC).

In general, the second test is now generally applied rather than the first but we need to consider both.[3] Guidance on the application of the second test was given in ***Botham* v *TSB Bank Plc*** (1997) 73 P & CR D1, where the Court of Appeal considered whether 109 different items in a flat were fixtures or fittings. These included baths, kitchen units, sinks, refrigerators, washing machines and dishwashers. Roch LJ stated that 'if the item viewed objectively is intended to be permanent and to afford a lasting improvement to the building, the thing will have become a fixture'.[4]

(i) The first article to consider is the greenhouse. If the greenhouse is not physically attached to the land and rests on the land by its own weight, it is unlikely to be considered a fixture and so as a fitting it will belong to Jean. If, it is physically attached to the land, it is likely to be a fixture and belong to Meg. However, if we apply the second test, it may be that the greenhouse is intended to be 'permanent and to afford a lasting improvement to the building' and so it will be a fixture. This is usually the case and so it is suggested that the greenhouse will be a fixture and will pass to Meg.[5]

(ii) Rare shrubs planted in the garden are certainly annexed to the ground and are likely to be considered fixtures especially as they are rare and as, on the basis of the test in ***Botham* v *TSB Bank Plc***, they will afford a lasting improvement to the building which, in this case, will include the garden.

[1] Do point this out: it is actually the normal practice in conveyancing for the contract to set out what is included in the sale.

[2] This is a vital fundamental point. Although in a particular case we may be able to tell with reasonable certainty if an article is a fixture or a fitting, there is no absolutely hard and fast rule to apply to these cases.

[3] Do not forget this: you will lose marks if you mention only the second test but you should stress that the first test has less significance.

[4] You need to mention these general points at the start but all of the others will emerge when you consider each article. If you spend too long outlining points of law in your introduction, you will not have time to apply the law to each specific point.

[5] Remember that if you do feel that it is possible to come to a conclusion you should state what its effect will be: fixtures to Meg and fittings to Jean.

(iii)   The miniature trees are in tubs. Thus, they are not annexed to the land, as presumably the tubs can be moved and so it seems likely that they are fittings and belong to Jean. In *Holland* v *Hodgson* Blackburne J stated that 'Articles not otherwise attached to the land than by their own weight are not to be considered as part of the land, unless the circumstances are such as to shew [*sic*] that they were intended to be part of the land'. In *Hulme* v *Brigham* [1943] KB 152 HC a printing machine which was secured by its own weight was held to be a fitting. However, it might be argued that this was intended to serve an activity carried on on the land but the tubs are intended to enhance the land itself. However, on balance it is likely that they are fittings.

(iv)   The garden seat secured to the land could be a fixture as it has been annexed to the land. One test is to ask if the seat has been fixed for its more convenient use as a seat, in which case it will be a fitting, or for the more convenient use of the building, in which case it will be a fixture. In *Leigh* v *Taylor* [1902] AC 157 HL a tapestry attached by tacks to wooden frames on a wall was held to be a fitting and not a fixture as the purpose of displaying the tapestry was to enhance it rather than the building. A similar approach was taken in *Berkley* v *Poulett* (1976) 241 EG 911 CA where in addition Scarman LJ suggested that, where an object cannot be removed without serious damage to or destruction to the realty, then it is likely to be a fixture. It is difficult to apply this test here but it is suggested that it would not be difficult to remove the seat and so it could be considered a fitting.[6]

[6] This is a good illustration of where you would lose marks if you came to a definite conclusion.

(v)   It is not clear if the statue of the Duke of Wellington is fixed to the ground. If it is not, then the case is similar to *Berkley* v *Poulett* where a white marble statue which weighed half a ton and was on a plinth was held not to be a fixture. If it is fixed then the question may depend on how difficult it is to remove it as suggested by Scarman LJ in *Berkley* v *Poulett* (above).

(b)   The gold bracelet which has been dated to 1470 may be treasure under the Treasure Act 1996 which provides that articles defined as treasure vest in the Crown. Section 1(1)(a) provides

[7] The moral here is obvious: always check the date of articles found as this information will be crucial to your answer.

that treasure includes objects, excluding single coins, at least 300 years old[7] which bear at least 10% precious metal, and other specified objects at least 200 years old. In this case the gold bracelet is over 500 years old and appears to contain at least 10% precious metal if not more. Thus, the gold bracelet belongs to the Crown although an *ex gratia* payment is generally made to the finder. The 12 coins will also count as treasure under section 1(1)(a) of the Treasure Act 1996 as there are at least ten of them and they are at least 300 years old. Indeed, in this case they are nearly 1,000 years old. Thus, they will also belong to the Crown.

The gold ring dating from 1947 is not of course treasure. If the true owner can be found and it is shown that he/she has not abandoned possession of the ring, then the true owner will have the best claim. If not, then we must apply the fundamental principle that a person who can establish a prior possession of a chattel has a better claim to it than anyone who possessed it later. (***Armory v Delamirie*** (1722) 5 Str 505 KB.) The question is whether Jean as the owner of the land had the intention to possess the gold ring.[8] It seems that the garden is not regularly open to the public and so Jean retains possession of the land and the ring belongs to her. If it had been open regularly, it would be arguable that Ted might have a right to the ring as in ***Parker v British Airways Board*** [1982] 1 QB 1004 CA.

[8] Notice here the emphasis of English land law on the concept of possession.

✓ Make your answer stand out

■ Read Wilkinson (1991) Farewell, Ladies Must We Leave You. *Conveyancer* 251, which is a short article on whether Greek goddesses at Woburn Abbey were considered fixtures or fittings. You could mention this in (a)(v) to add value to your answer.

■ You might introduce some discussion in part (b) on the consequences of abandonment as in Hudson (1984) Is Divesting Abandonment Possible at Common Law? *LQR*, 100: 110.

■ You could consider some of the situations in (a) together and so make room for a discussion of the historical development of the test for annexation of objects to the ground. See Luther (2004) Fixtures and Chattels: A Question of More or Less. *Oxford Journal of Legal Studies*, 24: 597.

! Don't be tempted to . . .

- Think that the law is absolutely definite in each case.
- Forget to mention that if the item is a fitting it will go to Jean and if it is a fixture it will go to Meg.
- Forget that in (b) the true owner, in principle, will have the best claim.

www.pearsoned.co.uk /lawexpressqa

 Go online to access more revision support including additional essay and problem questions with diagram plans, You be the marker questions, and download all diagrams from the book.

Registered and unregistered title to land

2

Attack the question

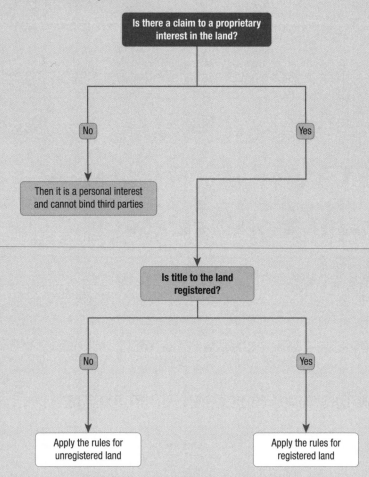

Is there a claim to a proprietary interest in the land?

No

Yes

Then it is a personal interest and cannot bind third parties

Is title to the land registered?

No

Yes

Apply the rules for unregistered land

Apply the rules for registered land

A printable version of this diagram is available from www.pearsoned.co.uk/lawexpressqa

 Question 1

'The register provides, in effect, a fairly accurate snapshot of title (to land) at any given moment.'
(Gray and Gray (2009) *Elements of Land Law* (5th edn))

Why do the authors consider that the 'snapshot of title' is only fairly adequate and could this picture be made clearer?

Answer plan

→ Outline what the land registration system is about.

→ Provide an explanation of where the register does provide an accurate 'snapshot'.

→ Consider cases where the snapshot is only fairly adequate – mainly existence of overriding interests. Explanation of how overriding interests fit into the scheme of the LRA 2002 and how the LRA 2002 has reduced the scope of overriding interests. Consider if they could be reduced further.

→ Look at other areas e.g. good leasehold title.

→ Conclusion by considering indeed the register does provide an accurate snapshot of the register.

Diagram plan

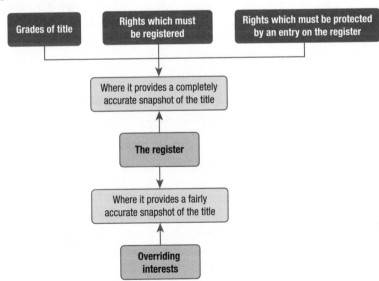

A printable version of this diagram plan is available from www.pearsoned.co.uk/lawexpressqa

Answer

[1] This paragraph, and in particular the last words, are vital as it ties your discussion into the question. Note that you could adopt a different approach and go at once to the situations where the register is not accurate, such as overriding interests. The objection is that your essay would lack balance as it would overemphasise the cases where the register is not accurate and not explain that in most cases it is accurate.

[2] Most students, faced with this question, would probably start with overriding interests and, indeed, might not mention anything else. However, by mentioning grades of title, which is a relevant but less obvious point, you immediately impress the examiner!

[3] Accurate terminology is essential for a good mark. Here we have not said 'the owner of the land' but used the accurate term 'registered proprietor'.

[4] Note the use of the term 'fee simple' rather than 'freehold' as there are other estates of freehold, although they are not legal estates and 'term of years' rather than lease. Accurate terminology will earn you those vital extra marks.

The reason why the authors consider that the register provides, in effect, a fairly accurate snapshot of title to land at any given moment is because, despite the mirror principle that the register is a reflection of title, this is not entirely true. There are situations where the register cannot be accurate due to the existence of overriding interests, which do not appear on the register at all, and where land is registered with good leasehold title. It is suggested that it is unduly harsh, however, to say that the register is, in effect, only fairly accurate and in this essay I will argue that it is very largely accurate and that the changes made by the Land Registration Act (LRA) 2002 have increased its accuracy.[1]

When title to land is registered, the Registrar awards a grade of title such as absolute, possessory and qualified.[2] The result is that the register does give an accurate indication of the status of the registered proprietor's[3] title. One instance where the register is only fairly accurate is where leasehold is registered with only 'good' leasehold title. This means that the freehold title has not been registered and so the land registry can say nothing about the freehold and, in effect, cannot give any snapshot of the freehold at all. This is not, however, a criticism of the land registration system. Instead it is an inevitable consequence of the process of time which it takes to get title to all land registered. When this is finally achieved, this problem will disappear as all good leasehold titles will be upgraded to absolute leasehold.

When title is registered estates and interests existing on the land are classified into three categories by the LRA 2002:

(a) Dispositions which must be completed by registration.

(b) Unregistered dispositions which override registered dispositions.

(c) Interests which must be protected by an entry against the title which they bind.

Taking (a) first, section 27(1) of the LRA 2002 lists dispositions which must be completed by registration such as transfers of the fee simple and also a grant of a term of years for seven years[4] from the date of the grant together with legal easements and profits (with some exceptions – see below) and the grant of a legal charge (mortgage) over the estate. Thus, if any disposition of any of the above is not completed by registration, the disposition will not take effect. By this means the register provides a completely accurate 'snapshot' of all these rights as the title of the question mentions.

I will deal with (c) first as (b) will require a more extended treatment. Category (c) comprises rights which have to be protected by an entry on the register to bind a purchaser. Thus they are treated differently from rights in (a) where the actual disposition must be registered but the effect is the same in that when a person buys land they need not be concerned about any of these rights unless they appear in the register and so, as far as they are concerned, the 'snapshot' is accurate. Examples of these are restrictive covenants, equitable easements and estate contracts.

The area which shows that the register only provides a fairly accurate snapshot of title to land is overriding interests. This term is not used in the LRA 2002 but it was used in the Law of Property Act (LPA) 1925 and is the most convenient short description of them. As mentioned above, they may not appear on the register but can still bind a purchaser.

[5] For some reason students forget to mention that the lease must be legal. Don't let it be you.

The first category is legal[5] leases not exceeding seven years. Section 118 of the LRA 2002 contains power to reduce this and it is suggested that it will eventually be reduced to three years. Under section 70(i)(k) of the Land Registration Act (LRA) 1925 the term was 21 years. Legal leases granted before 13 October 2003 and which were overriding before that date continue to override.[6] The reason why these leases override is that it would be unreasonable to expect short leases to be registered and that, if they were, the register would be cluttered up by them. This exception is found in other land registration systems (see e.g. the Queensland Real Property Act 1877).[7]

[6] The extra material on the leases which were overriding under the LRA 1925 retaining this status is what is expected if you are aiming for at least a 2.1.

[7] A short point showing a comparative approach will gain you marks.

The second category is the interests of persons in actual occupation of the land where these are coupled with an interest in land, and it is this category which has expanded greatly since it was introduced by the LRA 1925 and is the most controversial. It protects those who are in actual occupation under a legal or equitable interest in the land. The familiar example is where a person is in occupation under an equitable interest arising under a trust where they have contributed to the cost of acquisition of the land as in *Williams and Glyn's Bank v Boland* [1980] 2 All ER 408 HL where a wife who had contributed to the purchase price of their home had an overriding interest against the bank to whom her husband, who was the registered owner, had mortgaged it. As Denning MR put it in **Strand Securities v Caswell** [1965] Ch 373 Ch D a person in actual occupation 'is protected from having his rights lost in the welter of registration'. The justification is that occupation by itself should be obvious to a purchaser who should be alerted to the need to make enquiries even though the occupier's rights are on the register. Moreover an occupier might not realise that they had an interest which could be registered, and in addition it is socially right that a person in the position of Mrs Boland should have priority over a lender. However, Schedule 3 of the LRA 2002 has reduced the extent to which these interests can bind a purchaser on a subsequent registration of title so that a purchaser will not be bound if the occupation would not have been obvious on a reasonable inspection of the land at the time of the disposition.[8]

[8] Resist the temptation to go into too much detail – as here, give just enough to show the examiner that you know what you are talking about!

The third category of interests which override is a legal easement or a profit acquired by implied grant or by prescription, but Schedule 3 applies here too. It also provides that where the easement or profit has been exercised in the year before the disposition a purchaser will always be bound.

Finally, local land charges override but they should be discovered by a local land charges search carried out before purchase. An example is a tree preservation order.

It should be emphasised that the LRA has substantially reduced the number and extent of overriding interests. In addition to the instances mentioned above certain other interests, such as equitable easements, which did override under the LRA 1925, will not override if created on or after 13 October 2003. Moreover other interests, such as chancel repair liability, will cease to override on 13 October 2013. Thus the 'snapshot' is becoming more accurate.

[9] This type of conclusion, dealing directly with the actual words of the question and giving *your* view, is the hallmark of a really good answer.

Thus no purchaser can be confident that the register is completely accurate, as the register will not include overriding interests and there is the further exception of good leasehold. However, it is not the case that the actual register is inaccurate. It would perhaps be more correct to say that it is not comprehensive but, on the other hand, it is slowing becoming more so.[9]

✓ Make your answer stand out

- Clear, concise and appropriate use of case law to illustrate when interests of occupiers can override, e.g. more detail on *Wiliams and Glyn's Bank* v *Boland.*

- Refer to the Law Commission's Reports especially on the justification for overriding interests. See e.g. Law Commission (2001) *Land Registration for the 21st Century: A Conveyancing Revolution*, No. 271.

- Absolute clarity about which interests override, especially in the area of easements and profits.

- Reference to the distinction between interests which override on a first registration and those which override on a subsequent registration.

- Enhance your answer by referring to *Re North East Property Buyers Litigation* [2012] EWCA Civ 17 where properties had been sold by X to N under a buy-to-let scheme. Nominees of N had obtained a mortgage to enable it to purchase but defaulted and the mortgagees was held entitled to possession as against X. The contract of sale between X and N made no reference to the grant of a lease to X on completion and gave the clear impression that X would be selling without reserving any beneficial interests. Thus X did not have an overriding interest in the property. This is a very significant decision and you should watch for any appeal to the Supreme Court.

! Don't be tempted to . . .

- Just give lists of overriding interests.
- Go into too much detail on one area, such as Schedule 3 of the LRA 2002 or the cases on overriding interests of occupiers.
- Plough through the land registration system, mechanically describing it.
- Worse still, discuss the unregistered land system.
- Even worse, make simple errors, e.g. state that all easements override.

🔯 Question 2

'There are substantive differences between registered and unregistered land.' (Law Commission Report (1987) *Property Law – Third Report on Land Registration*, No. 158) Critically consider how significant these differences are.

Answer plan

→ Explanation of exactly what registration of title to land means and how it differs from the system of unregistered title – basis of title is the register.

→ Mirror principle: Compare and contrast how third party rights are protected under both systems.

→ Briefly mention the curtain principle.

→ Consider the insurance principle: Guarantee of title by land registry if title registered. Investigation of title simplified if title registered.

→ Conclusion – how significant are the differences?

Diagram plan

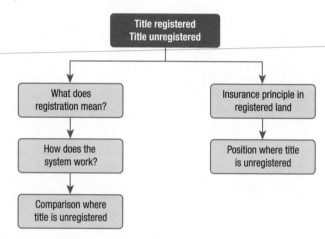

A printable version of this diagram plan is available from www.pearsoned.co.uk/lawexpressqa

Answer

The basic idea of the system of registration of title is simple. It means that both freehold title[1] to land must be registered and leaseholds which, at the time of the transfer, grant or creation have more than seven years to run (s. 4 LRA 2002). Both of these are registrable estates. The effect is that, when title to land is registered, the basis of the proprietor's title is the register and, when the land is transferred, conveyancing will be based on the Official Register Entries. When title is not registered, then the basis of the owner's title and of any conveyancing will be the deeds of the land.

[1] Do not say that 'freehold land must be registered' as you will lose marks. Technically it is *title* to land which must be registered. However, having made this point initially you can then later on just refer to registered land.

The system of land registration is generally considered to rest on three principles and a comparison will be made between the registered and the unregistered systems using these principles.

The mirror principle means that the register is intended to be a mirror which reflects to potential disponees[2] all the estates and interests which affect the land and it should be possible for purchasers, for example, to examine the register and gain an absolutely accurate picture of them. However, this is not so and there is a 'crack' in the mirror because of the existence of what the LRA calls 'unregistered dispositions which override registered dispositions' (overriding interests) and which are set out in Schedules 1 and 3 of the LRA.

There are three main categories:

(a) Legal leases not exceeding seven years.

(b) The interests of persons in actual occupation of the land.

(c) Certain legal easements and profits.

The extent to which these override depends on whether there is a first or subsequent registration of title.[3]

In fact the LRA has reduced the extent of this crack as, when title is subsequently registered, the number of legal easements and profits which can bind is reduced to those acquired by implied grant and prescription. Moreover in the case of these and also in the case of interests of persons in actual occupation any overriding interest will not bind in circumstances set out in Schedule 3 of the LRA 2002.[4] Moreover, by comparison with its predecessor, the LRA 1925, the LRA 2002 has reduced the number of overriding interests so that, for example, chancel repair liability will cease to be overriding in 2013.

The position where title is unregistered is more complex. There is no comprehensive register and so no question of a mirror. However, there is a register of land charges, a kind of mini land registration system, and if an interest is registrable as a land charge, exactly as with registered land, a purchaser will automatically take subject to it and, if it is not registered, it cannot bind a purchaser. Examples are second legal mortgages, equitable easements and profits, restrictive covenants and estate contracts. If an interest is not registrable as a land charge then whether a purchaser is bound depends on whether it is legal or equitable. If it is legal then a purchaser is always bound, for example in the case of a legal easement. If it is equitable then a

[2] A more accurate term than 'purchasers' as it includes those who acquire title by inheritance for example. However, given that the person is likely to be a purchaser, it would be pedantic to continue to use this term.

[3] At this point you could give a detailed explanation of exactly which legal easements and profits do override, but if you did you would not have time for other more relevant points. By mentioning the distinction between first and subsequent registration you have shown the examiner that you know something important about land registration, so why not leave it at that?

[4] There is just not time to set these rules out in detail but if you show the examiner that you are aware of their source, this gives a good indication that you know what they are.

purchaser is bound unless they are a bona fide without notice. An example of notice is **Kingsnorth Finance Co Ltd v Tizard** [1986] 2 All ER 54 HC.[5]

The curtain principle means that any trusts relating to the land are kept off the title and so any person dealing with the proprietor need not concern themselves with the rights of the beneficiaries under the trust as these will be overreached.

Overreaching occurs in this context when section 2(1)(i) of the LPA 1925 applies and the provisions of section 27 of the LPA 1925 are complied with. The effect is that if capital money arising on a sale (the purchase price) is paid to two trustees or a trust corporation then any interests of beneficiaries in the property are overreached and exist only in the proceeds of sale. It applies to both registered and unregistered land. Where there are two or more co-owners then they are trustees and so overreaching can operate. This can be seen in **City of London of Building Society v Flegg** [1987] 3 All ER 435 HL where two co-owners held a house by registered title to which the parents of one of them had contributed part of the purchase price.[6] The parents also occupied the house along with the trustees. The co-owners took out a mortgage without the knowledge of the parents and, when this could not be repaid, the lender sought repossession. It was held that, as the mortgage was in the names of two persons, they took it as trustees and so the rights of the parents were overreached.

Overreaching applies to both registered and unregistered titles. Where title is registered and there is a tenancy in common, then by section 44 of the LRA 2002 a restriction must be entered on the register so that on a sale overreaching will take place. Where title is unregistered overreaching can still take place but the mechanism provided in section 44 of the LRA will not be available.

The insurance principle means that if title to land is registered then if there is a mistake on the register which prejudicially affects the title of the registered proprietor[7] (Sched. 4 LRA 2002) then a claim to rectify the register may be made (see s. 66 of the LRA 2002 and Sched. 4). Moreover section 103 of the LRA 2002 makes provision for the payment of indemnities and the detailed provisions are in Schedule 8. This states that a person is entitled to be indemnified (i.e. paid compensation) if they suffer loss by reason of a variety of

[5] You need to support your answer with cases even though it is an essay and not a problem. However, you will probably find that you only have time to give the principle of the case and not the facts.

[6] In this instance it is appropriate to give the facts of the case, as overreaching is difficult to understand without a case example.

[7] It is vital not to just say that 'a mistake' can lead to a claim for rectification as there are some mistakes of an administrative kind which do not affect title and instead lead to alteration of the register as distinct from rectification. It is rectification which can lead to an indemnity.

[8] Better not to say; 'right to compensation' as there are situations (set out in Paragraph 5 of Schedule 8) where there will be no claim to compensation, such as where part of the loss was caused by the claimant's own fraud.

[9] Of course it is impossible to remember many statistics such as this one but try to recall just one or two – they really can illuminate an answer!

[10] Keep using this term rather than just the loose one of 'owner'.

cases, of which the main one is a rectification of the register. Thus registration of title carries with it the expectation[8] of compensation if in the course of registration a mistake is made which causes loss and, in a general sense, registration of title can be considered state insurance against that title being defective. For example, suppose that a person owns land but there was a forged transfer of that land to someone else so that the register states that the forger owns the land. There were 62 claims involving forgery in 2008–9.[9] This will lead to a claim for an indemnity as the registered proprietor[10] has suffered the loss of title to their land.

A comparison with the situation where title is not registered is difficult as mistakes arise when land is registered following a transfer although any transfer of an unregistered title will lead to it being registered. However, for the sake of example say that the forgery situation mentioned did occur then any claim would have to be brought against the forger and/or the person who now had title if the land had been sold on. In effect, although in the end the owner might win as for registered land, they would have to do all the work themselves.

In conclusion there are very substantial differences between registered and unregistered land which all derive from the point that in a registered title system the actual title to land is registered and if it is unregistered it is not, with the small but significant exception of land charges.

✓ Make your answer stand out

- Explain clearly at the start of the answer exactly what is meant by registered title. Having done this, an explanation of what unregistered title is should follow naturally.
- Make sure that there is a clear comparison throughout your answer between the registered and unregistered systems. Do not describe the registered system and then the unregistered system.
- Point out that there is an argument that the overreaching provisions are incompatible with the European Convention on Human Rights (e.g. Art. 8) but that in *National Westminster Bank Plc* v *Malhan* [2004] EWHC 847 Morritt VC indicated *obiter* that he did not agree.
- Clear explanation of the insurance principle as applied to registered land. This is often omitted by students or dealt with very briefly.

> **! Don't be tempted to . . .**
>
> - State the land registration rules in detail and then mention unregistered land fairly briefly at the end. It is surprising how many students do!
> - Ignore the differences between the systems of registered and unregistered land until you get to the end of your answer. Instead you should be comparing them throughout.
> - Give too much detail on overriding interests and not enough to perhaps less well known areas such as rectification and indemnity.
> - Ignore the insurance principle.

? Question 3

Six months ago Tim bought a freehold factory building, together with adjoining land, from Fred. The property was correctly registered at HM Land Registry with absolute title. Since the purchase was completed, the following matters have come to light:

(a) Quick Money Ltd claims that it has a legal mortgage over the land granted by Fred three years ago. it says that, as instalments are now considerably in arrear, it wishes to enforce its security.

(b) Eileen has produced a letter signed by both her and Fred in which Fred agreed to allow her to graze her goats over the land.

(c) Albert, who owns adjoining land, has produced an old deed which prevents any industrial activities taking place on Tim's land.

(d) Aidan, another adjoining landowner, says that he and his predecessors in title have used a path across Tim's land for at least the last 100 years and that he has evidence to prove this.

(e) Teresa claims that Fred allowed her to sit on the land to paint and she hopes that Tim will continue to do so.

Advise Tim on whether he is bound by any of these claims.

Answer plan

→ Provide a short introduction – explain the significance of registered title and that it is absolute. Also mention that this is a subsequent registration.

→ In each question assume that none of the matters appeared on the title and make this clear in your answer.

→ For each question identify the right claimed and then explain where it fits in the registered land system.

→ Then decide if Tim is bound.

Diagram plan

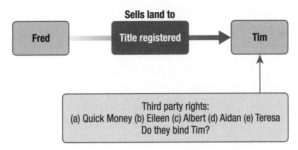

A printable version of this diagram plan is available from www.pearsoned.co.uk/lawexpressqa

Answer

There are three points to note at the start of this answer: first that Tim holds the freehold, second that that title is registered and so we must apply the land registration rules applicable on a subsequent registration, and third that it is registered with title absolute which is the best grade of title.[1] The assumption from the question is that none of the matters mentioned appeared on the register.

¹ Do make sure that at the start of any problem question on registered or unregistered land you address these three points. They are straightforward and usually easily answered and will get your answer off to a good start.

(a) Quick Money claims that it has a legal mortgage[2] but there was no mention of this on the register when Tim purchased. A legal mortgage is required by section 27(2)(f) of the LRA 2002 to be registered as a legal charge over the land. If it is not, as is the case here, then by section 29(1) of the LRA it will not bind a purchaser for valuable consideration. Tim did provide valuable consideration as he bought the property and so applying section 29(1) he is not bound by Quick Money's mortgage and they cannot enforce it against him.[3]

² It is much better to always follow the structure of the question and not to write a general answer. Often marks are allocated to each section.

³ Note that we have gone straight into the issues and have not given a general description of the land registration system. There is no time for this and it is not required. In addition there is no need to go back to the law of contract and discuss what 'valuable consideration' means.

(b) Eileen's claim to graze her goats over Tim's land is a claim to a profit à prendre as she is claiming the right to enter Tim's land and take something from it. A profit can be created by deed, in which case it will be a legal profit, but here it has been created by a letter and so it will be equitable provided that it satisfies the requirements of section 2 of the Law of Property (Miscellaneous) Provisions Act 1989. This provides that a contract for the sale or other disposition of an interest in land, which includes a profit, must be in writing, signed by the parties and the writing

[4] We are told that there was a letter but this may not contain a contract. You will gain marks by highlighting the areas of uncertainty rather than just making an assumption that there is a contract.

must incorporate all the terms agreed by the parties. We do not know that there was a contract[4] but if there was it was in writing and signed by both Fred and Eileen. However, we do not know if it incorporated all the terms. If the requirements of section 2 are satisfied then Eileen has a valid equitable profit, but to bind Tim it must be protected on the register as provided by section 32 of the LRA 2002 and if so section 29 of the LRA provides that it will have priority over any later disposition of the land. Thus, if Eileen had protected her interest by a notice, it would have bound Tim but, as she has not, he is not bound.

(c) The old deed produced by Albert contains a restrictive covenant. We can assume that it is valid and that it applies to Tim's land. However, restrictive covenants are equitable interests in land and, although they do not have to be substantively registered, they must be protected by a notice on the register as for equitable easements in (b) above. As it has not been protected, Tim will not be bound.

(d) Aidan's claim is to an easement as he is claiming the right to use the land of another. We can assume that it satisfies the requirements for a valid easement as laid down in **Re Ellenborough Park** [1955] 3 All ER 667.[5] A valid easement can be created by prescription which is long use and under section 2 of the Prescription Act 1832 a claim to an easement except one of light may be made on the basis of 20 years continuous use for the period immediately before the action on the easement. However, if the easement was enjoyed by the permission of the owner of the land, then the period is 40 years unless the permission was in writing in which case no easement by prescription can be claimed. Thus, oral permission will still allow a claim based on 40 years' continuous use. It seems that Aidan has a valid claim to an easement by prescription. There appears no evidence that permission was ever given for Aidan or his predecessors in title to use the path and, even if it was oral, the use here was for 100 years. Thus it seems that a legal[6] easement by prescription can be claimed. If so, this is an overriding interest under Schedule 3 Paragraph 3 of the LRA 2002 and so Tim may be bound even though it does not appear on the register. However, we need to look more closely at the conditions set out in Schedule 3 Paragraph 3. Paragraph 3(2) provides that, if the

[5] There is no need to go into detail on the requirements for an easement as the question does not lead us in this direction by giving any further information. However, a mention as above is essential.

[6] Watch for this point: if Aidan and his predecessors had used the path for, say, 100 years but had not used it at all for the period of two years immediately before the action was brought then there could not be a claim under section 2.

easement has been exercised in the period of one year ending with the day of the disposition, then Tim will be bound. Thus, if Aidan can show that he used the path in the year before Tim bought the land, Tim will be bound even though when he purchased he had no knowledge of the easement. If Aidan had not used the path in this time, then Tim will not be bound if he can show that when he bought he had no actual knowledge of the existence of the easement and it would not have been obvious on a reasonably careful inspection of the land at the time of the disposition. This is a question of fact on which we cannot come to a conclusion, but if a path had been used for 100 years then it is likely that there would be evidence of it[7] and so Tim would not be able to say that it would not have been obvious on a reasonably careful inspection. Thus it is likely that Tim will be bound by Aidan's claim.

[7] There is no case law on this point and so there is no harm in using your common sense to predict what the courts might do.

(e) Teresa's claim can only be to a licence. In ***Thomas v Sorrell*** (1673) Vaugh 330 HC Vaughan CJ held that: 'a licence properly passes no interest not alters or transfers property in any thing'. The effect is that a licence does not create an interest in land and so it cannot bind a third party such as Alf nor appear on the register. Thus in ***King v David Allen*** [1916] 2 AC 54 HL a licence to fix advertisements to the wall of a cinema did not bind a lessee of the cinema. Nor could Teresa claim that her sitting on the land amounted to occupation so as to give her an overriding interest and, in any event, any occupation must be under an interest in the land which she does not have. If Tim wishes to allow her to continue to sit on his land he may do so but he does not have to.

✓ **Make your answer stand out**

- Mention *Barclays Bank Plc* v *Zaroovabli* [1997] Ch 321 HC where a bank which had failed to register a mortgage was bound by a tenancy created after the date of the mortgage.
- Clear analysis of Eileen's letter.
- Clear analysis in Aidan's claim how Schedule 3 Paragraph 3 of the LRA 1925 applies to the situation.
- Possible mention in the case of Teresa of cases where a licence might bind a purchaser but point out that they will not apply here.

> **! Don't be tempted to . . .**
>
> - Include an introduction dealing with the issues in general.
> - Discuss whether the claimed easement by Aidan satisfies the requirements for a valid easement.
> - Speculate on whether Teresa's claim could be anything other than a licence. It clearly is not, for example, an easement as it is purely personal and nor is it a profit as she is not taking anything from the land.

❓ Question 4

In 2012 Alf bought a disused farm building, together with adjoining land, from Anita. Title to the property was not registered. Since the purchase was completed the following matters have come to light:

(a) Cheeploans Ltd claims that it has a legal mortgage over the land granted by Anita three years ago. It says that, as instalments are now considerably in arrear, it wishes to enforce its security.

(b) Roger has produced a letter signed by both him and Anita in which Anita agreed to allow him to graze his sheep over the land.

(c) Aaron, who owns adjoining land, has produced an old deed which prevents any industrial activities taking place on the land which Alf has bought.

(d) Liz, another adjoining landowner, says that she and her predecessors in title have used a path across Alf's land for at least the last 200 years and that she has evidence to prove this.

(e) Sam claims that Anita allowed him to sit on the land to sketch and he hopes that Alf will continue to do so.

Advise Alf on whether he is bound by any of these claims.

Answer plan

➡ Provide a short introduction – explain the significance of unregistered title as contrasted with registered title.

➡ For each question identify the right claimed and then explain where it fits in the unregistered land system: does it have to be registered as a land charge.

➡ Distinguish clearly between legal and equitable interests in cases where the interest does not have to be registered as a land charge.

➡ Then decide if Alf is bound.

Diagram plan

```
                    Sells land to
  ┌─────────┐   ┌──────────────────┐          ┌─────────┐
  │  Anita  │   │ Title unregistered│ ───────► │   Alf   │
  └─────────┘   └──────────────────┘          └─────────┘
                                                   ▲
                                                   │
                          ┌────────────────────────────────┐
                          │      Third party rights:        │
                          │ (a) Cheeploans (b) Roger (c)     │
                          │     Aaron (d) Liz                │
                          │      Do they bind Alf?           │
                          └────────────────────────────────┘
```

A printable version of this diagram plan is available from www.pearsoned.co.uk/lawexpressqa

Answer

The fact that title was unregistered when Alf bought the property means that we must consider in each case whether the right was registrable as a land charge and, if not, then whether the right is a legal or equitable interest in land and the rules applicable in each of these cases.[1]

[1] Begin every answer to a problem question on unregistered land in this way. You have identified the three stages: check if the right is registrable as a land charge, if not, is it legal, if not, is it equitable.

(a) A legal mortgage is a legal interest in land under section 1(2) of the LPA 1925. If the mortgagee (Cheeploans Ltd) had taken possession of the title deeds then this would have been a trigger to title to the land being registered. This is because a mortgage by deposit of title deeds is a protected legal mortgage by section 4(8) of the LRA 2002 and by the operation of section 4(1)(g) it will trigger registration of the title However, we are told that title has not been registered in this case and so this must be a second or subsequent legal mortgage (a puisne mortgage)[2] and as such it requires protection as a Class C(i) land charge. If this is not done, as seems to be the case here, then by virtue of section 4(5) of the Land Charges Act 1972 it is void against a purchaser of the land such as Alf. Furthermore section 199(l)(i) of the LPA 1925 provides that a purchaser is not prejudicially affected by notice of it so, even if Alf did have notice of the mortgage before he purchased, he would not be bound by it.

[2] This analysis, although it may seem complex, is vital. The essential point is that you cannot assume that the mortgage is either a first or subsequent mortgage.

(b) Roger's claim to graze his sheep over Alf's land is a claim to a profit à prendre as he is claiming the right to enter Alf's land and take something from it. A profit can be created by deed in which case it will be a legal profit, but here it has been created

33

by a letter and so it will be equitable provided that it satisfies the requirements of section 2 of the Law of Property (Miscellaneous) Provisions Act 1989. This provides that a contract for the sale or other disposition of an interest in land, which includes a profit, must be in writing, signed by the parties and the writing must incorporate all the terms agreed by the parties. We do not know that there was a contract[3] but if there was it was in writing and signed by both Roger and Anita. However, we do not know if it incorporated all the terms. If the requirements of section 2 are satisfied then Roger has a valid equitable profit but as it was created on or after 1 January 1926[4] it must be protected as a Class D(iii) land charge to bind Alf. If not then by section 4(6) of the Land Charges Act 1972 it is void against a purchaser for money or money's worth and we are told that Alf purchased the land which means that he gave money for it. Therefore he is not bound by Roger's claimed profit even if he had notice of it (section 199)(I)(i) LPA 1925.

(c) The old deed produced by Aaron contains a restrictive covenant. We can assume that it is valid and that it applies to Alf's land.[5] Restrictive covenants are equitable interests in land and the answer depends on the date when the covenant was originally entered into. If this was on or after 1 January 1926 then the covenant must be registered as a Class D(ii) Land Charge, otherwise it will not bind a purchaser of the land for money or money's worth such as Alf. If, however, this date was before 1 January 1926[6] then the covenant is not registrable as a land charge and instead whether Alf is bound depends on the rules governing equitable interests. Alf will be bound unless he is a bona fide purchaser of the land for value without notice of the interest. Alf certainly gave value for the land as he purchased it and there is no reason to suspect that he is not bona fide but did he have notice of it? It is clear that he did not have actual notice as we are told that the matter came to light after he purchased the land but did he have constructive notice? On the facts it is impossible to be certain. In ***Hunt v Luck*** [1901] Ch 45 it was held that a purchaser is bound by all matters which would be revealed by an examination of the land[7] but it is likely that no inspection of the land would have revealed the existence of this covenant. Nor does it seem that the deeds made any reference to it because, as pointed out above, the matter only

[3] You must not assume that there is a contract. You will gain extra marks if you follow this approach.

[4] In a question on unregistered land, check if you are told the date of creation of the equitable profit (or equitable easement or restrictive covenant as the rules are the same). If you are not, then you must examine the possibilities on the basis that it was created either on or after 1 January 1926 or, alternatively, before this date. See also footnote 6 below.

[5] Show the examiner that you are aware of the requirement that the covenant must apply to the land benefited but there is no need, or time, for detail on this.

[6] Note that you must not just say that a restrictive covenant must be registered as a land charge to bind a purchaser: it depends on the date of its creation.

[7] This is a crucial point in unregistered land.

came to light after the purchase. Thus it is likely that Alf will not be bound by the covenant.

(d) Liz's claim is to an easement as she is claiming the right to use the land of another. We can assume that it satisfies the requirements for a valid easement as laid down in **Re Ellenborough Park** [1955] 3 All ER 667 CA.[8] A valid easement can be created by prescription which is long use and under section 2 of the Prescription Act 1832 a claim to an easement except one of light may be made on the basis of 20 years' continuous use for the period immediately before the action on the easement. However, if the easement was enjoyed by the permission of the owner of the land then the period is 40 years unless the permission was in writing in which case no easement by prescription can be claimed. Thus oral permission will still allow a claim based on 40 years' continuous use. There appears no evidence that permission was ever given for Liz or her predecessors in title to use the path and even if it was oral the use here was for 200 years. Thus it seems that a legal easement by prescription can be claimed. A legal easement does not require registration as a land charge to bind a purchaser and so Alf will be bound on the fundamental principle that a legal interest in land binds all the world.

[8] We have no information on any matter which would enable us to decide if the requirements in *Re Ellenborough Park* have been met, so this is a sure indication that the examiner does not expect us to discuss this.

(e) Sam's claim can only be to a licence.[9] In **Thomas v Sorrell** (1673) Vaugh 330 HC Vaughan CJ held that: 'a licence properly passes no interest not alters or transfers property in any thing'. The effect is that a licence does not create an interest in land and so it cannot bind a third party such as Alf nor appear on the register. Thus in **King v David Allen** (1916) a licence to fix advertisements to the wall of a cinema did not bind a lessee of the cinema.

[9] This is a straightforward point and so you need not discuss it in detail.

✓ Make your answer stand out

- Clear explanation of rules where title is unregistered – do not mention registered land.
- Clear analysis of the position re the mortgage.
- Appreciation of the significance of the fact that in (c) we do not know the date of the restrictive covenant.
- Application of the rule in *Hunt* v *Luck* to the question of the restrictive covenant.

> **! Don't be tempted to . . .**
>
> - Include an introduction dealing with the issues in general.
> - Leave out a clear explanation of how the Land Charges Act works.
> - Forget that, if a claim is to a proprietary right, it which not registrable as a land charge, then you must ask if it is a legal or equitable interest and apply the appropriate law.

? Question 5

Maureen bought 'The Laurels', a freehold detached house, for herself and her partner Oliver to live in. The purchase price was £300,000. Oliver paid the 10% deposit and the balance of the price was funded by a mortgage taken out by Maureen with the Easypay Bank. The property was registered in Maureen's name. The purchase was completed in January 2011 and the property, together with the bank's charge to secure the mortgage, was registered in February 2011.

In January 2013 Maureen needed extra funds to pay for the care of her mother and so she took out a loan of £20,000 funded by a mortgage with the Shark Finance Co., secured by a another charge on 'The Laurels'. At this date 'The Laurels' was unoccupied as it was being renovated and Maureen and Oliver moved back in April 2013.

Maureen is now in financial difficulties and she cannot meet the repayments on either mortgage.

Oliver asks your advice on whether he has any interest in the property which binds:

(a)   the Easypay Bank;

(b)   the Shark Finance Co.

Answer plan

→   Does Oliver have an interest in the property?

→   What is his position regarding the acquisition mortgage?

→   What is his position regarding the second mortgage?

→   Detailed discussion of what is meant by 'actual occupation'.

→   Application of Schedule 3 Paragraph 2 of the LRA 2002.

Diagram plan

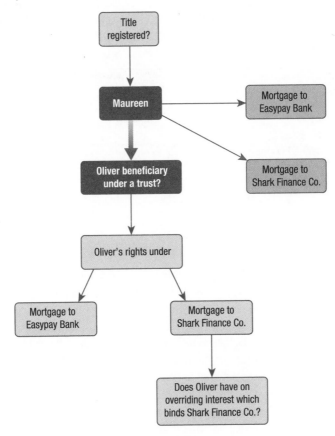

A printable version of this diagram plan is available from www.pearsoned.co.uk/lawexpressqa

Answer

[1] This must be your starting point. If Oliver does not have a beneficial interest then he has no rights in the property at all.

The first question is whether Oliver has an interest in 'The Laurels'.[1] The property is registered in Maureen's sole name and an interest of Oliver's can only be equitable on the basis that, by virtue of his payment of the deposit, Maureen holds the property for herself and him under a trust, thus giving him a beneficial interest in it. As Oliver's interest arose by way of contributions to the purchase price there is certainly a resulting trust (**Dyer v Dyer** (1788) 2 Cox Eq Cas 92) and it could also be argued that there is a constructive trust under the principles laid down by the House of Lords, in **Stack v Dowden** [2007] UKHL 17 HL and by the Supreme Court **Jones v Kernott** [2011] UKSC 53. The advantage of a constructive trust is that Oliver's beneficial interest in the property will not be limited to the extent of his contribution to the purchase price but the court can take into account other factors and in **Jones v Kernott** Lord Walker and Lady Hale said that reliance on contributions alone would be rare in a domestic context.[2] However, we are simply asked if Oliver has an interest in the property and the answer is that he does.

[2] It could be argued that any discussion of the extent of Oliver's beneficial interest is irrelevant as we are only asked if he has an interest at all. However, an examiner may expect some reference to this issue, but a long discussion is clearly not required as we do have enough information. If the question went into detail on the respective contributions of the parties then it would be relevant to discuss beneficial interests in more detail.

That being so, the next question is whether his interest binds the Easypay Bank[3] who provided the finance to acquire the property and who thus have an acquisition mortgage over it. Oliver's claim will be that, as title to the property is registered, he has an overriding interest under Schedule 3 Paragraph 2 of the LRA 2002. It should be noted that, as the property is already registered, this is the applicable schedule rather than Schedule 1 which applies on applications for first registration.[4]

[3] This must be your next point.

[4] This is a point almost universally missed by students and so if you include it you should certainly add to your marks.

In fact Oliver's claim will not have priority over that of the bank. In **Abbey National Building Society v Cann** [1990] 1 All ER 1085 HL the House of Lords held that in order to bind a purchaser there must be occupation under an interest in the land at the time of the disposition, which here means the time of the creation of the rights of the lender. This will have been at completion of the purchase. Here Oliver's right to occupy only arises after completion as his rights depended on Maureen holding the property on trust for him and she could not do this until title had been transferred to her following completion. The same result, but by a different route, is reached by following the decision in **Paddington Building Society v Mendelsohn** (1985) 50 P & CR 244 HC and holding that Oliver had, by implication, consented to the mortgage as he must have known that a mortgage was needed to complete the purchase. He was involved in the purchase as he paid the deposit and so he must have known that, if Maureen needed him to pay the deposit, she also needed assistance from a mortgage to fund the remainder of the cost of the house.

[5] Note that this is a crucial distinction. Watch for subsequent mortgages in questions of this kind.

The position is different with regard to the second mortgage with the Shark Finance Co. as this was a post-acquisition mortgage.[5] We need to distinguish between the question of whether Oliver was in actual occupation when the bank's interest was created and whether, assuming that he was in occupation, the Shark Finance Co.

can successfully argue that they are not bound by his overriding interest.

Was Oliver in occupation when the bank's interest was created? If he was then he will have an overriding interest. However, Oliver (and Maureen) were not physically present at the property when the mortgage was taken out as the house was being renovated and unoccupied. In *Williams and Glyn's Bank v Boland* [1980] 2 All ER 408 HL Lord Wilberforce said that 'actual' in the phrase 'actual occupation' merely emphasised that what was required was physical presence.[6] Although Oliver was not physically present, the builders engaged on renovation could be regarded as in actual occupation and, if they can be regarded as agents of Oliver, can their occupation be regarded as that of Oliver? In *Lloyds Bank Plc v Rosset* [1989] 1 Ch 350 Nichols LJ regarded the builders as agents of the wife, who was in Oliver's position.

This is supported by *Thomas v Clydesdale Bank Plc* [2010] EWHC 2755[7] where, as here, the owners were absent due to the renovation of the house when the bank's interest arose. The court held that the degree of occupation had to take into account the fact that the house was not being used as a residence on the date of disposition.

In both *Lloyds Bank Plc v Rosset* and *Thomas v Clydesdale Bank Plc* the owners frequently visited the property; in *Thomas* they were there almost every other day and Ramsey J pointed out that 'the degree of occupation must take into account the fact that the house was not being used as a residence'.

We are not told whether Oliver visited the property when it was being renovated but, even if he did not, it is submitted that the occupation by the builders would be regarded as his and so he was in actual occupation when the bank's interest was created.

If Oliver is in actual occupation then we must apply Schedule 3 Paragraph 2 of the LRA[8] which deals with when a purchaser can be bound by the overriding interest of an occupier. A purchaser, here the Shark Finance Co., will not be bound by the interest of Oliver as an occupier in two cases:

(a) If his occupation would not have been obvious on a reasonable inspection of the land. Here it is suggested that the presence or

[6] This phrase is still usually taken as the starting point of any discussion.

[7] There have been a number of recent cases on overriding interests of occupiers, of which this is one. Make sure that you keep up to date with them.

[8] This is the crucial link: if he is not in actual occupation then there is no point in applying Schedule 3 Paragraph 2.

not of Oliver assumes particular significance. Schedule 3 Paragraph 2 refers specifically to 'his' occupation and so it is the occupation of Oliver which must be obvious. In **Thomas v Clydesdale Bank Plc** Ramsey J referred to the need for 'relevant visible signs of occupation upon which a person who asserts an interest by actual occupation relies' and one of these signs in that case was the visits of the occupier. In **Thomas v Clydesdale Bank Plc** Ramsey J was unwilling to add a requirement that the person inspecting should make reasonable enquiries, which might have revealed Oliver's occupation. In conclusion it could be argued that a reasonable inspection would not have revealed Oliver's occupation and so Shark Finance Co. would not be bound. However, it is not possible to come to a definite conclusion.[9]

[9] Avoid giving dogmatic conclusions unless the answer is really clear. Here it is not and so a dogmatic conclusion would lose marks.

(b) If he failed to disclose his rights over the property when he could reasonably have been expected to do so. There is no evidence that the Shark Finance Co. ever asked Oliver if he had an interest in the property, and indeed that they knew he even existed, and so this will not apply.

✓ Make your answer stand out

- Start with a clear (but not too detailed) analysis of whether Oliver has an interest in the property at all. If he does not then he cannot have an overriding interest.
- Some reference to academic debate on, for example, the question of when a constructive trust as opposed to a resulting trust can arise and the distinction between them.
- Clear analysis which goes from beneficial interest – occupation – Schedule 3 Paragraph 2 LRA 2002.
- Mention that in *Thompson* v *Foy* [2009] EWHC 1076 there was some discussion on whether the provisions of the LRA 2002 had changed the position in *Abbey National* v *Cann* that actual occupation was required at the time of the disposition and the time of registration. Look at the wording of section 29 of the LRA 2002 and of Schedule 3 Paragraph 2 and at the judgment of Lewison J.
- Make sure that you are up to date with the developing case law on Schedule 3 Paragraph 2 of the LRA 2002. Look at the article by Bogusz (2011) Defining the Scope of Actual Occupation under the LRA 2002: Some Recent Judicial Clarification. *Conveyancer* 268.

! Don't be tempted to . . .

- Ignore the initial question of whether Oliver has an interest in the property at all. If he does not then he cannot have an overriding interest and so there would be no point in answering the rest of the question.

- Forget to include an analysis of how the operation of Schedule 3 Paragraph 2 of the LRA 2002 affects the claim. This is a crucial issue and if you ignore this your marks will be reduced considerably. So do learn this area!

- Include cases on overriding interests which do not bear directly on the question.

- Give a very dogmatic answer to the question. There isn't one!

www.pearsoned.co.uk/lawexpressqa

 Go online to access more revision support including additional essay and problem questions with diagram plans, You be the marker questions, and download all diagrams from the book.

Co-ownership of land

3

How this topic may come up in exams

The standard question on this area is a problem which asks you to consider various methods of severance of a joint tenancy. This may be linked with a question on the Trusts of Land and Appointment of Trustees Act 1996 (TLATA), or a TLATA question may appear separately.

Essay questions may ask you about the historical basis of the law on trusts of land, dealing with trusts for sale and strict settlements, and also about the debate on whether it should no longer be possible for an equitable joint tenancy to exist and in all cases of joint ownership there should be a tenancy in common.

Attack the question

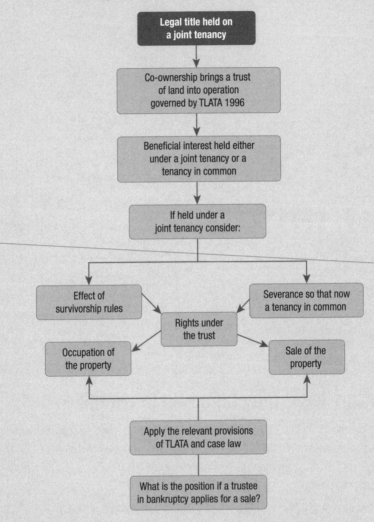

Legal title held on
a joint tenancy

Co-ownership brings a trust
of land into operation
governed by TLATA 1996

Beneficial interest held either
under a joint tenancy or a
tenancy in common

If held under a
joint tenancy consider:

Effect of
survivorship rules

Severance so that now
a tenancy in common

Rights under
the trust

Occupation of
the property

Sale of the
property

Apply the relevant provisions
of TLATA and case law

What is the position if a trustee
in bankruptcy applies for a sale?

A printable version of this diagram is available from www.pearsoned.co.uk/lawexpressqa

❓ Question 1

In 2010 Jim and his wife Amy, who had separated, then bought a restaurant for £600,000. Their finances were of course kept separate and they both contributed equally to the price. The property was held in their joint names but the transfer did not record the beneficial interests.

The business ran successfully but later the strain of working with her estranged husband proved too much for Amy and she left. She then wrote to Jim saying that she would like to have the business sold so that she could realise her share of it especially as she now has a son by her new partner, Don, and she wishes to make provision for him. Jim was reluctant to agree to this as he felt that the business was doing well.

Advise Amy on whether she has an interest in the restaurant and, if so, in what share. In addition you are asked to advise her on any procedures which she would need to follow in order to enforce a sale if Jim persists in refusing to agree to one.

Answer plan

→ Decide if the beneficial interest held as joint tenants or as tenants in common by looking at all the relevant factors not forgetting to apply the reasoning of the majority in *Stack* v *Dowden*.

→ If it is held as joint tenants, consider if Amy has severed her interest and then identify and apply the relevant method of severance.

→ Explain the law on applications to the court for a sale and the principles to be applied.

→ End by outlining what Amy could do if her application for a share was refused.

Diagram plan

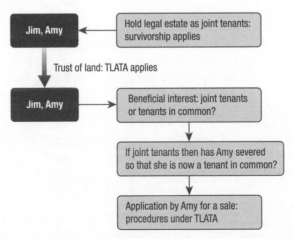

A printable version of this diagram plan is available from www.pearsoned.co.uk/lawexpressqa

Answer

Under section 34(2), Law of Property Act (LPA) 1925 where land is conveyed to co-owners who are of full age they must be joint tenants and so Jim and Amy will hold the legal estate as joint tenants.[1] The question is then whether they hold the beneficial interests in equity as joint tenants or as tenants in common. If they hold as joint tenants, then neither will have a separate share and survivorship will apply so that on the death of the first the beneficial interest will pass automatically to the survivor. If they are tenants in common then they do have separate shares which can, for instance, be sold and which will form part of their estate when they die.

We are told that the transfer did not record the beneficial interests and so we must turn to equitable principles.[2] There are no words of severance indicating a separate share and so a tenancy in common but we are told that Jim and Amy, although still married, were separated when they bought the restaurant. There is an equitable presumption against a joint tenancy where there is a relationship of a commercial character such as partnership property (**Re Fuller** [1933] Ch 652) and it is suggested that, as they are separated, the relationship is commercial and not domestic and that they will be tenants in common and have a separate share. On the other hand they contributed equally to the purchase price which in itself indicates a joint tenancy.[3] The decision in **Stack v Dowden** [2007] UKHL 17, which held that the courts could hold that there is a tenancy in common even where there is a declaration that they hold the legal title as joint tenants, will not apply here[4] as it was made clear that it was concerned, in Lady Hale's words 'with people living together in an intimate relationship' and not with, as she put it 'commercial men'. Here Amy and Jim have separated and so the relationship should be viewed in a commercial context.[5]

The conclusion must be that, as the matter is uncertain, this answer will be on the basis that it could be either, although my view is still that a tenancy in common is the most likely.[6] Whichever it is there seems no reason why their beneficial interests[7] should not be equal.

Here Amy has written to Jim saying that she would like to have the business sold and the question is whether this amounts to a severance of any joint tenancy. If Amy holds as a tenant in common with

[1] An answer on co-ownership should always start by identifying this point. The beneficial interests should be dealt with second once you have dealt with the legal estate.

[2] This is vital: see if you are told what the actual transfer says about the beneficial interests. It may say that the parties are to hold as joint tenants, and if so, this is really telling you that this will almost certainly be a question on severance of that joint tenancy. Here the question is less straightforward, as we shall see.

[3] This type of approach always picks up marks: you are carefully looking at the issue from two different angles: here the argument in favour of a tenancy in common and now that of a joint tenancy.

[4] You will certainly pick up marks by mentioning Stack v Dowden but equally you will also pick up marks by quickly spotting that in this scenario it will not apply.

[5] You could come to the opposite conclusion on this point although this one seems the more likely.

⁶ This is a crucial sentence on which the rest of the answer hangs: you have spotted that there could be either a joint tenancy or a tenancy in common and so you are going to answer on the basis of both possibilities. A poor answer would plump for one of these and so lose lots of marks. Always be confident enough to say, as here, that the application of the law to the facts is uncertain and so consider more than one possibility.

⁷ Beware here: it would be easy to slip into saying 'shares' but if so you would lose marks as we have not made up our minds if indeed it is a joint tenancy (no separate shares) or a tenancy in common (separate shares).

⁸ The significant words, which you could quote, are that Amy 'would like to have the business sold', not that she wants to have it sold.

⁹ This is a basic point on applications for a sale and should be mentioned at the start.

¹⁰ Although this criterion turns out not to be relevant, you should mention it as we are told that Amy has a son and so it could have been relevant!

Jim then of course there is nothing to sever as she already has a separate share. However, if the property is held as joint tenants then the question is whether Amy has severed her interest by her letter saying that she would like to have the business sold so that she could realise her share of it. By section 36(2) of the LPA 1925 a joint tenancy in equity can be severed by a notice in writing to the other joint tenants and by section 196(3) of the LPA a notice is sufficiently served if it is left at the last known place of abode of the person to be served. This looks more like the opening of negotiations between them than an actual notice of severance[8] and so Amy would be well advised to serve a formal notice of severance on Jim which complies with section 196(3) of the LPA 1925. This would safeguard her position in the event, for example, of Jim dying before negotiations were concluded.

The question is then what procedures Amy would have to follow to force a sale in the event of Jim not agreeing to one as Jim feels that the business is doing well. Amy has no right to insist on a sale and all that she can do is to apply to the court which has a discretion.[9]

Section 14 of the Trusts of Land and Appointment of Trustees Act (TLATA) 1996 allows any person interested in the trust to apply to the court for an order, which could be, for example, for a sale or authorising what would otherwise be a breach of trust. The term 'any person interested' includes trustees, beneficiaries, remaindermen and secured creditors of beneficiaries and so here it clearly includes Amy as a trustee and also a beneficiary.

Section 15 sets out the following criteria to which the courts must have regard when settling disputes:

(a) The intentions of the settlor.

(b) The purposes for which the property is held on trust.

(c) The welfare of any minor who either occupies, or might reasonably be expected to occupy, the land as his home.

(d) The interests of any secured creditor of any beneficiary.

It should be noted that these criteria are not in any order of importance. Of them, (c) is not relevant here as, although Amy has a son, who presumably is a minor, there seems to be no intention that he should occupy the land as his home especially as there appears to be no living accommodation.[10] Nor is a sale sought by a creditor such as a mortgagee, which would have involved (d). Thus, the only relevant criteria are (a) and (b), which amount to the same because Amy and Jim are the settlors as they created the trust and they also decided why the property was to be held on trust, in this case, for it to be run as a restaurant.

In **Re Buchanan–Wollaston's Conveyance** [1939] Ch 738, land was bought by four co-owners to prevent it from being built on. One later wished to sell but the others did not. As the original purpose remained, the court refused to order a sale. On this basis Jim would have a strong case to resist an application by Amy for a sale as the restaurant, according to him, is doing well and so there is no reason to sell it. This decision pre-dates TLATA (1996) and was based on its predecessor, section 30 of the LPA 1925,[11] but it is submitted that as section 15 of TLATA does specifically refer to the purposes for which the property was acquired this decision is still good law and can be applied in this case.

[11] You will lose marks if you quote pre-1996 cases in a question on TLATA unless you show, as here, that they can still be relevant.

If Amy cannot force a sale then she still remains a joint tenant in law with Jim and so her consent will be needed to a sale and she will be able to ensure that she receives her entitlement at that point. If she does not want to wait that long, she could sever her joint tenancy (if that is what she has) in equity by a sale to another, including Jim, as this is one of the equitable methods of severance set out in **Williams v Hensman** (1861) John & H 546.

✓ Make your answer stand out

- Note this quote from Lady Hale in *Stack* v *Dowden*: 'Parties may not intend survivorship even if they do intend their shares to be equal'. You could use this to bolster your argument that the parties are tenants in common.
- More detail on what can constitute severance. See Garner (1977) Severance of a Joint Tenancy. *Conveyancer* 77.
- Look at the facts of *Burgess* v *Rawnsley* [1975] Ch 429 and contrast with those in this problem.
- Read the judgment of Greene MR in *Re Buchanan–Wollaston* [1939] Ch 738 at 747 on the principles which should govern the exercise of the court's discretion in applications for a sale. Although this of course pre-dates TLATA 1996, his remarks are still relevant.

> **!** **Don't be tempted to . . .**
>
> - Assume at the start that there is either a joint tenancy or a tenancy in common and failing to spot that there is a doubt.
> - Forget to mention *Stack* v *Dowden* – as the latest decision of the highest court on this area it must be considered.

? Question 2

Sam, Ben, Ed and Sue, who worked at a firm of City of London solicitors as litigators, bought 'The Nest' in 2011 to provide a home for themselves whilst they were working at the firm. They remembered their Land Law and were registered as joint owners of the property in law and equity. There was a restriction entered on the register at the insistence of Sam providing that 'The Nest' could not be sold without his written consent.

In 2012 Ben was short of money and so he sold his interest in 'The Nest' to Sue. Ben later died leaving 'all my rights' in 'The Nest' to his girlfriend Nesta.

Later that year Ed decided to leave the firm and work for a country firm of solicitors as a conveyancer, which he thought would be less stressful. He orally agreed with Sam and Sue that Emma, a mutual friend, would 'take my place' but Ed died before the agreement could be formalised. Ed died intestate, leaving only a brother as a close relative.

It is 2013 and Emma has moved into 'The Nest'. Sam and Emma have quarrelled and Sam says that Emma should leave the property. Meanwhile Emma, Nesta and Sue all want the property to be sold but Sam refuses his consent. Advise the remaining parties on:

(a) Who now holds the legal title to the property?

(b) Who now has a beneficial interest in the property?

(c) Whether Emma can be required to leave the property.

(d) Whether Emma, Nesta and Sue can insist that the property is sold.

Answer plan

→ Explain how the legal title will be held.

→ Move on to decide how the beneficial interests will be held.

→ Assuming that they are held as joint tenants have they been severed so that they are now held as tenants in common? Identify and apply the relevant law.

→ Now explain how the law on the rights of occupation of beneficiaries can apply to this question.

→ Outline the position regarding the restriction on the register.

→ End by considering the law on applications to the court for a sale.

Diagram plan

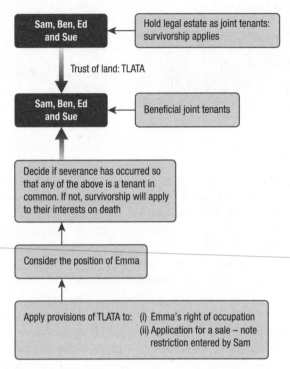

Sam, Ben, Ed and Sue → Hold legal estate as joint tenants: survivorship applies

Trust of land: TLATA

Sam, Ben, Ed and Sue → Beneficial joint tenants

Decide if severance has occurred so that any of the above is a tenant in common. If not, survivorship will apply to their interests on death

Consider the position of Emma

Apply provisions of TLATA to: (i) Emma's right of occupation
(ii) Application for a sale – note restriction entered by Sam

A printable version of this diagram plan is available from www.pearsoned.co.uk/lawexpressqa

Answer

[1] Do remember that where there are co-owners there *cannot* be a tenancy in common of the legal estate and the legal estate must always be held on a joint tenancy. If you make a mistake on this it will throw the rest of your answer out and lose you a lot of marks.

[2] Note that the term 'beneficial interests' means the same as equitable interests, i.e. the interests of the beneficiaries.

Under section 34(2), LPA 1925 where land is conveyed to co-owners who are of full age they must be joint tenants[1] and there cannot be more than four. Thus the legal title to 'The Nest' will vest in Sam, Ben and Sue and clearly they are of full age as a minor cannot hold a legal estate in land (s. 1(6) LPA 1925).

As the land is held by joint tenants, by section 36(2) of the LPA it must be held on trust which now means a trust of land governed by the Trusts of Land and Trustees Act (TLATA) 1996.

We next need to decide how the beneficial interests[2] under the trust will be held. The choice is between joint tenancy and tenants in common.[3] The property was conveyed to them with a declaration that they were joint tenants, in both law and equity, and this is decisive. It seems that they had not remembered their land law revision very well as a tenancy in common would have been more appropriate here as there is no apparent connection between them apart from work. The result is that the doctrine of survivorship will apply to the legal estate, which is inevitable, and also to the beneficial interest, which need not have happened.

The restriction entered on the register that the property cannot be sold without Sam's consent has been entered under section 40(2) of the LRA 2002 which provides that a restriction can prohibit the making of an entry in respect of any disposition. Thus if the property is sold without Sam's consent the actual transfer will be valid[4] but the new owners will not be able to be registered as such and the effect is to prevent any transfer without Sam's consent.

[4] Note carefully exactly what the effect of a restriction is. A clear and accurate explanation will earn you much credit as this is not a straightforward point.

In 2012 Ben sold his interest in 'The Nest' to Sue, thereby effecting a severance of his interest in equity under one of the rules set out in **Williams v Hensman** (1861) John & H 546 that a joint tenancy can be severed in equity by the act of one joint tenant 'operating on his own share' as this destroys one of the four unities, that of title. Although technically he has no share, it seems that the very act of sale or other disposition brings about a severance. The curious position is that Sue is now a tenant in common of the share acquired from Ben but a joint tenant with regard to her interest which she holds as a joint tenant with Sam and Ed. However, Ben's legal joint tenancy is not affected and will pass by survivorship on his death to the remaining joint tenants, Sam, Sue and Ed. His will leaving 'all his rights' in the property to Nesta has no effect as section 3(4) of the Administration of Estates Act 1925 provides that the interest of a joint tenant ceases at death and so Ben has no 'rights' to leave.

[5] This is the point to pick up on. If there was a written formalised agreement then the answer would be easy as there would be severance. However, here you need to think if an oral agreement will suffice.

Ed has orally[5] agreed with Sam and Sue that Emma will 'take his place'. Even though the agreement is not formalised, it is likely that Ed has severed his beneficial joint tenancy (**Williams v Hensman** (1861)) as the agreement does not have to be a specifically enforceable contract (**Burgess v Rawnsley** [1975] Ch 429). Thus Emma takes Ed's share as a tenant in common and when Ed dies his interest in the legal estate goes to Sam and Sue by survivorship.

The next question is whether Emma can be required to leave the property.

Section 12 of TLATA 1996 gives a right of occupation to beneficiaries who are entitled to an interest in possession in the land, provided that the trust so allows, but no right of occupation arises if the land is either unavailable or unsuitable for occupation by the beneficiary in question. The property was originally purchased as a home for the original four joint tenants whilst they were working at the same firm in London but all we know of Emma is that she is a 'mutual friend'. So it could be argued that the land is in this sense unsuitable for occupation by her.[6]

[6] Here you need to refer back to the start of the question and remind yourself of the reason why the property was purchased. Students often forget to do this. Remember to make a note right at the start of your answer of why the property was purchased to remind you to refer back to it later.

Even if she continues to live there, section 13 of TLATA 1996 allows the trustees to exclude or restrict her right to occupy but the power must not be exercised unreasonably. Section 13(4) sets out matters to which the trustees must have regard when exercising their powers to restrict or exclude the right to occupy, and a relevant one here is the purposes for which the land is held on trust which, as mentioned above, does not seem to include occupation by Emma. So there seems no reason why the trustees could not exclude her from occupation but section 13(7) provides that a person in occupation of the land, whether or not in occupation under section 12, shall not be evicted except with their consent or a court order.[7] The court, when deciding whether to evict, may, by section 13(8) have regard to the matters set out in section 13(4).

[7] This is important and often forgotten. It not only gives protection from eviction to those who are entitled to occupy under section 12 of TLATA (i.e. beneficiaries under the trust) but also to any others in occupation.

If Emma is to be allowed to stay, or at least pending a court order that she must leave, conditions may be imposed on occupation and section 13(5) sets out examples: paying outgoings and complying with obligations, e.g. ensuring that any planning permission is complied with. Thus Emma could, for example, be obliged to contribute towards gas and electricity bills and council tax.

[8] Note this point, especially of course where there are more than two trustees. The reason for requiring the consent of at least two is to enable overreaching to take place. Check that you are clear on what overreaching means.

Finally, under section 10(2) of TLATA, the consent of any two trustees of land[8] to a disposition of the land is sufficient in favour of a purchaser and here there are only two remaining, Sam and Sue. In deciding whether to sell, section 11 of TLATA provides that all the beneficiaries have a right to be consulted by the trustees, who should give effect to the wishes of the majority. However, if Sam still refuses to consent then, as the restriction entered on the register means that any disposition requires his consent, an application to the court under section 14 of TLATA is needed. An application can be made by any person interested in the trust and the term 'any person interested' includes trustees and beneficiaries. This includes Sue, Sam and Emma but not Nesta who has no interest in the property.

Section 15 of TLATA sets out criteria to which the courts must have regard when settling disputes and the relevant one here is (b): the purposes for which the property is held on trust. It is suggested that as only one of the original four owners, Sam, still wishes the property to be held for its original purpose then, using the analogy with section 11 and giving effect to the wishes of the majority, the property should be sold, but it must be emphasised that this will be in the discretion of the court.

✓ **Make your answer stand out**

- Include further discussion of the principles on which the court can order a sale under section 15 of TLATA as set out in the cases.
- Mention section 15(3) of TLATA: the court must have regard to the wishes of the beneficiaries of full age and in cases of dispute the wishes of the majority according to the value of their combined interests. Thus, there is a kind of majority rule but not by numbers but by the value of interests.
- Look at the article by Hopkins (1996) The Trusts of Land and Appointment of Trustees Act 1996. *Conveyancer* 267, which was written when this Act was passed and contains a valuable survey of its provisions, although obviously it needs to be looked at in the light of developments since then.
- Explain exactly what overreaching means in the context of section 10(2) of TLATA.

! **Don't be tempted to . . .**

- Plunge in without first setting out how both the legal title and the beneficial interests are held.
- Ignore the effect of the restriction.
- Spend too long on either section: devote roughly equal time to the question of how the interests are held and then the question of rights under TLATA of occupation and sale.
- Fail to apply each of the relevant provisions of section 13 of TLATA to this question.

Question 3

What are the essential features of a joint tenancy as contrasted with a tenancy in common? In your answer critically evaluate the argument that it should no longer be possible to have a joint tenancy in equity and instead there should always be a tenancy in common.

Answer plan

→ Explain the distinguishing features of a joint tenancy – the four unities, survivorship, undivided shares.

→ Now move on to look at the distinguishing features of a tenancy in common – lack of the four unities, separate shares and no survivorship.

→ Common law preferred joint tenancies, equity preferred tenancies in common – explain why this was so.

→ Survivorship rule can produce unfairness – explain in detail why this is so with case examples.

Diagram plan

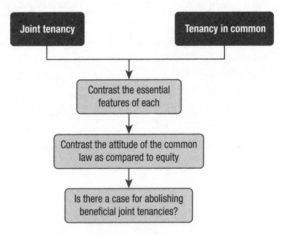

A printable version of this diagram plan is available from www.pearsoned.co.uk/lawexpressqa

Answer

The essential feature of a joint tenancy is that all joint tenants are co-owners who are not regarded as having separate shares but together own all. It is often said that they own an 'undivided share'. Four unities are necessary for a joint tenancy to exist:

(a) Time: the interests of all must vest at the same time.

(b) Title: all must derive their title from the same document.

(c) Interest: all must have the same interest.

(d) Possession: all must be equally entitled to possession of the whole land.

Even if the four unities exist, there will not be a joint tenancy if there are words of severance, i.e. words which indicate that the parties are to hold separate shares. Examples are: 'in equal shares' *Payne v Webb* (1874) LR 19 Eq 26, 'equally' *Lewen v Dodd* (1595) Cro Eliz 443 and 'to be divided between' *Peat v Chaman* (1750) 1 Ves Sen 542.[1]

[1] There are many more examples of words of severance but these have been included to illustrate the point that words of severance mean separate shares.

As joint tenants own an undivided share, their interest ceases on death (s. 3(4) Administration of Estates Act 1925) and so they cannot leave any part of their joint tenancy by will nor does it pass under the intestacy rules. Instead it passes to the surviving joint tenants under the right of survivorship – jus accrescendi. Where the deaths of joint tenants occur in circumstances making it uncertain which died first then the younger shall be deemed to have survived the elder (s. 184 of the LPA 1925). This was applied in *Hickman v Peacey* [1945] AC 304 where deaths occurred simultaneously in a bomb blast.

The right of survivorship is the feature of joint tenancies which distinguishes them from tenancies in common. With a tenancy in common the only unity required is possession. Each is entitled to a separate share and can dispose of this share either during life or on death.[2] Sometimes the four unities are present but there are words of severance and therefore there is a tenancy in common.

[2] Note the clear comparison between the two types.

Where there are co-owners the legal title must be held by joint tenants (s. 34(2) LPA 1925), but no more than four, and the legal estate can never be held by tenants in common. However, the beneficial interests can be held either as joint tenants or as tenants in common.

[3] This mention of feudal dues is useful in adding depth to your answer and you could research this – most major text books have a section on the history of land law. Students usually skip this but you should not as it will give valuable background detail.

The common law preferred joint tenancies. One reason was that the existence of a joint tenancy meant that, with survivorship, the land would ultimately be vested in one person and this would facilitate the performance of feudal dues.[3] In addition, as one of the objects of the Law of Property Act 1925 was to simplify conveyancing, the advantage of providing that the legal estate was to be held by joint tenants was obvious as, on the death of one joint tenant, the survivor is able to convey the legal estate and only needs to show the buyer the death certificate of the deceased joint tenant to prove title to the land.

Equity has always leaned against joint tenancies as it feels that not the accident of one co-owner living longer than the others should by itself entitle them to that person's interest in the land.

Beneficial joint tenancies are open to two objections. One is that, as Bandali (1977) puts it 'when used in relation to beneficial ownership its effect is to produce fortuitous and intended enrichment of a surviving joint tenant'. Moreover the parties may be unaware of the existence of survivorship and make a will leaving their 'share' (which of course does not exist) to another person. As noted above section 3(4) of the Administration of Estates Act 1925 makes this ineffective.

An example of the problems caused by a beneficial joint tenancy is *Campbell* v *Griffin* [2001] EWCA Civ 990[4] where Campbell was a lodger in a house and had taken care of the owners, an elderly couple. The husband executed a codicil to his will leaving Campbell a life interest in the house, but as the house was held by the couple as legal and beneficial joint tenants, the gift failed by survivorship. In fact the situation was rescued by applying proprietary estoppel to give Campbell a charge over the property. However, if the couple had had a beneficial tenancy in common, the husband would have been able to leave what would then have been his share to Campbell and this expensive litigation would have been avoided.

It is of course possible to sever a joint tenancy so that it becomes a tenancy in common but the parties may think that they have severed when they have not.[5] For example, it is of course possible to sever by written notice addressed to all the other joint tenants (s. 196 LPA 1925). Alternatively severance in equity can be effected by agreement with all the other joint tenants (*Williams* v *Hensman* (1861) John & H 546). The agreement does not have to be a specifically enforceable contract (*Burgess* v *Rawnsley* [1975] Ch 429 but in *Slater* v *Slater* (1987) 4 BPR 9431 it was held that there must be an intention to sever 'irrespective of the outcome of the negotiations'. What is not acceptable is an oral declaration by one joint tenant that she wishes to sever, despite the suggestion that it would be by Denning MR in *Burgess* v *Rawnsley*.[6] This makes perfect legal sense as, if severance by oral declaration was possible, there would

[4] This is absolutely crucial in gaining those extra marks. An average answer would have just set out the survivorship rule and how it works with perhaps an example. This answer has gone further and backed this up with a case which is, in fact, not very well known and so needed some research to find it. Perfect!

[5] A poor to average answer would simply go through the methods of severance but here you are using your knowledge of the law on severance to answer the question.

[6] A small point of detail but which shows that there are views on this.

[7] It is vital to bring in the practical aspect of the law and show how it works in practice. It is usually best to do this after you have stated what the law actually is, though.

[8] A mention of this decision, in addition to being relevant, will add to your marks as *Stack* v *Dowden* is usually studied in the area of trusts of the home and not here. So a mention of this case will show the examiner that you can think laterally across the subject: always a plus point. You could also add in some references to the debate on this case.

[9] You could, of course, take the opposite view and gain an equally good mark. It is quite reasonable to argue that beneficial joint tenancies should survive. What matters of course is how you justify your view.

be no need for the provisions of section 196 of the LPA 1925 governing severance by written notice. However, from the practical point of view an oral declaration by one party is exactly what may happen. That party will think that they have severed and perhaps execute a will leaving their (non-existent) share on death. In fact the will has achieved nothing. If there was always a tenancy in common there would be no need for severance.[7]

It could be said that the law is moving in favour of a tenancy in common anyway. Equity has always held that a tenancy in common will be presumed where the parties have contributed unequally to the purchase price (**Lake v Gibson** (1729) 1 Eq Ch Abr 290. However, in **Stack v Dowden** [2007] UKHL 17 it was held that there can be a tenancy in common even where there is a declaration that the parties hold the legal title as joint tenants.[8] Whilst this is true it does not do away with the situation where the parties have expressly declared that they hold the beneficial interests as joint tenants but then wish to sever. It is suggested that the end of beneficial joint tenancies would be a very useful reform of our law.[9]

 Make your answer stand out

- There has been a great deal of academic debate on the question of whether beneficial joint tenancies should continue to exist. Start with Bandali (1977) Injustice and Problems of Joint Tenancy. *Conveyancer* 243 and then move on to Thompson (1987) Beneficial Joint Tenancies. *Conveyancer* 29 which agrees with Bandali. For a contrary view see Pritchard (1987) Beneficial Joint Tenancies: A Riposte. *Conveyancer* 273 and also Piska (2008) Revisiting Resulting Trusts. *Conveyancer* 441.

- Add some references to the debate on *Stack* v *Dowden* and *Jones* v *Kernott* – see Chapter 4.

- There is evidence that the parties do not realise the implications of a joint tenancy especially where one has contributed more to the purchase than the other – see Douglas, Pearce and Woodward (2008) Cohabitation and Conveyancing Practice: Problems and Solutions. *Conveyancer* 365. This is obviously evidence against the existence of beneficial joint tenancies.

- Look at *Bindra* v *Mawji* [2009] EWCA Civ 203 – an interesting angle on this area where the Court of Appeal upheld an arrangement whereby a tenancy in common in life was to become a joint tenancy of the proceeds of sale of the property on death. Inclusion of this case will add depth to your answer.

> **!** **Don't be tempted to . . .**
>
> ■ Just list the ways in which joint tenancies can be severed – integrate the methods of severance into your answer and you will give your marks a real boost.
> ■ Spend too long on the first area and neglect the more challenging issue raised by the second part of the question.

◤ Question 4

Dixon ((2012) *Land Law* (8th edn)) considers that case law on section 15 of the Trusts of Land and Trustees Act 1996 has 'not been consistent in those cases . . . in which the rights of creditors are in contest with the rights of co-owners'.

Critically consider this view.

Diagram plan

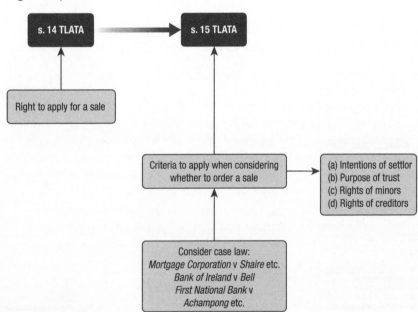

A printable version of this diagram plan is available from www.pearsoned.co.uk/lawexpressqa

Answer plan

→ Set out the criteria in section 15 and explain how they are exercised on an application under section 14.

→ Briefly mention the previous law to evaluate if and how the law has changed.

→ Consider *Mortgage Corporation* v *Shaire* and in particular Neuberger J's views on the application of section 15.

→ Evaluate how subsequent courts have dealt with applications under section 15: consider each decision and contrast the approaches taken by each court.

→ Emphasise that the approach has to be flexible and so the statement in the question is not in fact a criticism of the law.

Answer

Section 15(1) of the Trusts of Land and Trustees Act (TLATA) 1996 sets out criteria to which the courts must have regard when settling disputes over whether land should be sold, together with other disputes. The use of section 15(1) is triggered by an application for sale under section 14 of TLATA. The criteria are:

(a)   The intentions of the settlor.

(b)   The purposes for which the property is held on trust.

(c)   The welfare of any minor who either occupies, or might reasonably be expected to occupy, the land as his home.

(d)   The interests of any secured creditor of any beneficiary.

These criteria are not ranked in order of importance and so the fact that the rights of creditors are placed below those of co-owners does not say anything about their relative importance. It is also worth stressing that, in order to give a complete picture of how the criteria work, we need to consider criterion (c), the welfare of minors. Thus it is not just a tug between creditors and co-owners.[1]

In addition, it was held in **Bank of Ireland Home Mortgages Plc v Bell** [2001] 2 FLR 809 that, in the words of Peter Gibson LJ, the above criteria are 'not exclusive but inclusive' and so other factors can be taken into account where appropriate.[2]

One of the first examples of a contest between the rights of creditors and those of co-owners under section 15(1) to reach the courts was the county court decision in **TSB Bank Plc v Marshall** [1998] 2 FLR 769 where it was held that the interest of the chargee in a matrimonial

[1] This is a good point: you have shown that you are *thinking about* the words of the question and relating them to the actual criteria under section 15(1) of TLATA.

[2] This point is not usually made and so you will gain credit for doing so!

home would prevail over the interests of an innocent spouse save in exceptional circumstances. Here, although there were children resident at the property, there was no clear evidence to suggest that the purpose to provide a home for them was intended to survive once they became adults which they all now were.

However, it is arguable that the judge here was influenced too much by the predecessor to section 15(1) of TLATA, section 30 of the LPA 1925, which gave a wide discretion to the courts and did not set out any criteria.[3] Instead as the judge put it in *TSB* v *Marshall*: 'section 30 enabled the court to do what was equitable, fair and just'.

[3] This is one of those areas where an outline (but no more) of the previous law does add depth to your answer as here there has been more of a change in emphasis in the law rather than a radical alteration.

The first detailed consideration of section 15(1) by the higher courts was in *Mortgage Corporation* v *Shaire* [2000] Ch 743. The house was held by X and Y as joint tenants. It was bought to provide a home for them and Y's son by a previous marriage. X owned a 25% share in equity and Y a 75% share. X mortgaged the house by forging Y's signature and after X's death the mortgagee sought a sale. The court refused. Here Neuberger J emphasised that the law had changed under TLATA and that, by comparison with section 30 of the LPA, Parliament in section 15(1) of TLATA had intended to 'tip the scales more in favour of families and against banks and other chargees'. Neuberger J also made the obvious but necessary point that, if the law was to stay the same, then why had it been necessary to pass TLATA? Pascoe (2000) has described the approach of Neuberger J in this case as 'wiping the slate clean and starting afresh with secured creditors as the likely casualties of the new approach'.

[4] In this question we have a line of cases none of which differ from each other radically but which show subtle differences of approach. This means that you will gain marks by paying very close attention to the actual facts and how the decision in each case depended partly on its facts and partly on a different approach.

However, in *Bank of Ireland Home Mortgages Plc* v *Bell* (2001) the Court of Appeal, whilst apparently approving of Neuberger J's approach in the above case, did not follow the same bold approach.[4] The family home was owned jointly by the husband (H) and wife (W) in law but the wife had only a 10% beneficial interest. H forged W's signature on a mortgage and then left W. She remained in the house with their son for 10 years after H stopped making mortgage repayments and, when the bank sought possession, W was in poor health. The mortgage debt was now £300,000. The court recognised that the law had now changed as the courts were now required to have regard to particular factors set out in section 15 but nevertheless it held that a sale would be ordered here as a 'powerful consideration' was 'whether the creditor is receiving proper recompense for being kept out of his money'. This was clearly not the case. This case appears to show that, as the quotation in the question points out, the case law has apparently not been consistent. However, another way of putting it would be to say that the courts, being given a set of criteria, all of equal importance, are obviously going to reach decisions on the facts of each case.[5]

First National Bank Plc v Achampong [2003] EWCA Civ 487 shows the way in which the courts try to balance the interests of the different parties in applying the factors under section 15(1) of TLATA when the creditor applies for a sale. The house was purchased as the matrimonial home but at the time of the application the marriage had broken down and the parties had not been in contact for many years. Thus the court held that the purpose for which the property was acquired (s. 15(1)(b)) was no longer relevant. One child of the marriage was grown up and no longer in occupation but the other child had a mental disability and, although an adult, still lived at the house. However, there was no clear evidence that her disability meant that she had to continue to live there. There were infant grandchildren in occupation and the court was prepared to regard this as relevant but it was not clear how their interests would be adversely affected if an order for sale was made.[6] Therefore the court held that it would order a sale bearing in mind that if it did not the bank 'will be kept waiting indefinitely' for its share of the property.

In **Edwards v Lloyds TSB Bank Plc** [2004] EWHC 1745 the court dealt with an application by the creditors for a sale of the matrimonial home by granting a postponed order for sale that allowed the wife to continue living in the house until the youngest child reached full age.

Omar (2006) says that disputes between owners and creditors still tend to be resolved in the creditor's favour. However, the decision in **Edwards v Lloyds TSB Bank Plc** certainly took account of the needs of the family[7] and that in **First National Bank Plc v Achampong** might have been different if more evidence had been produced to the court on the situation of members of the family.

It is submitted that Omar's view is too pessimistic and that, although the statement in the question is true, it is not a criticism that the courts have 'not been consistent in those cases . . . in which the rights of creditors are in contest with the rights of co-owners but simply a recognition that there is no one right answer in these cases but instead a number of factors which have to be balanced.[8]

[5] These two sentences do two things: first they remind the examiner that you have not forgotten what the question is asking you about and secondly they make a new point which you now need to follow through in your answer.

[6] As section 15(1) of TLATA sets out a number of criteria for the courts to apply if you are to score highly you need to really research these cases. This passage shows that the cases have been read in detail.

[7] Notice how we have referred to the views in an article and then go on to link this to a case. This approach will really impress your examiner. So many students just pick out a quote from an article, mention it and do not show how it is relevant. Do not be one of them!

[8] It is important that a conclusion brings the arguments together in a succinct way.

✓ **Make your answer stand out**

- It is interesting that in several of the cases (*Bank of Ireland Home Mortgages Ltd* v *Bell* and *First National Bank Plc* v *Achampong*) the county court judge had held very strongly that no order for sale should be made and this was reversed by the Court of Appeal. Have a look at at least one of these county court judgments and contrast it with the approach of the Court of Appeal.

- Mention that in *Mortgage Corporation* v *Shaire* Neuberger J referred to the Law Commission Report (1989) *Transfer of Land, Trusts of Land*, No. 181, which had led to the passage of TLATA, and referred to Para. 12.9, which stated that its aim was not only to consolidate the law but also to rationalise it.

- Read Omar (2006) Security over Co-owned Property and the Creditor's Paramount Status in Recovery Proceedings. *Conveyancer* 157. Although it does not consider the case law under TLATA in much detail, it does provide useful material on the approach in other jurisdictions and this will improve your answer.

- Note that where one of the co-owners is bankrupt then his estate vests in the trustee in bankruptcy (s. 306 Insolvency Act 1986) and he may apply for a sale under s. 14 of TLATA. Mention briefly at the end how this might affect the position – see e.g. *Re Citro* [1991] Ch 142.

- Possible application of the Human Rights Act – Art. 8 Respect for Private and Family Life – see *Barca* v *Mears* [2004] EWHC 2170.

- Note *Bank of Baroda* v *Dhillon* [1998] 1 FLR 524 which deals with the relationship between section 14 and section 15 of TLATA and overriding interests.

! **Don't be tempted to . . .**

- Just set out a list of cases on section 15(1) of TLATA and say nothing on the principles.

- Spend too much time on the facts of the cases and not relate them to principles and in particular the criteria in section 15(1) of TLATA.

- Leave out a mention of what the law was before TLATA.

❓ Question 5

John and Jane are co-habitees and are joint tenants in law and equity of 'Southlands', a detached house. They have one child, Amy, who has a learning difficulty and cannot live independently.

Jane ran a hairdressers' business but, due to some rash expansion plans failing in the recession, she was declared bankrupt in July 2012 and her assets have vested in her trustee in bankruptcy.

It is now May 2013 and Jane has heard that the trustee in bankruptcy is applying for a sale of 'Southlands'.

Advise John and Jane on the likelihood of the trustee in bankruptcy being able to force a sale.

Answer plan

→ Identify ownership of the legal and beneficial interests in the property.

→ Explain the relevant provisions of the Insolvency Act 1986 and apply them to the facts.

→ Stress the different provisions which apply where there is an application for a sale more than one year after the bankruptcy.

→ Consider the possible application of Article 8 of the ECHR.

Diagram plan

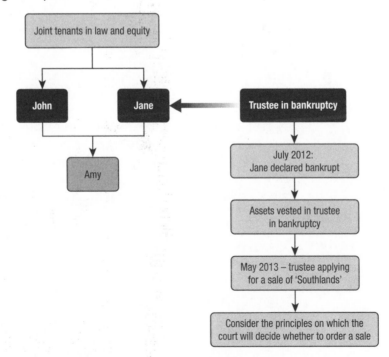

A printable version of this diagram plan is available from www.pearsoned.co.uk/lawexpressqa

Answer

[1] You will not be expected to examine the extent of Jane's beneficial interest in the property but in this opening paragraph you simply need to explain clearly where Jane's assets are in the property.

[2] The point is that as this is not a dispute between the two co-owners we do not need to decide the extent of their respective beneficial interests.

[3] This is an important point and you will lose marks for omitting it: it is obviously sensible to see if a sale can be negotiated before going to court.

[4] This is a typical point which arises in these questions. Check at the very start of your answer if the parties are married/civil partners or not.

The first question is to identify what assets Jane has in the property.[1] She is a legal joint tenant with John and also a joint tenant in equity. An equitable joint tenancy implies that the beneficial interest is in equal shares but since **Stack v Dowden** [2007] UKHL 17 it is possible to displace this presumption in certain cases. However, in this question we are simply required to identify that she has assets.[2] The trustee in bankruptcy has a duty to realise Jane's assets in order to pay off her creditors.

The first step will be that the trustee will see if Jane and John are opposed to a sale.[3] We assume that they will be as if there is a sale they will lose their home and they also have their daughter to consider.

If so the trustee in bankruptcy will have to apply for a sale under section 14 of the Trusts of Land and Trustees Act (TLATA) 1996 which provides that any person who has an interest in property subject to a trust of land may make an application to the court for an order under this section and, as the assets of Jane have vested in the trustee in bankruptcy, they will count as such a person.

On applications for a sale of property the considerations which the court must have regard to are set out in section 335A(2) of the Insolvency Act 1986, which was inserted into this Act by TLATA 1996. This provides that on such an application the court shall make such order as it thinks just and reasonable and then sets out a number of factors which involve trying to balance the needs of the creditors, and the bankrupt and others who may be affected by a sale. The factors which the court must have regard to differ depending on whether the parties are married or civil partners or not, and here John and Jane are not married.[4] In all cases, by section 335A(2)(a) the court must naturally have regard to the interests of the bankrupt's creditors. Section 335A(2)(b) does not apply here as it only applies where the application is made in respect of land which includes a dwelling house which is or has been the home of the bankrupt or the bankrupt's spouse or civil partner or former spouse or former civil partner. Here the parties are co-habitees. If section 335A(2)(b) had applied, then the court could have had regard to a number of factors including the conduct of the parties and the needs and financial resources of the parties and their children. And here the parties have a child, Amy. It would be astonishing and grossly unfair if Amy's needs were not considered and it is suggested that they would be under section 335A(2)(c) which allows the court to consider all the circumstances of the case other than the needs of the bankrupt.[5] Moreover in **Re Citro** [1991] Ch. 142 it was held that the predecessor to section 335A(2), section 336(3) of the Insolvency Act 1986, did apply to unmarried couples.

[5] This is another familiar point in these questions.

The general principle as laid down in **Re Solomon** [1967] Ch 573 HC was that in these cases 'the voice of the trustee in bankruptcy is one which ought to prevail' (Goff J). Here it should be noted that Jane was declared bankrupt in July 2012 and it is now May 2013. It seems unlikely that the trustee in bankruptcy will apply for a sale within a year of the bankruptcy.[6] If he does not then section 335A(3) applies and the court shall assume, unless the circumstances of the case are exceptional, that the interests of the bankrupt's creditors outweigh all other considerations. Thus the principle laid down in **Re Solomon** is in effect applied even more strongly.

[6] Do make a note of when the bankruptcy occurred and the date of the question so that you can see if this point applies. In practice it is generally the case that the application is made after a year of the bankruptcy.

The question is then what are exceptional circumstances.[7] In **Dean v Stout** [2005] EWHC 3315 HC it was held that typically these related to the personal circumstances of one of the owners, such as a medical or mental condition. However, exceptional circumstances were not to be categorised and the court was to make a value judgment after looking at the circumstances. Thus it would not be an exceptional circumstance for a wife with children to be faced with eviction in circumstances where the realisation of her beneficial interest would not produce enough to buy a comparable home. The problem is that although this tells us what will not be exceptional it does not tell us what will be exceptional.

[7] It is vital that you identify this point and show how it has been applied in the case law.

In this case the fact that the parties will lose their home is clearly not exceptional.[8] As Nourse LJ put it in **Re Citro** such cases are 'the melancholy consequences of debt and improvidence with which every civilised society has been familiar'.[9] One arguably exceptional circumstance is that Jane and John have a daughter, Amy, who has a learning difficulty and cannot live independently. The nearest parallel is **Barca v Mears** [2004] EWHC 2170 Ch D where it was argued that a sale should be postponed where the parties had a son with special educational needs. In this case the son was, however, able to live independently and the issue was whether a sale of the house

[8] This does need to be stressed, even if you do not agree!

[9] This is a very useful quotation to include especially as it relates to the possible application of Article 8 of the ECHR as explained below.

would require him to leave his present school. On the facts it would not and indeed a sale was ordered. In this case there is no evidence, unlike in **Barca v Mears**, that the relationship between John and Jane has broken down and it may be that they have sufficient capital to enable them to obtain another home and live as a family. If this was not so and John and Jane would be homeless then this might well count as an exceptional circumstance as Amy then would have to live apart from them, presumably in residential accommodation and be separated from her parents.

The case against a sale will be strengthened if it can be argued that, under the Human Rights Act 1998, Article 8 of the European Convention on Human Rights applies.[10] This provides that 'Everyone has the right to have respect for his private and family life, his home and his correspondence'. In **Barca v Mears** the court held that the approach of the courts to the effect on a sale on family life might not be compatible with Article 8. Thus a shift in emphasis in the interpretation of the Insolvency Act 1986 section 335A, section 336 and section 337 might be necessary to achieve compatibility with a bankrupt's rights under the European Convention on Human Rights 1950. The effect would be that eviction from the family home might sometimes be relied on under the Insolvency Acts as exceptional circumstances.

[10] This is one of the few cases where the Human Rights Act has had an impact on Land Law. You must mention this point in any answer on this topic. However, you should first state the relevant domestic law before turning to the ECHR.

✓ Make your answer stand out

- Clear identification of the crucial statutory provisions and an ability to show how these have been applied in the case law.
- Mention *Re Holliday* [1981] Ch 405 which is one of the very few cases where a sale has not been ordered in an application by a trustee in bankruptcy in this type of case.
- Refer to the Cork Committee (1982) *Insolvency Law and Practice* Cmnd. 8558, especially Paragraphs 1114–1123, and consider if the attitude of the committee is reflected in the provisions of the Insolvency Act 1986 and in the case law.
- Instead of giving details of the facts in *Barca* v *Mears*, just give the decision, which is obviously vital, and then mention other cases which have considered the possible application of the ECHR in these cases. An example is *Nicholls* v *Lan* [2007] 1 FLR 744.

! Don't be tempted to . . .

- Ignore the significance of the application for a sale being likely to be more than a year after the bankruptcy.
- Fail to mention the provisions of the Insolvency Acts before you deal with the cases.
- Forget that the cases are applying the statute law.
- Mention too many cases on this area without explaining the principles.

www.pearsoned.co.uk/lawexpressqa

Go online to access more revision support including additional essay and problem questions with diagram plans, You be the marker questions, and download all diagrams from the book.

Trusts and the home

■ Attack the question

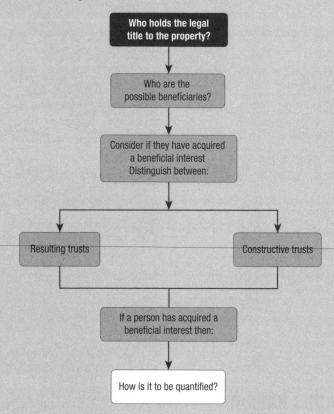

A printable version of this diagram is available from www.pearsoned.co.uk/lawexpressqa

 Question 1

In *Jones* v *Kernott* [2011] UKSC 53 (SC) Lord Wilson said, in reference to disputes as to the beneficial interest in the family home: 'Where equity is driven to impute the common intention, how can it do so other than by a search for the result which the court itself considers fair?'

Discuss.

Answer plan

→ Explain the ways in which the courts have used the word 'intention'.

→ Distinguish between resulting trusts and constructive trusts in relation to the word 'intention'.

→ Look back at cases where intention has not been found e.g. *Burns* v *Burns* and mention *Lloyds Bank* v *Rosset*.

→ Look in detail at the speech of Lady Hale in *Stack* v *Dowden*.

→ Note Lord Neuberger's dissent.

→ Round off by looking at *Jones* v *Kernott*.

Diagram plan

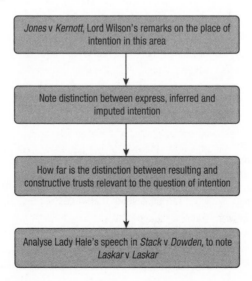

Jones v Kernott, Lord Wilson's remarks on the place of intention in this area

↓

Note distinction between express, inferred and imputed intention

↓

How far is the distinction between resulting and constructive trusts relevant to the question of intention

↓

Analyse Lady Hale's speech in *Stack* v *Dowden*, to note *Laskar* v *Laskar*

A printable version of this diagram plan is available from www.pearsoned.co.uk/lawexpressqa

Answer

The question of whether the courts can base rights to a beneficial interest in the home on the intentions of the parties has bedevilled this area of law. The starting point was ***Pettit v Pettit*** [1970] AC 777 and ***Gissing v Gissing*** [1971] AC 886[1] where the House of Lords attempted to lay down principles governing the acquisition of beneficial interests in the home under an implied trust where previously claims had been based on a purchase money resulting trust.

[1] There is no time in this essay to give details of these cases but you should show the examiner that you are aware of the context of *Stack v Dowden* and *Jones v Kernott.*

Lord Walker in ***Stack v Dowden*** [2007] UKHL 17 HL (para. 17) felt that the crucial issue was 'whether the court must find a real bargain between the parties, or whether it can (in the absence of any sufficient evidence as to their real intentions) infer or impute a bargain'.[2] The problem is with the extended meaning given to the word 'intention' as Lord Walker referred to what the courts could do in the absence of any sufficient evidence as to the real intentions of the parties. Here he first mentioned the possibility of inferring an intention. This appears to link to actual intentions as it means where the court could, in effect, tease out the parties' intentions from their words and conduct. Imputing an intention goes further and seems to allow the courts to say what the intentions of the parties were, even though there is no evidence that that is the case.[3] If we have reached this stage then, as Lord Wilson says, we have reached the stage where the court is simply deciding what is a fair result.

[2] This is the fundamental point around which all the debate really revolves and so it needs to be stressed near the start of an answer of this kind.

[3] The idea of an imputed intention is crucial.

The place of intention in trusts of the home rests to some extent on the question of whether the beneficial interests arise under a constructive trust, a resulting trust or both.[4] Under resulting trusts the beneficial interests of the parties are ascertained by reference to their intentions at the time of acquisition of the property, and these are generally fixed by reference to monetary contributions at that time. The difficulty is that in cases where, for example, cohabiting couples acquire property, they may have given no thought at all to this question. Under the principles of constructive trusts wider factors than merely monetary contributions are considered and the court is not restricted to considering only factors present at the time of purchase.

[4] Although this is not a trusts exam, you do need to be aware of the fundamental difference between resulting and constructive trusts. In addition a mention of this point helps to lift your answer, as mediocre answers will just plough through the case law. You are showing that you are aware of fundamental principles.

In fact an emphasis on the need to discover the parties' intentions can lead to what is arguably injustice. This is seen in ***Burns v Burns***

[1984] Ch 317 CA where the claimant had lived with the defendant for 17 years. They were not married and the house was in the name of him (the defendant). The claimant had not made any direct contribution to the cost of acquisition nor was there evidence of any common intention that the claimant should have a beneficial share. The court held in the absence of either that the claimant had no entitlement to a beneficial interest. The reason for this was the insistence by the court of the need to find a common intention by the parties that the claimant should have a beneficial interest and this was stressed in *Lloyds Bank Plc v Rosset* [1991] 1 AC 107 HL[5] where Lord Bridge said that there were two ways in which this could be demonstrated, both resting on what he called the common intentions of the parties.[6]

There is much common sense in the remarks of Waite J in *Hammond v Mitchell* [1992] 2 All ER 109 HC that the parties were 'too much in love at this time either to count the pennies or pay attention to who was providing them'.[7]

In *Stack v Dowden* it is clear from the speech of Lady Hale, with whom the majority agreed, that she preferred the broader approach of the constructive trust and so would not place the same emphasis on finding the intentions of the parties. She said that 'in law, "context is everything" and the domestic context is very different from the commercial world. Each case will turn on its own facts. Many more factors than financial contributions may be relevant to divining the parties' true intentions' (para. 69). Moreover in *Jones v Kernott* [2011] UKSC 53 (SC)[8] Lord Walker and Lady Hale expressly rejected any presumption of a resulting trust arising from the parties having contributed to the deposit or the rest of the purchase price in unequal shares.

The question is how to find those intentions and here the decision in *Stack v Dowden* begins to unravel.[9] Lady Hale (para. 69) said that the search for intention 'does not enable the court to abandon that search in favour of the result which the court itself considers fair' and she gave a lengthy, and helpful, list of factors which the courts could use to find intention. However, earlier (at para. 59) she said that 'The search is to ascertain the parties' shared intentions, actual, inferred or imputed, with respect to the property in the light of their whole course of conduct in relation to it.' The use of the word 'imputed', as explained above, seems to mean that the court can impute an

[5] You should not spend too long on *Burns* v *Burns* but use it to provide a vivid illustration of how the law can work. It is also important to then move on to consider *Lloyds Bank* v *Rosset* as this gives you a yardstick against which to assess *Stack* v *Dowden*.

[6] Note that we have not said what these two ways are. This is simply for reasons of space and as the law has moved on so much since *Rosset* we have to jettison something to make room for newer cases.

[7] This is a nice vivid quote and easily remembered!

[8] Be sure to include a mention of this case as well as *Stack* v *Dowden* as it is the latest case in this area.

[9] This is a good critical point.

intention to the parties which they may not have had. This looks very much like the notion of 'fairness' which Lady Hale had earlier rejected. Lord Neuberger, however, strongly preferred the resulting trust analysis referring (para. 145) to what he regarded as 'the forbidden territories of imputed intention and fairness'. Indeed in the later case of *Laskar* v *Laskar* he applied the resulting trust principle in a case where property was bought by two members of a family as an investment rather than as a home on the basis that *Stack* v *Dowden* only applied in domestic situations.[10]

[10] Lord Neuberger took a different line from that of Lady Hale in *Stack* v *Dowden* and so it is essential for a good mark to mention his views. Here we have gone one better and shown how his views were applied in a case subsequent to *Stack* v *Dowden*.

Jones v *Kernott* concerned a family home which had been bought in the joint names of an unmarried cohabiting couple who were both responsible for any mortgage, but without any express declaration of their beneficial interests.[11] Thus the normal rule would be that they had a 50:50 beneficial share. This was the same situation as in *Stack* v *Dowden* and thus differed from *Burns* v *Burns* where the claimant was not the owner. The Supreme Court held that the primary search was for what the parties had actually intended and their common intention was to be deduced objectively from their words and conduct. However, where such common intention could not be found, then each party was entitled to that share which the court considered fair having regard to the whole course of dealings between them in relation to the property. This looks like resting the decision on general principles of fairness and indeed the majority did later refer to 'factors which might enable the court to decide what shares had been intended by the parties or were fair'.

[11] It is vital to make it clear that *Stack* v *Dowden* and *Jones* v *Kernott* are different types of cases from e.g. *Burns* v *Burns*.

[12] Here the conclusion arises naturally from the foregoing discussion. Something to aim for!

Lord Wilson, as the question shows, and Lord Kerr, who agreed with him, thought that this whole idea of imputing intention would have been better based simply on fairness. It is difficult to disagree.[12]

✓ Make your answer stand out

- If you have studied family law, or can research it, then why not see how the courts deal with distribution of assets on a divorce or end of a civil partnership. Have we reached the same stage with cohabitees and, if not, should we? Look at *White* v *White* [2001] 1 AC 596. It is arguable that Lady Hale in particular, with her background in family law, is attempting to introduce a similar regime in cases involving cohabitees.

- Dixon (2007) The Never-ending Story: Co-ownership after *Stack* v *Dowden*. *Conveyancer*, 71: 456 – a clear analysis of the case in which the author feels that 'there is little that can be worse' than the law which has resulted.

- Harding (2009) Defending *Stack* v *Dowden*. 73 *Conveyancer* 309. Written from an Australian perspective, the author considers liberal and communitarian approaches and looks at the Australian decision in *Cummins* v *Cummins* (2006) 227 CLR 278.

- Mee (2012) *Jones* v *Kernott*: Inferring and Imputing in Essex. *Conveyancer*, 2: 167.

- Lee (2012) 'And the Waters Began to Subside': Imputing Intention under *Jones* v *Kernott*. *Conveyancer*, 5: 421. This looks at the application of *Jones* v *Kernott* in the later case of *Aspden* v *Elvy* [2012] EWHC 1387.

! Don't be tempted to . . .

- Just give an account of the cases – go for the underlying principles.
- Ignore Lord Neuberger's dissenting speech in *Stack* v *Dowden*.
- Go into the answer without explaining fundamental principles, especially the differences between resulting and constructive trusts.
- Fail to distinguish between acquisition of a beneficial interest and quantification of that interest.

? Question 2

Ted bought 'The Laurels' as a home for himself and his partner Mel. The house was registered in Ted's name and so the mortgage was in Ted's name also as he was the wage earner. It was agreed that as the house was only barely habitable Mel would stay at home and organise the repairs. The other household bills would be paid partly out of Ted's income and partly out of Mel's savings. It was the intention of both of them that, when the repairs were completed, Mel would start work and her income would then go to help paying the household bills and perhaps the mortgage.

Two years later their son Robert was born but as he was disabled Mel needed to spend all her time looking after him and was unable to return to work.

They needed further help in looking after Robert and so it was agreed that Mel's mother Dot would come and help to look after him. An extension was built onto the house to accommodate her and, as Ted and Mel were short of money, Dot agreed to finance this herself.

The relationship between Ted and Mel has broken down and Mel, Robert and Dot wish to leave 'The Laurels' and find another home.

Advise Mel and Dot on whether they have any interest in 'The Laurels' and, if so, on any principles which could be used to determine its extent.

Answer plan

→ Note that the property is registered in Ted's name only and so the claimants can only have a beneficial interest.

→ Mel's claim: application of the factors set out by Lady Hale in *Stack* v *Dowden*.

→ Would the principles set out in *Lloyds Bank* v *Rosset* give a different result?

→ Dot's claim: Are the rules different? Is this a resulting trust claim?

→ Principles used to decide quantification of the beneficial interest: note *Oxley* v *Hiscock* and contrast with those set out in *Stack* v *Dowden*.

Diagram plan

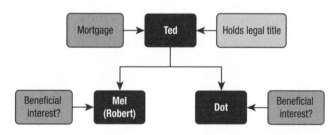

A printable version of this diagram plan is available from www.pearsoned.co.uk/lawexpressqa

Answer

It should first be pointed out that as the parties are unmarried[1] any claim will be under trusts law whereas if they were married it would be under the Matrimonial Causes Act 1973. 'The Laurels' is registered in Ted's name only and so any claim by Mel and Dot can only be to

[1] This will usually be the case in a trusts question but you will gain credit for pointing it out. Note, though, that if the dispute is between the parties and a *third party* such as a mortgagee (as in *Midland Bank v Cooke* [1995] 4 All ER 562), then they may be married or registered civil partners.

[2] This must be your first point in any question on trusts of the home: identify who holds the legal title and, when you have done this, you will be able to see where any trusts will exist.

[3] Almost certainly there will not be an express trust but logically you should first check if there is and you will lose marks if you do not.

[4] This should always be your next one.

[5] And this is the fourth one. This opening paragraph ticks four boxes and, in just over 100 words, you have mentioned five good points and not only earned a lot of marks but neatly cleared the ground for the discussion which follows.

[6] This is an excellent point and will impress the examiner.

[7] You need to show awareness of the two possible types of trust in view of the importance of this issue and the continuing debate.

[8] Before you consider the factors set out by Lady Hale in detail you need to set out the general principle in these cases.

a beneficial interest under a trust.[2] There is no express declaration of trust[3] and indeed if there was it would need to be in writing or evidenced in writing to satisfy section 53(1)(c) of the Law of Property Act (LPA) 1925.[4] As there is no express trust any trust will be implied and, by section 53(2) of the LPA resulting, implied or constructive trusts are exempted from the requirement of writing.[5] Thus in this case it is permissible to look for evidence of a trust other than in written documents. There is some debate on exactly how a trust can be proved in these types of cases.[6] We shall look at the principles set out in **Stack v Dowden** [2007] UKHL 17 first and then apply those in **Lloyds Bank Plc v Rosset** [1991] 1 AC 107. Although the actual decision in **Stack v Dowden** concerned a claim on the quantification of the beneficial interest where the house was held in joint names, the principles set out in particular by Lady Hale, who was in the majority, do seem to be applicable to all claims to the acquisition of a beneficial interest. This was accepted by the Privy Council in **Abbott v Abbott** [2007] UKPC 53 PC.

In this case Mel did not make any contributions to the cost of acquisition nor did she make any contribution to the repayment of the mortgage. In **Stack v Dowden** Lady Hale preferred the constructive trust rather than a resulting trust[7] based on monetary contributions to the cost of acquisition and here this claim will by necessity have to be under a constructive trust.

Lady Hale held that the search is 'for the result which reflects what the parties must, in the light of their conduct, be taken to have intended' and she emphasised that it is not for the court to impose 'its own view of what is fair upon the situation'.[8] In this case there is no evidence of any express discussions between Ted and Mel but, as Lady Hale pointed out, it is possible for a trust to be inferred. Factors mentioned by Lady Hale were 'the purpose for which the home was acquired' and 'the nature of the parties' relationship'. Here it is clear that Ted and Mel intended 'The Laurels' to be a home for them both, as it was agreed that Mel would stay at home and see to the repairs to make the house habitable.[9] Moreover they came to an agreement about payment of the household bills, which shows that the parties arranged their finances together, which was another criterion set out by Lady Hale. Another factor was 'how the purchase was financed, both initially and subsequently' and here, although the

[9] You will lose marks if you simply set out a long list such as the list of possible relevant factors in the speech of Lady Hale. Instead, if you want to impress your examiner, you will spend a short time glancing through the facts of this problem and then thinking about exactly which of the factors could be relevant.

purchase was initially financed by Ted, it was the intention of both of them that when the repairs were completed Mel would start work and her income would then go to help paying the household bills and perhaps the mortgage. It was the fact that their son was disabled which meant that Mel was unable to do this but this does not detract from what their intention was. Moreover another factor of Lady Hale's was 'whether they had children for whom they both had responsibility to provide a home' and the fact that they did have a child and that Mel stayed at home to look after Robert is further evidence that they regarded themselves as a family unit.

Thus on the basis of the majority in **Stack v Dowden** it is submitted that clearly Mel does have a beneficial interest in 'The Laurels'.

Dot's claim is different as she paid for an extension to be built on to the house so that she could come and help look after Robert. There is no doubt that Dot's claim is clearer than Mel's and that there is a presumption that she will have an interest under a resulting trust as she has, in effect, contributed to the present value of 'The Laurels'.[10]

[10] The significant point is that Dot's claim is really a resulting trust one so do make this clear.

Thus any increase in the value of the house attributable to the extension will result back to her on trust. This presumption can be displaced by evidence that only a loan was intended (**Dyer v Dyer** (1788) 2 Cox Eq Cas 92) but here the evidence is that Dot was not just coming to live at 'The Laurels' but joining in the tasks of the household.

[11] Students often ask if they should remember dates of cases. The answer is in general no but here is an example of where an answer is improved by at least knowing the *order in which decisions occurred.*

In **Thomson v Humphrey** [2009] EWHC 3576, which of course post-dated **Stack v Dowden**,[11] the court applied **Lloyds Bank v Rosset** where Lord Bridge held that a constructive trust would be implied if, at any time prior to acquisition or exceptionally at some later date, there was any agreement, arrangement or understanding between the parties that the property was to be shared beneficially. However, **Stack v Dowden** was followed by the Supreme Court decision in **Jones v Kernott** where the approach in **Stack** was followed. Thus it is most unlikely that **Rosset** is still good law.

[12] You must deal with this issue in any question on trusts of the home but of course you must first decide if any interest has been acquired. So this point will often come towards the end of your answer.

Finally, there is the question of the quantification of Mel and Dot's beneficial interests.[12] In **Oxley v Hiscock** [2004] EWCA Civ 546 Chadwick LJ in the Court of Appeal spoke of 'what would be a fair share for each party having regard to the whole course of dealing between them in relation to the property?' In **Stack v Dowden** Lady Hale approved the statement of the Law Commission (2002) in

[13] Although this report has, for the moment anyway, been shelved, there is still the possibility of legislation and you should mention it.

Sharing Homes, A Discussion Paper, para. 4.27, referring to a 'holistic approach' to quantification,[13] undertaking a survey of the whole course of dealing between the parties and taking account of all conduct which throws light on the question what shares were intended. This approach was followed by the Supreme Court in *Jones* v *Kernott* [2011] UKSC 53 (SC). Thus all the factors mentioned in considering if Mel had a beneficial interest at all will be relevant here also.

✓ Make your answer stand out

- Remember to deal first with whether Mel, and later Dot have a beneficial interest at all.
- Look at *Jones* v *Kernott* and at what the Supreme Court decided as well as the judgments of Lords Kerr and Wilson, whose reasoning differed from the majority.
- Mention in relation to Dot's claim the decision in *Re Sharpe* [1980] 1 WLR 219 which would reinforce her claim.
- Read Gardner (2004) Quantum in *Gissing* v *Gissing* Constructive Trusts. *LQR*, 120: 541. This article deals with the decision in *Oxley* v *Hiscock* on quantification of the beneficial interests and is valuable as most articles on this area deal with acquisition of a beneficial interest.
- Consider the argument in the above article that in these types of cases as Gardner puts it: 'the true driver of these trusts is and should be the ethic of the parties' relationship'. This would contrast with a search for the intentions of the parties.

! Don't be tempted to . . .

- Mechanically list all the factors listed by Lady Hale in *Stack* v *Dowden* as being of possible relevance to the question of whether a beneficial interest was acquired. Instead select the relevant ones and apply them to the question.
- Make it clear that first you are going to look at acquisition of the beneficial interests.
- Ignore the question of the quantification of the beneficial interests.
- Remember to deal with the two claims (Mel and Dot) separately.

Question 3

Critically evaluate the different directions which English law on beneficial interests in the family home might take in the future.

Answer plan

→ Evaluate possible developments along the lines of *Stack* v *Dowden*.

→ Consider, by contrast, a possible return to the resulting trust idea.

→ Evaluate the possibility of statute law taking over from the law of trusts: look at the proposals of the Law Commission (2007) in *Cohabitation: The Financial Consequences of Relationship Breakdown*, No. 307.

→ Evaluation of how other jurisdictions deal with this – Canada, Australia, New Zealand.

→ Summing up.

Diagram plan

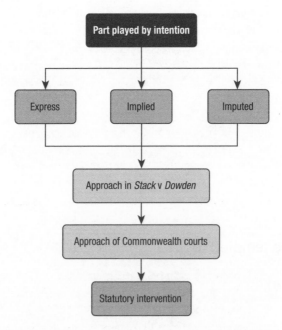

A printable version of this diagram plan is available from www.pearsoned.co.uk/lawexpressqa

Answer

There is no doubt that English law has found it extremely difficult to find a satisfactory way of dealing with claims to a beneficial interest in the home. The search began forty years ago[1] with the decisions of the House of Lords in *Pettit and Pettit* [1970] AC 777 and *Gissing* **v Gissing** [1971] AC 886 and then continued through a restatement of the law, again by the House of Lords, in ***Lloyds Bank Plc* v *Rosset*** [1991] 1 AC 107 and then to the decision, also by the House of Lords, in ***Stack* v *Dowden*** [2007] UKHL 17, followed by that of the Supreme Court in ***Jones* v *Kernott*** [2011] UKSC 53. Yet there is still debate.

The fault lines are really between those who would argue for an approach based on the intentions of the parties, whether express or implied, and an approach based on wider considerations such as imputed intention.[2] Another way of looking at the debate is to ask if the law should be founded in rewarding the consequences of a relationship or should be based on the intentions of the parties. (See Gardner (1993)). Harding (2009) seeks to refocus the debate around the concepts of liberal and communitarian approaches. He argues that a liberal approach means upholding personal autonomy and in this context means promoting the concept of reasonable expectation. By contrast a communitarian approach would mean that, as he puts it, 'the basis on which a person makes a claim to her home against her cohabiting partner is different from the basis on which such a person may make such a claim against a stranger'. Thus a communitarian approach would emphasise precisely community. In terms of the law of trusts, an approach based on the intentions of the parties would indicate the use of a resulting trust and an approach based on wider considerations would indicate the use of a constructive trust.

The present approach set out by Lady Hale in ***Stack* v *Dowden*** is, in her words, to search 'for the result which reflects what the parties must, in the light of their conduct, be taken to have intended' and she emphasised that it is not for the court to impose 'its own view of what is fair upon the situation'.[3] This looks like an approach based on intention or, as Harding would put it, a liberal approach. However, it is not clear that this is so, as Lady Hale also said earlier 'The search

[1] Although some may object that we should, in this question, be looking to the future and not the past, it is of course impossible to do this without saying something about the problems which the law has had in this area. If there had been no problems, this question would probably not have been asked!

[2] A poor answer would at once take refuge in a recital of cases but if you are aiming for a really good pass you need to first sketch in the general background to the debate and this paragraph seeks to do that. You then have a structure for your answer as you can look at the cases through the prism of the two approaches set out here.

[3] Note that we have not set out the facts of *Stack* v *Dowden* as they would not assist the argument. Instead we have picked out what seems to be the ratio of Lady Hale's speech but then, later in the same paragraph, pointed out that elsewhere she said something which seemed to indicate a different *ratio*. This analytical approach will gain you marks so adopt it whenever you can.

is to ascertain the parties' shared intentions, actual, inferred or imputed, with respect to the property in the light of their whole course of conduct in relation to it.' The use of the word 'imputed' seems to give power to the courts to impute an intention to the parties which they may not have had. This point was made by Lords Kerr and Wilson in the subsequent Supreme Court decision in **Jones** v **Kernott** and the result is that the present law in England is unclear.[4] Are we in fact moving to a jurisdiction based on fairness and is the talk of 'imputed intention' just a cover for this?

[4] Do not just say that the law is unclear but give evidence for this view as here.

To decide where the law might go in future we can turn to Canada[5] where the leading case is **Pettkus** v **Becker** (1980) 117 DLR (3rd) 257 where a farm had been bought out of the man's savings but this was only possible because his partner had paid all their living expenses out of their joint earnings and had also contributed to the running of the farm. Dickson J, who delivered the majority judgment, held that 'The principle of unjust enrichment lies at the heart of the constructive trust'. In this context he was referring to the remedial constructive trust based on a general power of the court to 'achieve a result consonant with good conscience' (**Rathwell** v **Rathwell** (1978) 83 DLR (3rd) 289. A later case (**Peter** v **Beblow** (1993) 101 DLR (4th) 621) shows the application of this principle to the provision of domestic services by the woman as 'housekeeper, homemaker and stepmother' and the court ordered that, as these services were an enrichment to the man, the home should be transferred into the woman's name.

[5] This question is clearly asking you to look at what approach is used in other jurisdictions. Although it is only possible to give a snapshot, this answer has selected three jurisdictions and in each case selected a leading case and, most important, the principle of law which is applied.

In the Australian case of **Baumgartner** v **Baumgartner** (1987) 62 ALJR 29 an unmarried couple pooled incomes to meet their living expenses and the purchase of a house which was put in the man's name. They separated and the court held that the woman was entitled to a 45% share, corresponding to the amount of pooled income which she had contributed. The *ratio* of the decision was unconscionability and the court referred to **Muchinski** v **Dodds** (1985) 160 CLR 583 where Deane J referred to the principle of joint endeavour: this means that where there is a joint endeavour which has failed and one party has contributed money or other property to the endeavour which it was not intended that the other should retain, then equity will not permit him to do so. The New Zealand decision in **Gilles** v **Keogh** [1989] 2 NZLR 327 is based on the concept of meeting the reasonable expectations of the parties reinforced by evidence of direct or indirect contributions of either a monetary or non-monetary kind.

In all these cases there is a much wider approach than has been adopted by the courts in England, with the relationship of the parties as the starting point rather than a narrow search for what they intended. This is therefore one direction where English law might develop.[6]

The other possibility is that statute law might eventually take over from case law.[7] There are precedents for this, for example, the De Facto Relationships Act, a New South Wales statute of 1984, provides that the basis of the jurisdiction of the courts is whether it would be just and equitable to make an order adjusting the interests of de facto partners in property.

Legislation did at one time seem likely in England following the Law Commission Report (2007) *Cohabitation: The Financial Consequences of Relationship Breakdown*. This proposed a scheme where parties to a relationship could claim a share in property on the basis of economic advantage or disadvantage.

The effect would have been to widen the net for possible claimants but the Government announced that it was delaying any implementation of the scheme until it had assessed research findings on the effect of the Family Law (Scotland) Act 2006 which has similar provisions.[8]

What is clear is that none of these schemes, whether statutory or based on case law, use the intention approach as a model. The conclusion must be that the law is likely to develop in a broadly based direction with the relationship of the parties at its centre.

[6] At this stage you need to sum up the approaches of the courts in other jurisdictions and then relate this to the question.

[7] The examiner is obviously expecting you to deal with statute law also especially as some statutory regulation of this area still remains a possibility in England.

[8] The decision in *Stack* v *Dowden* has also made it less likely that there will be legislation on the basis that if the courts are developing the law satisfactorily then why bother with legislation?

✓ Make your answer stand out

■ There have been many academic articles on this area. There is obviously not the time to include references to all of them in this answer but here are some suggestions for how to make your answer stand out:

  □ Look at Gardner (1993) Rethinking Family Property. *LQR*, 109: 263. Although the law has moved on a great deal since then this article does provide an excellent analysis of the law as at that date and in particular of Commonwealth decisions. →

- ☐ See Rotherham (2004) The Property Rights of Unmarried Co-habitees: A Case for Reform. *Conveyancer* 268. You could follow the article by Gardner by this one. It was written when the idea of statutory intervention in this area was much more likely than it is now.

- ☐ Law Commission Report (2007) *Cohabitation: The Financial Consequences of Relationship Breakdown*, No. 307. You must look at this if you want to be prepared to attempt this type of question. The summary is a good place to start – but not to end!

- ☐ Etherton (2008) Constructive Trusts: A New Model for Equity and Unjust Enrichment. *CLJ* 265 and Etherton (2009) Constructive Trusts and Proprietary Estoppel: The Search for Clarity and Principle. *Conveyancer*, 73: 104 are both essential for a good mark. These look at how these types of cases should be classified and at their relationship with resulting trusts, constructive trusts, proprietary estoppel and unjust enrichment'.

- ☐ Harding (2009) Defending *Stack* v *Dowden*. *Conveyancer*, 73: 309 has some excellent material on recent Australian decisions, especially the important one of *Trustees of the Property of Cummins* v *Cummins* (2006) CLR 278 which you could integrate into your answer.

! Don't be tempted to . . .

- ■ Plunge into an account of the present law without setting the scene.
- ■ Forget to mention the Law Commission Report No. 307.
- ■ Omit discussion of the theoretical issues. Instead you should try to integrate them into your answer.
- ■ Forget to give the facts of some (but not all) of the cases you mention to show how the law works.

www.pearsoned.co.uk/lawexpressqa

 Go online to access more revision support including additional essay and problem questions with diagram plans, You be the marker questions, and download all diagrams from the book.

Licences and estoppel

5

How this topic may come up in exams

There have been two very important House of Lords decisions on estoppel and so be prepared for either or both essay or problem questions on this. A problem question on estoppel will involve a discussion of the concept of detriment, as well as other points, and detriment can also appear as a topic on its own for a essay question.

Licences lend themselves to an essay on the extent to which licences are interests in land, and on the extent to which they can be enforced against third parties. Licences and estoppel can, of course, appear in the same question.

■ Attack the question

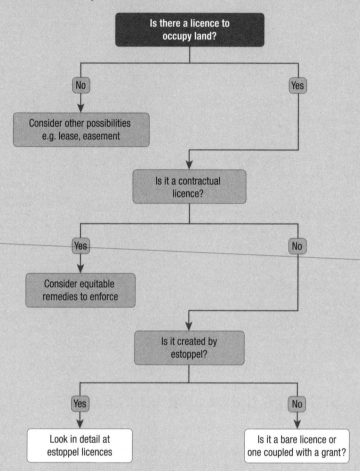

A printable version of this diagram is available from www.pearsoned.co.uk/lawexpressqa

❓ Question 1

John runs a car breaker's yard, and in 2007 he was given a licence by Steve to use part of Steve's land to store cars. The licence was in writing and was stated to run for 10 years at an annual fee of £1,000. John then erected a shed to store some of the cars. Steve saw the shed and said, 'That looks a nice building'.

In 2010 Steve decided that he needed the land as he was expanding his own business and he told John that he would need to vacate the land in three months.

John wishes to remain and asks your advice.

Would your answer differ if Steve had sold the land to Roger in 2009 and it was Roger who wished to terminate the licence?

Answer plan

➡ Identify the main features of licences and mention the possibility of a lease.

➡ Outline the rules on termination of a licence and assess the equitable remedies to restrain a breach.

➡ Is there the possibility of estoppel?

➡ Explain why the licence does not bind Roger.

➡ Conclusion.

Diagram plan

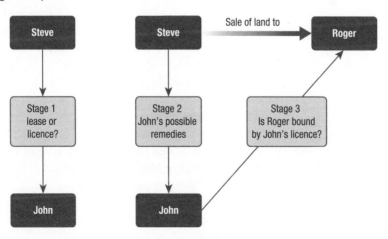

A printable version of this diagram plan is available from www.pearsoned.co.uk/lawexpressqa

Answer

Steve has granted John a licence but it is worth checking first if it could amount to a lease.[1] However, John's licence only extends to part of the land and so John does not have exclusive possession. In **Street v Mountford** [1985] AC 809 HL this was identified as one of the essential indications of a lease and so it is submitted that John only has a licence. This is important, as a licence only confers a personal right in the land and not, as in the case of a lease, a proprietary right. Exceptions are where the licence is coupled with a grant, for example, if John had been granted a profit, which does not apply here or where a licence arises by estoppel,[2] which is a possibility here and which will be considered later. At the moment, we will proceed on the basis that John has a contractual licence as his consideration is the payment of an annual fee of £1,000.[3]

In 2010 Steve told John to vacate the land in three months although the licence is due to expire in 2017, having been granted in 2007 for ten years. This is obviously in breach of the licence, but what remedies does John have? As a licence does not confer a proprietary interest, John has no interest in the land itself and so his remedies must be contractual. In **Wood v Leadbitter** (1845) 13 M & W 838 HC it was held that, at common law, a licence can be revoked at any time even though this is in breach of the licence. Thus Steve, on this basis, need not give John three months' notice. If Steve did actually eject John, John would have no right to claim for damages for assault as this was the claim which failed in **Wood v Leadbitter**. However, John would be able to claim damages for breach of contract (**Kerrison v Smith** [1897] 2 QB 445 HC). These would be assessed on the normal basis for contractual damages as laid down in **Hadley v Baxendale** (1854) 9 Exch 341 HC.[4] Moreover, he is entitled to reasonable packing up time[5] and so does not become a trespasser at once. (See Lord MacDermott in **Winter Garden Theatre (London) Ltd v Millennium Productions Ltd** [1948] AC 173 HL.) Thus, if Steve tries to eject John without giving him any time to remove his property and, possibly, make alternative arrangements for their storage, John will have a claim against him in tort for, for example, assault if Steve tries to forcibly eject him.

However, John may be able to remain on the land until 2017 if he is able to utilise equitable remedies. The status of a contractual

[1] A mention of the possibility of a lease shows the kind of intelligent lateral thinking that will earn you extra marks. It is best to mention it at the start as it enables you to bring out the essential feature of a licence, which you need to mention for your answer, and contrast it with a lease.

[2] It is worth raising these two possibilities, if only briefly, as if a licence fell into either of these categories the answer would be different. As it is, point out now that estoppel could be relevant but leave it till later.

[3] A small point: if you just say: 'John has a contractual licence' the examiner will ask 'Why?'. A mark lost. So say why!

[4] Rather than speculate unprofitably on just what damages John might claim on the facts (we do not have enough information) gain marks by referring to another area of law, in this case, contract, which you have probably studied.

[5] This point is often missed by students so a mention of it will certainly improve your marks!

licensee has improved with the availability of equitable remedies in all courts following the Judicature Acts 1873–5. In ***Winter Garden Theatre (London) Ltd v Millennium Productions Ltd*** [1948] AC 173 HL it was recognised that at common law there can be an implied term that a licence will not be revoked until the end of the specified period unless the licensee is in breach of the licence. Thus, if the licence is wrongfully revoked, the court can restrain this by the grant of an injunction.[6] This term was not implied in the ***Winter Gardens*** case as there was an express term allowing termination on one month's notice which the court regarded as reasonable. Here there seems to be no express term allowing revocation on notice and so, as there is no evidence of breach by John, he can seek an injunction to restrain the termination of the licence by Steve until 2017. The court does have discretion whether to grant an injunction; it did not do so, for example, in ***Thompson v Park*** [1944] KB 408 HC[7] where breach of a personal sharing arrangement was not restrained by injunction, but this is a commercial arrangement and there seems no reason why one would not be granted. Specific performance is also available (***Verrall v Great Yarmouth Council*** [1981] QB 202 HC) but this would be more appropriate where, for example, Steve had made the agreement to grant the licence but had not carried it out. There would also be the possibility of equitable damages in lieu of an injunction (Chancery Amendment Act 1858).

If Steve had sold the land to Roger, the law on termination of the licence is the same but there is the preliminary question of whether the licence binds Roger. As we mentioned above, contractual licences do not create a proprietary interest in land and so, in general, they are not binding on third parties. An example is ***King v David Allen*** [1916] 2 AC 54 HL where a licence to place advertisements on the wall of a cinema did not bind a third party. In ***Errington v Errington*** [1952] 1 All ER 149 CA it was held by Denning LJ that where, in that case, a person took land with notice of a contractual licence, he or she could be bound by it in equity. But the decision on that point[8] has been held to be wrong. John may have more success if he relies on authority starting with ***Bannister v Bannister*** [1948] 2 All ER 133 CA and continued by ***Binions v Evans*** [1972] Ch 359 CA that equity may impose a constructive trust if he can show that on the sale of the land by Steve to Roger there was a clear intention that Roger should give effect to John's

[6] It is vital to link these two points: the courts cannot simply grant an injunction. There must be evidence, in this context, of an actual or threatened breach of contract. The development of the implied term supplies this.

[7] This point is often forgotten by students especially if they are not studying equity. If you mention equitable remedies at any point then you will lose marks if you do not also mention that they are discretionary. The addition of a case here which is relevant but in fact not well known will boost your marks.

[8] Where there is more than one issue in a case, it is important to single out the one which applies to your answer and to only deal with that, as we have done here.

[9] There is no need to mention the reasoning of Denning MR in *Binions* v *Evans* as this was disapproved by the Court of Appeal in *Ashburn*. Instead a good student will mention the explanation of the decision in *Binions* by Fox LJ in *Ashburn* as this represents the law.

[10] The facts of *Binions* v *Evans* are not needed – just this point.

[11] A quick reading of the question will show you that an estoppel claim is very unlikely to succeed, but the mention of the building of the shed by John is enough to show that you are expected to mention it.

[12] It would be tempting to refer to section 116 in more detail but time is likely to be lacking! At least show that you are aware of the position concerning registered and unregistered land.

licence[9] (see Fox LJ in ***Ashburn Anstalt* v *Arnold*** [1988] 2 All ER 147 CA). It would help John if Roger paid a reduced price for the land, as happened in ***Binions* v *Evans*** precisely because part of it was occupied by John.[10] If equity does impose a constructive trust, John could argue that, if title to the land is registered, then he has an overriding interest as he is an occupier who has an equitable interest in the land. If title is unregistered, he could argue that Roger is bound by his equitable interest as he is a purchaser for value with notice.

Finally, there is the question whether John can claim that he has a licence by estoppel.[11] Estoppel requires persons claiming it to show that they acted on a representation by the other party to their detriment. Although John built a shed on the land and Steve saw it and approved of it, there is no evidence that he was in any way encouraged to build it by Steve and so John did not act on any representation by Steve. It is submitted that estoppel does not apply. If it did, and if title is registered, John could claim that Roger is bound by the estoppel under section 116 of the LRA 2002. If title is unregistered John would claim that Roger is bound if he purchased with notice.[12]

Accordingly, John may claim damages for revocation of his licence by Steve and may be able to claim an injunction to actually prevent its revocation at all. Whether Roger is bound will depend on establishing the existence of a constructive trust.

Make your answer stand out

- Discuss exclusive possession as a requirement for a valid lease.
- Clearly discuss the current law as stated in *Ashburn Anstalt* v *Arnold*.
- Discuss the need for a representation in estoppel in the light of *Thorner* v *Major*.
- Include the possibility of future developments which might lead to an occupational contractual licence having the status of a proprietary interest.
- Read the judgment of Fox LJ in *Ashburn* where you will see that he thought that the decision in *Errington* could be justified on three other possible grounds. There is no need at this stage to examine these but you will increase your marks if you show that at least you are aware of this.

! **Don't be tempted to . . .**

- Confuse the right of the licensee to reasonable packing up time with a right to reasonable notice of termination of the actual licence.

- Discuss *Hurst* v *Picture Theatres Ltd* [1915] 1 KB 1 CA which tried to use the idea of a licence coupled with a grant to extend the status of contractual licences. This is no longer good law.

- Mix up common law remedies with equitable ones.

- Divert your answer into a discussion of the facts and detailed reasoning in *Binions* v *Evans*.

- Overlook the different rules which apply if title to the land is registered or unregistered and estoppel is claimed.

- Miss out estoppel altogether or spend too long on it.

Question 2

'Just how proprietary is the modern licence? There is no entirely clear or complete answer to this controversial question.' (Gray and Gray (2005) *Elements of Land Law* (4th edn) p. 312)

With reference to decided cases, discuss the principles of law governing the extent to which a licence may be considered to be a proprietary interest in land.

Diagram plan

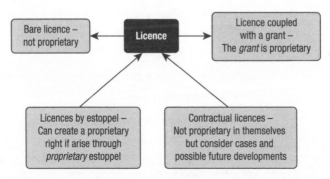

A printable version of this diagram plan is available from www.pearsoned.co.uk/lawexpressqa

Answer plan

→ Explain the traditional view that a licence is not an interest in land.

→ Contractual licences – can they be an interest in land?

→ Explore the cases where licences have been enforced through the mechanism of a constructive trust.

→ Explain how section 116, LRA 2002 affects estoppel licences.

→ Conclusion – can a licence ever be an interest in land?

Answer

The fundamental point is that English law arrived at a list of proprietary interests in land many years ago and is reluctant to add to that list. This explains why licences are not regarded as proprietary despite many attempts to make them so. In this essay I will argue that this reluctance of English law should be overcome and that some types of licences should have the status of proprietary interests in land.[1] A proprietary interest in land has the capacity to bind a purchaser of the land but by contrast a mere personal interest cannot do so. Thus a right arising only by contract is personal. The argument is then that in some circumstances a licence should be capable of binding a purchaser.

[1] The effect of granting proprietary status would be that the right bound third parties. The main area where this is significant is contractual licences where there is a right of occupation.

The traditional view is that this is not so (***Thomas v Sorrell*** (1673) Vaugh 330 HC). In ***Street v Mountford*** [1985] 2 All ER 289 HL Lord Templeman said, 'A licence does not create an estate in the land to which it relates but only makes an act lawful which would otherwise be unlawful.' The effect is that a licence simply prevents the licensee from being regarded as a trespasser. Thus, in ***King v David Allen*** [1916] 2 AC 54 HL a licence to place advertisements on the wall of a cinema did not bind a third party.

However, there are different types of licence and it is submitted that this statement is not necessarily true in relation to all of them.

It is true that bare licences cannot confer any proprietary interest in the land. A bare licence is merely a personal permission of the owner of land to enter the land to, for example, attend a party, and it would be extraordinary if it conferred any proprietary interest. On the other hand, a licence coupled with the grant of an interest in the land, such as a licence to enter on land to exercise a profit à prendre, certainly does have a proprietary character but this arises because of its link with a recognised proprietary right rather than because of its status as a licence. The question is really concerned with two other types of licence, contractual licence and licence arising by estoppel.[2]

[2] It would be easy here to simply plough through the categories of licences and say in each case if they amounted to a proprietary interest. This would be a waste of time which could be better spent on gaining marks in discussing the cases where there is the possibility of a licence amounting to a proprietary interest. So in this paragraph we have quickly disposed of two categories where the position needs little discussion.

A contractual licence arises where the right to enter land arises by contract. The rights of a contractual licensee have gradually increased as a result of the availability of equitable remedies since the Judicature Acts (1873–5). In *Wood* v *Leadbitter* (1845) 13 M & W 838 HC it was held that at common law a contractual licence could be revoked at any time and the licensee had no remedy, but in *Verrall* v *Great Yarmouth Council* [1981] QB 202 HC the equitable remedy of specific performance was granted to restrain the decision of the council to cancel the licence of a hall. Although this development does not mean that licences have a proprietary status, it does show how equity can intervene to improve the rights of a licensee and we will return to this point later.[3]

[3] Do not leave the examiner guessing. Show that your answer is thought out by flagging up that you know what to write later on.

At the same time, there have been attempts to argue that a contractual licence should have proprietary status. In *Errington* v *Errington* [1952] 1 All ER 149 CA a daughter and son-in-law occupied a house under a contractual licence where the father promised that, if they paid off the mortgage on it, he would transfer it to them. After his death the daughter continued to occupy the house and her licence was held binding on the mother who had inherited the house.[4] Denning LJ held that the couple had 'a contractual right, or at any rate, an equitable right, to occupy the house to remain as long as they paid the instalments'. Thus, he lifted contractual rights into equitable rights which of course, can create an interest in land. As title in the house was unregistered and the mother had notice of their equitable right, it followed that it bound her.

[4] Concentrate on the essential point that the licence bound a third party, i.e. the mother.

This decision was disapproved by the Court of Appeal in *Ashburn Anstalt* v *Arnold* and in *Camden LBC* v *Shortlife Community Housing Ltd* (1992) 90 LGR 358 CA, Millett LJ considered the idea that a contractual licence could bind third parties as 'heretical'. Thus, it can be concluded that a contractual licence in itself does not confer a proprietary interest in the land.

In **Binions v Evans** [1972] Ch 359 CA, Denning MR tried the different argument that a contractual licence could be held subject to a constructive trust so as to create a proprietary interest and bind third parties. Here Mrs Evans had been allowed to occupy a house under a contractual licence but it was then sold, although the buyers paid a reduced price as they took subject to her licence. This payment of a lower price meant that that Denning MR's decision was considered correct on the facts by Fox LJ in **Ashburn Arnold v Anstalt** on the general basis that equity can impose a constructive trust to prevent unconscionable conduct but the use of a constructive trust to elevate a contractual licence to a proprietary interest has been disapproved.[5]

The one area where a licence can be said to create a proprietary interest[6] is where that licence arises through proprietary estoppel as in **Inwards v Baker** [1965] 1 All ER 446 CA. This has added significance where title to the land is registered. Section 116 of the LRA 2002 provides that, where the court determines that an estoppel has arisen, it takes effect from the moment it arises and so if a person is in occupation under a licence they may have an overriding interest which can[7] bind a purchaser. This confirms that, in this situation, estoppel licences can be regarded as having a proprietary nature. However, whether equity by estoppel exists is in the discretion of the court (see e.g. **Jennings v Rice** [2002] EWCA Civ 159 CA) and it is open to a court to hold that a licence cannot be enforced against a third party.

The conclusion must be that this is an unsatisfactory area of the law. There is the possibility that in time a contractual licence may evolve into a proprietary interest in the same way as restrictive covenants did with the decision in **Tulk v Moxhay** (1848) 2 Ph 774 HC.[8] We have already seen that the law has extended the rights of contractual licensees to the grant of equitable remedies to prevent the revocation of a licence in breach of contract. Could the law now go further and provide that where the licence gives rights of occupation it confers a proprietary interest in the land?

At the moment the quotation in the question is correct. There is no 'clear or comprehensive answer' to the question of whether a licence creates a proprietary interest in land.[9]

[5] Try to bring out the distinction between Denning MR's reasoning that, in effect, the starting point is the need to enforce a contractual licence (unorthodox) and the general principle that a constructive trust may be imposed where there has been unconscionable conduct (orthodox). If you are clear on this, it will certainly add to your marks.

[6] Note that we always come back to the phrase 'proprietary interest' – this is the phrase in the question and so we must continually link our answer to it.

[7] Note that we have not said 'will' bind a purchaser as this will depend on the operation of Schedule 3, Paragraph 2 of the LRA 2002. (See Chapter 2.) A small point but one which an examiner will pick up on!

[8] This kind of point will certainly impress the examiner. You are showing that you have researched this area and also you are demonstrating the capacity to think laterally across the syllabus by mentioning another area.

[9] Do not forget to end with a reference to the words of the question.

✓ Make your answer stand out

- Refer to academic discussion on the enforceability of licences and their status as proprietary interests. An excellent article is that by Dewar (1986) Licences and Land Law: An Alternative View. *MLR* 741.

- Discuss the significance of section 116 of the LRA in asserting the proprietary character of estoppel licences – see Law Commission Report (2001) No. 271 (paras 5.29–5.32).

- Consider statute law which treats a contractual licence, especially one to occupy, on the same level as a lease, e.g. section 3(2A) and 2(B) of the Protection from Eviction Act 1977.

- Emphasise the contribution of equity and the availability of equitable remedies in all courts in improving the position of licensees.

- Mention possible use of Art. 8(1) of the ECHR (right to respect for the home) by a contractual licensee whose residential licence is terminated without notice.

! Don't be tempted to . . .

- Give a list of types of licence without discussion of the underlying issue.
- Start without explaining exactly what is meant by a 'proprietary interest'.
- Fail to distinguish between the extent to which types of licences can create a proprietary interest.
- Assume that the decisions in all the cases still represent the law. If you read the answer, you will see that they may not, e.g. *Errington* v *Errington*. Make this clear.
- Leave out a reference to the significance of section 116 of the LRA 2002.

❓ Question 3

Doris lived alone in a large house 'Redlands'. Her husband, Arthur had died and she asked her son, Jim, and his wife, Sally, to come and live with her. They agreed and sold their own house. When they moved into 'Redlands' Jim and Sally gradually started to care more for Doris as she got older and Sally gave up her full-time job and took a part-time one to enable her to do this. Doris often said to Jim and Sally: 'You are very good to me. When I am gone you will have a home of your own'. Jim and Sally took this to mean that Doris would leave them 'Redlands' and Jim started to do some work on the house such as installing a stair lift at his own expense when Doris found climbing the stairs difficult.

Doris has died and her will leaves all her property to the League of Friends of Sick Cats. Redlands is valued at current prices at £500,000.

Advise Jim and Sally on their chances of success in an action to claim that the house should belong to them.

Answer plan

→ Explain the principle that there is no enforceable promise at common law and so we need to rely on estoppel.

→ Was there a representation?

→ Did Jim and Sally rely on it to their detriment? Would it be unconscionable for it to be withdrawn?

→ Possible award by the court.

→ Possibility of a claim based on a remedial constructive trust.

Diagram plan

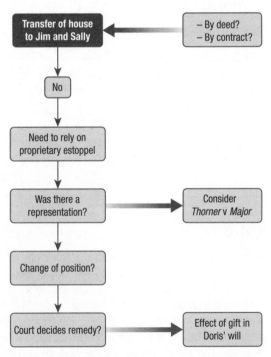

A printable version of this diagram plan is available from www.pearsoned.co.uk/lawexpressqa

Answer

Under section 52 (1) of the LPA 1925 a deed is required to convey a legal estate or interest in land and there is no evidence that Doris executed a deed during her lifetime conveying the house to Jim and Sally. Nor was there any contract, which in any event needs to satisfy the requirements of section 2 of the Law of Property (Miscellaneous Provisions) Act 1989. Therefore, in order to claim the house, Jim and Sally must rely on equity and, in this case, the doctrine of proprietary estoppel.[1]

The first element of an estoppel claim is to show that there was a representation, express or implied, by Doris to Jim and Sally that they would inherit the house.[2] Doris often said to Jim and Sally: 'You are very good to me. When I am gone you will have a home of your own'. Is this a sufficient representation by Doris? We are told that Jim and Sally took this to mean that Doris would leave them: 'Redlands' but was it reasonable for Jim and Sally to think this?

The leading case is **Thorner v Major** [2009] UKHL 18 HL where D had worked at P's farm for no payment from 1976 onwards and, although no express representation had ever been made, D relied on various hints and remarks made by P over the years, which he claimed led him to believe that he was to inherit the farm. Also, in 1990 P had handed D a bonus notice relating to two policies on P's life, saying 'that's for my death duties'.

Lord Walker said in **Thorner v Major** that what is sufficient is 'hugely dependent on context' and here it was held that, as this was a family-type case and moreover between 'taciturn farming folk', the lack of an absolutely clear representation did not matter as in the context it was clear that P intended D to have the farm. In this case the context is[3] that Doris asked Jim and Sally to come and live with her and they then sold their own house which meant that they had no home of their own. Could it be argued that at that stage there was an implicit representation[4] by Doris that she would leave them her house and that this implicit representation only became explicit later when Doris said: 'When I am gone you will have a home of your own'? The recent case of **Bradbury v Taylor** [2012] EWCA Civ 1208 was clearer, as a representation was actually made by the owner of the house to his relatives that if they moved to the property

[1] This kind of opening paragraph is essential. Never, in a problem question on estoppel, start with estoppel itself. Instead explain that we need to use estoppel because one or more identified formalities have not been satisfied. Then go on to estoppel. It is vital to identify that estoppel is an equitable principle as we can then bring in the concept of unconscionability later and explain that the remedy is discretionary.

[2] You could, at this stage, list the elements of estoppel, but why? You will be mentioning them separately and analysing them as you go on so avoid repetition when you could be bringing in new points and gaining extra marks.

[3] There is considerable analysis and discussion in this answer of the facts of the problem. This is essential in estoppel cases as 'context is everything' – see *Thorner* v *Major*. However, you must tie your discussion into the basic principles.

[4] Use the word 'representation' and not, e.g., promise in estoppel questions.

with their family he would leave it to them in his will, provided various conditions were met.

At this point we must proceed on the basis that there was a sufficient representation for an estoppel.[5] However, it is worth pointing out that in at least two cases decided after *Thorner* v *Major*, *Cook* v *Thomas* [2010] EWCA Civ 227 and *MacDonald* v *Frost* [2009] EWHC 2276, family-type claims did fail through lack of a clear representation so Jim and Sally's claim may fail on this ground.[6]

The next element of estoppel is for Jim and Sally to establish that they have changed their position in reliance on Doris's alleged representation such that it would be unconscionable for Doris's promise of the house to be withdrawn.[7] There needs to be what Robert Walker LJ in *Gillett* v *Holt* [2001] Ch 210 CA called 'a sufficient casual link' between the representation and the change of position and in *Greasley* v *Cooke* [1980] 1 WLR 1306 CA it was held that as soon as it can be shown that the representation was calculated to 'influence the judgement of a reasonable man' then it is presumed that the reliance was as a result of the representation.[8] Here there seem to be two clear cases of possible detrimental reliance: Sally gave up her full-time job and took a part-time one to enable her to care for Doris and Jim started to do some work on the house such as installing a stair lift at his own expense when Doris found climbing the stairs difficult. It seems clear that Jim's work was done in reliance on what Doris had said, but it is not clear if Sally's giving up of her full-time job was linked to Doris' statement. Jim and Sally seem to have left their house and moved in with Doris before any clear representation was made but, as indicated above, there may have been an implied representation.

If Jim and Sally succeed in proving detrimental reliance then it is for the court to decide the remedy necessary to 'feed the estoppel'[9] and so Jim and Sally may not actually receive the house. In *Jennings* v *Rice* [2002] EWCA Civ 159 CA the owner of a house had represented to his gardener that he would be left his house or possibly the entire estate and the gardener had not been paid for his work after then. The house was valued at £435,000 and the whole estate at £1.3 million. It was emphasised that it may be very difficult to quantify the value of care provided where the claim is brought by a

[5] This is a classic example of exam technique. We cannot take this point further so we simply assume that there is a sufficient representation so that we can go on and address the other issues. If we do not address them we will lose marks.

[6] Gain extra marks by showing that you are up to date with recent cases but do not mention them in detail as *Thorner* v *Major* is the main authority.

[7] Note the two points: change of position, and also that it would be unconscionable for the representation to be withdrawn. Apply both to the question.

[8] An important point often missed: in effect this deals with the burden of proof.

[9] It is vital to mention this – do not assume that if Jim and Sally win on the estoppel issue she will automatically receive what Doris represented to her that she would.

carer and Robert Walker LJ held that it would only rarely be appropriate to look at, for example, hourly rates of pay that might have been received. In **Jennings v Rice** an award of £200,000 was upheld which was the cost of full time nursing care.

[10] The law reports contain a continual flow of cases on estoppel. Be selective in the use you make of them as in some cases the matter is purely one of fact and not law. However, here we have a case which does contain a helpful explanation of a point and so a discussion of it will add to your marks.

In **Suggitt v Suggitt** [2012] EWCA Civ 1140 the Court of Appeal clarified the principle in **Jennings**.[10] It did not mean that there had to be a relationship of proportionality between the level of detriment and the relief awarded, but rather that if the expectations were extravagant or out of all proportion to the detriment suffered, the court should recognise that the claimant's equity should be satisfied in another, generally more limited way. In this case much will depend on whether the court accepts the leaving of their home by Jim and Sally was in reliance on a promise by Doris to leave them her house. If it does, then they may succeed in a claim to the house. If, however, they have to rely on their other acts, the court may hold that to expect a house valued at £500,000 would be out of proportion to the detriment suffered and only award them a monetary sum.

[11] Mention this point after the discussion on remedies as if Jim and Sally were not awarded the house this issue would not arise.

If Jim and Sally's claim to the house does succeed[11] then the leaving of the house by will to the League of Friends of Sick Cats will not affect their claim (**Gillett v Holt**). Instead the League will take the house under the will but subject to the estoppel in favour of Jim and Sally.

 Make your answer stand out

- An answer which combines a close analysis of the facts with an ability to relate those facts to the principles of proprietary estoppel.
- Check the possibility of a claim for unjust enrichment as in *Cook* v *Thomas*.
- Look at the possibility of a remedial constructive trust as suggested in *Thorner* v *Major*.
- Examine the possibility of Jim and Sally registering their estoppel as a notice under section 116 of the LRA 2002 if title to Redlands is registered.
- Reference to academic debate on what constitutes a representation in cases of estoppel. See e.g. McFarlane (2009) Apocalypse Averted: Proprietary Estoppel in the House of Lords. *LQR*, 125: 535.

> ❗ **Don't be tempted to . . .**
>
> - Explain why we need to rely on estoppel at all.
> - Spend too long on outlining the facts of cases and not enough on the principles.
> - Mention estoppel cases in detail which do not really relate to this question. *Inwards* v *Baker* is a possible example – an excellent illustration of estoppel but the facts do not help here.
> - Fail to spot that we do not have enough information to decide if there was a sufficient representation and come to too definite a conclusion on this point.
> - Forget to mention the burden of proof.

 # Question 4

'Proprietary estoppel should not become the penicillin of equity.' (Dixon (2009) Proprietary Estoppel: A Return to Principle? *Conveyancer* 260)

Do you agree?

Answer plan

→ Distinction between proprietary estoppel and promissory estoppel.

→ Estoppel based on unconscionability – Court of Appeal and House of Lords in *Yeoman's Row* v *Cobbe*.

→ Further example of unconscionability as the basis of estoppel: *Pascoe* v *Turner*.

→ Restriction on availability of proprietary estoppel to representations – comparison of Lord Scott's view in *Yeoman's Row* with the decision in *Thorner* v *Major*.

→ Proposed requirement that claimants must believe that they have been made an irrevocable promise.

Diagram plan

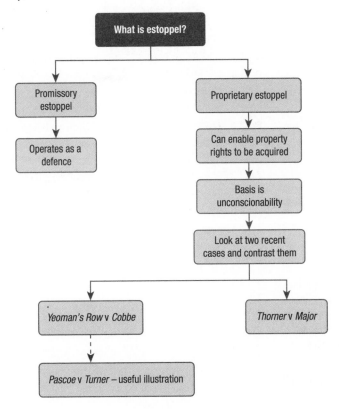

A printable version of this diagram plan is available from www.pearsoned.co.uk/lawexpressqa

Answer

[1] Promissory estoppel and proprietary estoppel are so different that a definition covering them both would be too wide to be of use especially in an essay like this. Better to say at once that there are two types, which then leads you on to discuss proprietary estoppel in detail, which is what this question is about.

The idea behind this quotation is that estoppel can be seen as a cure for many hardships which could result from a too rigid application of principles of common law or statute law. Is this true?

This essay will argue that estoppel needs to steer a middle ground. It must not be so governed by its own principles that it is unable to undertake its main function nor so wide and general that it is impossible to see what that function is. In short it should be penicillin but not a universal one.

There are two distinct types of estoppel.[1] As Martin (2009) points out: 'Each has a separate origin and history' (p. 926). Promissory estoppel applies in contractual relationships and essentially operates as a defence to prevent a party from going back on a promise. Its best-known application was in **Central London Property Trust v High Trees Houses Ltd** [1947] KB 130 HC. This doctrine does not create a new cause of action; instead it prevents a party going back on a representation, as in High Trees itself. Proprietary estoppel, by contrast, is a sword: it enables rights, especially property rights, to be acquired when none existed before. It involves a representation by one person (X) to another (Y) which X intends Y to rely on and where Y's actual reliance is reasonable in the circumstances. An objective test applies: thus the question is whether a promise by X can reasonably be understood as a commitment by X to Y. If so, then X will be estopped from going back on the representation and asserting their strict legal rights.

Provided that the above elements are present, the basis of the doctrine can be seen as unconscionability: would it be unconscionable for X, when Y has relied on X's promise to his detriment, to then depart from that promise?[2]

This question was prompted by recent cases involving proprietary estoppel not promissory estoppel and so this essay will concentrate on this.[3]

The first issue is to ask if proprietary estoppel should be available where conduct has been unconscionable even though the essential elements of it are not present.

In **Yeoman's Row Management Limited v Cobbe** [2008] UKHL 55 HL an oral agreement between the company and Cobbe provided that a block of flats owned by the company would be demolished and Cobbe would apply for planning permission to erect houses in their place with any excess of the proceeds over £24 million shared equally with the company. After planning permission had been obtained, the company went back on the oral agreement and demanded more money as it now realised that the land was worth much more. Cobbe claimed that the company was estopped from going back on the agreement.

Lord Scott asked: What is the fact that the company is estopped from asserting? There was no question that the oral agreement was unenforceable and Cobbe did not claim a specific property right, merely a hope of entering a contract. He held that the Court of Appeal, which held in Cobbe's favour, had been influenced too much

[2] Your discussion of the issue raised in the question will be much clearer if you have started by stating what the essential elements of estoppel are.

[3] However, as we will see later the mention of promissory estoppel is not wasted even though the question is primarily about proprietary estoppel.

by the fact that it regarded the behaviour of the company as unconscionable, and in effect as penicillin, without requiring the essential
elements of proprietary estoppel to be present. It is submitted that
another case where estoppel acted too much as a general penicillin
is **Pascoe v Turner** [1979] 1 WLR 431 CA.[4] The claimant and
defendant had lived in the claimant's house. The defendant told the
claimant that the house was hers and everything in it. In reliance on
this the claimant, to the defendant's knowledge, spent money on the
house. She was given notice to quit by the claimant but the court
ordered the house to be conveyed to her although it was clear that
her acts of reliance were only on the basis that she had a licence to
live there for life.

[4] This case is outside the current debate but adds another angle to it. Mention of it ought to add to your marks.

However, although the courts should require that a proprietary estoppel
claim satisfies the criteria set out above, there is also a danger of the
courts going too far the other way and setting out criteria which
would mean that proprietary estoppel would no longer apply to
promises of future intentions such as promises to leave by will.[5]

[5] This is a crucial paragraph which links the first part of the answer to the second. You are showing that you are actually engaging with the question and writing a balanced answer which looks at two points of view – the type of paragraph which really adds to your marks!

In **Yeoman's Row Management Limited v Cobbe** Lord Scott
considered that proprietary estoppel should be restricted to representations of specific facts or mixed law and fact by X which stood
in the way of a right claimed by Y.[6] This seemed to mean that
proprietary estoppel was no different to promissory estoppel: it only
applied as a defence to an action where those specific representations had been gone back on, and not to enable an independent right
to be asserted. In cases of promises to leave by will Lord Scott would
use the remedial constructive trust.

[6] This is an essential point: the view of Lord Scott needs to be carefully stated.

The problem is that proprietary estoppel has always applied to
representations of what will happen and not just to specific present
facts as where there is a representation to someone that they will
acquire property on the death of the representor, as in **Gillett v Holt**
[2001] Ch 210 CA and in cases such as **Dillwyn v Llewelyn**
(1862)[7] 4 de GF and J 517 HC, where a father's encouragement to
his son to build a house on the father's land meant that on the father's
death the land built on was ordered to be conveyed to the son.

[7] This is important: if Lord Scott's analysis was adopted then it would not only mean that promises to leave on death would be outside the scope of estoppel but others too. *Dillwyn* v *Llewellyn* is a good case to mention as it has always been regarded as a classic estoppel case and it would seem startling if this type of case was no longer to be decided under estoppel.

However, in **Thorner v Major** [2009] UKHL 18 HL the majority did
not accept that estoppel should be confined to representations of
present fact. D had worked at P's farm for no payment from 1976
onwards, and, by the 1980s, hoped that he might inherit the farm.

No express representation had ever been made, but D relied on various hints and remarks made by P over the years. The House of Lords held that these amounted to an estoppel.

Furthermore, the idea of Lord Walker in **Yeoman's Row** that the claimant must believe that they have been made an irrevocable promise was not accepted.[8] This would inevitably have meant that promises to leave by will would not be covered by promissory estoppel as a will can be revoked. However, in **Thorner v Major** it was held that the question is whether a party has reasonably relied on an assurance by the other as that person's conduct.

[8] This rounds off the answer as it mentions a slightly different point from that made by Lord Scott. It shows that you have really looked at what the judges actually said in these cases and will add to your marks.

In conclusion, estoppel should be a penicillin which applies in as wide a variety of situations as possible, but which only applies if certain criteria are met.

✓ Make your answer stand out

- Discuss the remedial constructive trust.
- Make clear the extent to which promissory estoppel has moved on from the *High Trees* decision.
- Further point made by Lord Scott – the need for certainty of subject matter as to the subject of the representation.
- Academic literature – in addition to the article mentioned in the question and the one mentioned in Question 5, look at Sloan (2009) Estop Me If You Think You've Heard It. *CLJ*, 68(3): 518, which is a concise summary.
- Cases following *Thorner* v *Major*, e.g. *Cook* v *Thomas* [2010] EWCA Civ 227, can be mentioned to show how the principle in *Thorner* v *Major* has been applied.

! Don't be tempted to . . .

- Just describe estoppel.
- Go into the question without distinguishing between proprietary and promissory estoppel.
- Just reel off cases on estoppel without looking at the underlying issues.
- Miss the point that there are two distinct issues raised by the discussion of *Yeoman's Row* v *Cobbe* and *Thorner* v *Major*.

Question 5

The decision in *Thorner* v *Major* means that estoppel 'can thus perform its vital role as a broad and flexible doctrine focused on the need to prevent a party (B) suffering detriment as a result of his reasonable reliance on another (A)'. (McFarlane (2009) Apocalypse Averted: Proprietary Estoppel in the House of Lords. *LQR*, 125: 535)

Consider this statement in the light of recent decisions of the House of Lords.

Answer plan

→ Explanation of basic idea of proprietary estoppel.

→ Actual decisions in *Yeoman's Row Management Ltd* v *Cobbe* and *Thorner* v *Major*.

→ Estoppel in cases of representations about future rights over property.

→ Does the representee need to believe that the representation was binding and irrevocable?

→ Where proprietary estoppel is today. Cases since these two HL decisions.

Diagram plan

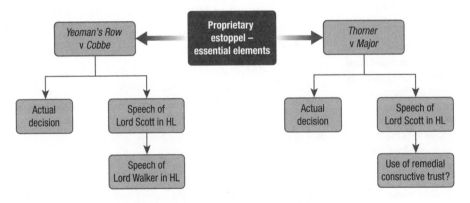

A printable version of this diagram plan is available from www.pearsoned.co.uk/lawexpressqa

Answer

This question concerns proprietary rather than promissory estoppel. Promissory estoppel applies in contractual relationships and essentially operates as a defence to prevent a party from going back on a promise. Proprietary estoppel applies in property as well as contractual situations and can give rights where none existed before.[1]

5 LICENCES AND ESTOPPEL

[1] Here we have simply pointed out that the question concerns one type of estoppel rather than the other as the actual quotation did not say this. It is also important to explain what promissory estoppel is as later on the essay discusses the views of Lord Scott which would, in effect, almost assimilate proprietary and promissory estoppel.

[2] Your discussion of the recent cases will be much clearer if you have started by stating what the essential elements of estoppel are.

[3] This sentence is vital: it sets the scene for the discussion in the light of the question.

[4] The quotation in this question is not suggesting that the Court of Appeal in *Yeoman's Row* was right and that estoppel should be an extremely broad-based doctrine founded on unconscionability. On the other hand, the argument is that some of the remarks in *Yeoman's Row* could, to put it in a nutshell, take estoppel too far in the opposite direction of excessive rigidity. You need to be very clear on this point.

[5] This is the essential point on which this essay hangs. If you get an essay on recent case law on estoppel then you must get this point over clearly.

The essential elements of proprietary estoppel are a representation by one person (A) to another (B) which A intends B to rely on and where B's actual reliance is reasonable in the circumstances. An objective test applies: thus the question is whether a promise by A can reasonably be understood as a commitment by A to B.

Provided that the above elements are present, the basis of the doctrine can be seen as unconscionability: would it be unconscionable for A, when B has relied on A's promise to his detriment, to then depart from that promise?[2]

This question concerns the extent to which two recent decisions of the House of Lords have affected this doctrine.[3]

In ***Yeoman's Row Management Limited v Cobbe*** [2008] UKHL 55 HL an oral agreement between the company and Cobbe provided that a block of flats owned by the company would be demolished and Cobbe would apply for planning permission to erect houses in their place with any excess of the proceeds over £24 million shared equally with the company. After planning permission had been obtained, the company went back on the oral agreement and demanded more money as it now realised that the land was worth much more. Cobbe claimed that the company was estopped from going back on the agreement.

Lord Scott asked: What is the fact that the company is estopped from asserting? There was no question that the oral agreement was unenforceable and Cobbe did not claim a specific property right, merely a hope of entering a contract. The Court of Appeal had held in favour of Cobbe but Lord Scott observed that it had been influenced by the simple fact that they regarded the company's behaviour as unconscionable and this by itself was not a sufficient basis for proprietary estoppel. Thus, estoppel did not apply. At this point the decision is straightforward.[4]

Lord Scott then broadened his argument and considered that proprietary estoppel should be restricted to representations of specific facts or mixed law and fact by X which stood in the way of a right claimed by Y.[5] This seemed to mean that proprietary estoppel was no different to promissory estoppel: it only applied as a defence to an action where those specific representations had been gone back on and not to enable an independent right to be asserted.

The problem is that proprietary estoppel has always applied to representations of what will happen and not just to specific present facts. This happens where there is a representation to someone that they will acquire property on the death of the representor, as in *Gillett* v *Holt* [2001] Ch 210 CA. It also applies in cases such as *Dillwyn* v *Llewellyn* (1862)[6] 4 de GF and J 517 HC where a father's encouragement to his son to build a house on the father's land meant that on the father's death the land built on was ordered to be conveyed to the son.

[6] *Dillwyn* v *Llewellyn* is a good case to mention as it has always been regarded as a classic estoppel case and it would seem startling if: as a result of Lord Scott's view being accepted this type of case was no longer to be decided under estoppel.

Lord Walker's reasoning also posed problems as he seemed to require proof that the claimant believed that he had been irrevocably promised a proprietary right. On the facts, Cobbe knew that the agreement was not binding and his hope that the company would stick to its promise was insufficient. How does this affect promises to leave by will? A representee must believe that a representation is legally binding, and of course, a will can be revoked. This was what bothered the court in *Taylor* v *Dickens* [1998] 1 FLR 806 HC which held that in these cases the representor must, to be estopped, encourage a belief that he would not change his mind. However, in *Gillett* v *Holt* it was held that this was too rigid a view. Lord Walker's view in *Yeoman's Row* seems to take us to where we were before *Gillett* v *Holt*. It is suggested that the law needs to strike a middle course between not enforcing mere hopes, on the one hand, as in *Yeoman's Row*, and on the other not requiring the representee to believe that the promise is irrevocable.

The second important recent estoppel case is *Thorner* v *Major* [2009] UKHL 18 HL. D had worked at P's farm for no payment from 1976 onwards, and, by the 1980s, hoped that he might inherit the farm. No express representation had ever been made, but D relied on various hints and remarks made by P over the years. Also in 1990 P gave D a bonus notice relating to two policies on P's life, saying 'that's for my death duties'.

The House of Lords held that the handing over of the bonus notice in 1990 should not be considered alone, and the evidence had demonstrated a continuing pattern of conduct by P for the remaining 15 years of his life sufficient to amount to an estoppel.

[7] This takes us back to our explanation of estoppel at the start.

It is clear that the majority did not accept that estoppel should be confined to representations of present fact as of course this case depended on assurances of future intentions. The idea of Lord Walker in *Yeoman's Row* that the claimant must believe that they have been made an irrevocable promise was not accepted. The question instead is whether a party has reasonably relied on an assurance by the other as to that person's conduct.[7] Thus context is important and this explains why here it was accepted that there had been estoppel on the facts despite the lack of an express statement by P to D.

Lord Scott dissented. He was particularly concerned about the lack of certainty of the exact subject matter of the representation. He pointed out 'Farm boundaries are not immutable'. He held that proprietary estoppel should only relate to cases where there was a representation as to an 'immediate, or more or less immediate, interest in the property in question' and in others such as this one the approach should be to ask if a remedial constructive trust could be imposed instead of estoppel.[8] However, in later cases such as **Cook v Thomas** [2010] EWCA Civ 227 CA the courts have not been inclined to use the remedial constructive trust approach.

[8] This is the final major point but must be included for a good pass. In effect, Lord Scott having abolished proprietary estoppel in cases of promises of future intentions must now replace it with something else.

[9] Note how the vital word in the article has been picked up at the end.

In conclusion, the quotation in the question is correct if we regard 'apocalypse'[9] as the adoption of the analysis by, in particular Lord Scott in *Yeoman's Row* which would have confined proprietary estoppel to cases of representations of existing law and fact and would have ended it as a remedy for those relying on promises of future intentions.

✓ Make your answer stand out

- Need for certainty of subject matter in trusts.
- Differences between rights under estoppel and under constructive trusts.
- Where the remedial constructive trust stands in trusts law – developments since the 1970s.
- Refer to academic literature in addition to the article mentioned in the question, e.g. Dixon (2009) Proprietary Estoppel: A Return to Principle. *Conveyancer* 260.

! Don't be tempted to . . .

- Just run through the idea of estoppel and give general examples.
- Overload your answer with cases – estoppel is very rich in case law but you must make the principles stand out from the cases.
- Ignore what the judges actually said in the cases.
- Fail to mention any academic articles.
- Minimise the essential points of difference between the approaches of the judges in these two cases.

Leases

How this topic may come up in exams

You will need to check your syllabus to see the extent to which the detail of the law on leases is examined. Problem questions are likely, which can be challenging but equally give a lot of scope to earn extra marks.

An essay or problem question may ask you about the distinction between a lease and a licence (see also Chapter 5) and there is an old standard essay question on the distinction between legal and equitable leases. Another area for a problem question is the creation of legal and equitable leases: this may be linked to other areas and require knowledge of material in Chapter 2.

■ Attack the question

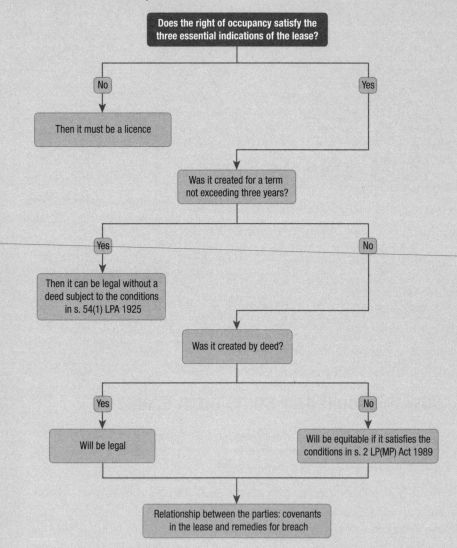

A printable version of this diagram is available from www.pearsoned.co.uk/lawexpressqa

❓ Question 1

Earlier this year, Bert purchased 1 High Street Downstairs from Vera. The freehold title to the property is registered at HM Land Registry. The property is divided into a flat and living accommodation for the owner upstairs.

When Bert purchased the property the flat was already occupied by Joan under a document signed by Joan and Vera headed 'Residential Property Occupation Licence'. This allows her to occupy the flat for four years for a payment of £250 a month. The agreement includes clauses declaring that it was not intended to create a lease and provides that Joan can be required to leave the flat and move to other premises provided by the landlord at any time.

The agreement also provides that the landlord agrees to do all of Joan's laundry and retains a key, so that he can enter the flat to collect and return the laundry. At the date of the sale of the freehold to Bert, Joan was away visiting her daughter in Germany.

Bert wishes to evict Joan so that he can turn the flat into an office. Ignoring any question of security of tenure, advise Bert whether the agreement with Joan is binding on him and whether he is entitled to take steps to evict Joan.

Answer plan

→ Explain the distinction between a lease and a licence.

→ Analyse the question of whether a licence can bind third parties in relation to this question.

→ Identify and explain the three criteria for indicating the existence of a lease.

→ Apply the facts of the problem to these criteria.

→ Consider the position if it is a lease. Is it legal by deed, equitable or a legal periodic tenancy and how does this affect the question of whether the lease binds third parties?

Diagram plan

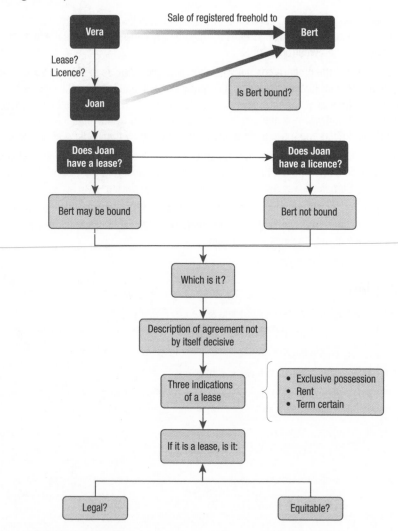

A printable version of this diagram plan is available from www.pearsoned.co.uk/lawexpressqa

[1] Note the wording: we have not decided, assuming that it is lease, if it actually does bind a third party. We must just say at this point that it is capable of doing so.

Answer

The question is whether Joan holds a lease or a licence. If she holds a lease, she has a proprietary right in the land which is capable[1] of binding a third party such as Bert. A licence does not in general

2 There is an earlier authority *Thomas* v *Sorrell* (1673) Vaugh 330 but especially as this is a problem question we only need one.

3 The average student would simply say that a licence does not bind third parties but the good student would mention the one type of case where a licence might do so.

4 This point is often missed by students so a mention of it will certainly improve your marks!

5 A vital word: these are not absolute rules and in particular if there is no requirement to pay rent this will not necessarily mean that there is no lease.

create a proprietary right. In **Street v Mountford** [1985] 2 All ER 289 HL[2] Lord Templeman said: 'A licence does not create an estate in the land to which it relates but only makes an act lawful which would otherwise be unlawful.' In **King v David Allen** [1916] 2 AC 54 HL a licence to place advertisements on the wall of a cinema did not bind a third party. So, unless Joan can show that her licence arose through proprietary estoppel,[3] it would not bind Bert. All that she could argue is that she is entitled to reasonable packing up time[4] and so does not become a trespasser at once. (See Lord MacDermott in **Winter Garden Theatre (London) Ltd v Millennium Productions Ltd** [1948] AC 173 HL.) Thus if Bert tries to eject Joan without giving her any time to remove her property and, possibly, make alternative arrangements for their storage, Joan will have a claim against Bert in tort for, for example, assault if Bert tries to forcibly eject her.

The document is called a 'Residential Property Occupation Licence' but the use of the word 'licence' is not decisive. However, this does not mean that the description given by the parties to the agreement should be ignored. In **Antoniades v Villiers** [1990] 1 AC 417 CA Bingham LJ said:

A cat does not become a dog because the parties have agreed to call it a dog. But in deciding if it is a cat or a dog the parties' agreement that it is a dog may not be entirely irrelevant.

So if other evidence points to a licence, the word 'licence' in the agreement could be taken into consideration.

The three indications[5] of a lease were stated by Lord Templeman in **Street v Mountford** (1985) as an intention to grant exclusive possession, for a fixed term, in consideration of periodical payments (rent). In **Bruton v London and Quadrant Housing Trust Ltd** [2000] 1 AC 406 HL Lord Hoffman indicated that the first two are essential but referred to 'usually' the payment of rent. In this case there are periodical payments of £250 a month. Although the agreement is for a fixed term of four years; Joan can be required to leave the flat and move to other premises provided by the landlord and this appears to mean that it is not for a certain term and so cannot be a lease. We cannot be sure.

This leaves the question of exclusive possession.

[6] It always adds to marks if you can mention, if only briefly as here, any underlying principle behind a point of law.

The rationale[6] of requiring exclusive possession for a lease is that without it the tenant would not be able to use the premises for the purposes of the letting (***Odey v Barber*** [2008] Ch 175 HC). The agreement provides that the landlord can require her to move to other premises at any time. The question is, in the words of Oliver LJ in ***AG Securities v Vaughan*** [1990] 1 AC 417 HL is this 'a sham . . . designed to conceal the true nature of the transaction'? On the evidence it is impossible to say.

Although the landlord retains a key, this does not prevent there being a lease (***Aslan v Murphy*** [1990] 1 WLR 766 HC). Donaldson MR in that case emphasised that one must look at why the landlord retains a set of keys. In this case it is to allow Vera to collect and return Joan's laundry and once again we must ask if this actually happened. If not then it may be just a sham. We cannot say if Joan has a licence or a lease.[7]

[7] Do not be afraid to say that you do not have enough information to come to a definite conclusion. You then gain marks by exploring both possibilities.

If Joan does not have a lease and only a licence then, as stated above, it will not bind Bert, but if it is a lease then it is capable[8] of doing so. This depends on whether the lease is legal or equitable. As the lease is for four years, it must be created by deed to be legal (s. 52(1), LPA 1925) as the exception in section 54 of the LPA 1925 allowing the creation of legal leases without a deed only applies to leases for a term not exceeding three years. The question uses the word 'document' and not deed and by section 2 of the Law of Property (Miscellaneous Provisions) Act 1989 the document must describe itself as a deed. If it is not in a deed, it may be an equitable lease under the principle in ***Walsh v Lonsdale*** (1882) 21 Ch D 9 HC. Section 2 of the Law of Property (Miscellaneous Provisions) Act 1989 provides that any contract for the sale or disposition of an interest in land, which includes an equitable lease, must be in writing, signed by the parties and contain all the terms. Although we know that the agreement is in writing and that it was signed by both parties, we do not know if it contains all the terms[9] and so we cannot be certain if it is a valid equitable lease. If it is, then it will bind Bert if it is registered as an estate contract. If not, then as Joan is in actual occupation at time of the sale to Bert, she may have an overriding interest under Schedule 3, Paragraph 2 of the LRA 2002, which applies as this is a subsequent registration.[10] The fact that at the time of the sale Joan was away in Germany does not deprive her of her overriding interest as temporary absence does not deprive one of

[8] The word 'capable' is important as you will lose marks if you say at this point that the lease will bind Bert. This is the point which we have to investigate.

[9] There will not be time in an exam to set out all the terms of the agreement and so remember that you will not be able to come to a definite conclusion.

[10] A good point for extra marks: you show the examiner that you know the distinction between a first and a subsequent registration.

[11] You should always watch for this in this type of question. First ask if the lease could be validly created by deed and so legal, then if it could be a valid equitable lease, and if you cannot come to a definite conclusion on this, ask if it could be a valid periodic tenancy. If, however, rent has not been actually paid at regular periodic intervals, it cannot be a periodic tenancy.

[12] Do remember that it is three years here. Students often forget.

occupation (***Chhokar v Chhokar*** [1984] FLR 313 CA). However, under Schedule 3, Paragraph 2 of the LRA 2002 an occupier may lose an overriding interest if their occupation was not obvious on a reasonably careful inspection of the land at the time of the disposition to them or if they did not disclose their interest when it would have been reasonable to do so. If either of these applies then Bert will not be bound by Joan's interest.

Even if Joan does not have a valid equitable lease, she may have a legal periodical tenancy based[11] not on her agreement but on the regular payment of rent. As she pays rent monthly she can have a periodic monthly tenancy which – as it is for a term not exceeding three years[12] – does not require writing. Moreover, as it is a legal lease for less than seven years then under Schedule 3, Paragraph 1 of the LRA 2002 it counts as an overriding interest by which Bert is bound.

✓ Make your answer stand out

- Refer to the speech of Lord Hoffman in *Bruton* v *London and Quadrant Housing Trust Ltd* on what he suggested was a distinction between a lease as a contractual relationship and the notion of a lease conferring a proprietary interest in land.
- Read Bright (2000) Leases, Exclusive Possession and Estates. *LQR*, 116: 7 on this issue.
- Mention the previous view on the relevance of the intentions of the parties in *Marchant* v *Charters* [1977] 1 WLR 1181.
- Discuss the position if there is only a licence is some detail: students often rush to the conclusion that there is a lease.
- Read and refer to Wallace (1990) The Legacy of *Street* v *Mountford. Northern Ireland Legal Quarterly*, 41: 143, who argues against an undue emphasis on exclusive possession in deciding if there is a lease.

! Don't be tempted to . . .

- Just say that because the agreement says that it is a licence then it is a licence.
- Come to a definite conclusion that the agreement is a lease or a licence.
- Leave out any discussion of Joan's position if it turns out that she only has a licence.
- Say that there is an equitable lease – we cannot know this.
- Leave out discussion of overriding interests.

Question 2

'Whether the lease is principally a contract or principally an estate in land is a question that casts a long shadow over the law of landlord and tenant.' (Lower (2010) The *Bruton* Tenancy. *Conveyancer*, 1: 38–56)

Examine the idea of the 'contractual tenancy' and how it might be applied in practice.

Answer plan

→ Explain what the question is about: nature of a lease.

→ Explain the facts of *Bruton* in relation to this issue.

→ Analyse the views of the Court of Appeal in *Bruton*.

→ Analyse the views of the House of Lords in *Bruton*, especially those of Lord Hoffman.

→ Explore the practical consequences of the recognition of a new species of 'contractual tenancy'.

Diagram plan

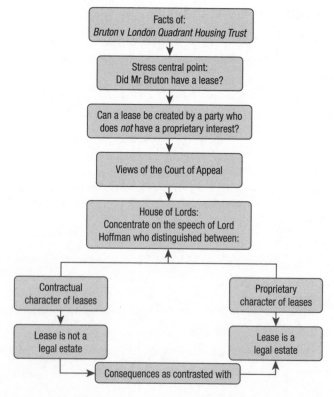

A printable version of this diagram plan is available from www.pearsoned.co.uk/lawexpressqa

Answer

The decision of the House of Lords in **Bruton v London & Quadrant Housing Trust** [2000] 1 AC 406 HL raised questions about the nature of leases[1] with which this question is concerned.

The facts were[2] that Lambeth Council granted London & Quadrant Housing Trust a licence to use a number of its properties to provide temporary housing pending redevelopment. The Trust agreed with the local authority that it would not give security of tenure to any tenant without the local authority's consent and that no occupier would acquire security of tenure whilst in the property. The Trust then gave Mr Bruton the right to occupy one of the properties, a flat, 'on a weekly licence'. In fact, the planned development was abandoned and by the time the case reached the House of Lords Mr Bruton had been living in the flat for ten years.

The essential point was simple: did Mr Bruton have a lease as he claimed? The case was not concerned with security of tenure but with whether the Trust was subject to the repairing obligations imposed upon landlords by the Landlord and Tenant Act 1985, section 11, which applies only to 'leases'.[3]

What lay in the way of the claim to a lease was simple; if a lease creates a proprietary interest in the land by way of a legal estate then a lease cannot be created by a party who does not themselves have a proprietary interest, and the Housing Trust did not as it only had a licence.[4] This was stressed by Millett LJ in the Court of Appeal[5] who pointed to the link with the fundamental requirement for a tenancy that there must be exclusive possession: 'If the grantor has no power to exclude the true owner from possession, he has no power to grant a legal right to exclusive possession and his grant cannot take effect as a tenancy.' So as the Trust did not have exclusive possession, it could not give the right of exclusive possession to Mr Bruton. There was an alternative argument based on tenancy by estoppel but the Court of Appeal held that, as the trust had never purported to actually grant a tenancy, there could be no tenancy by estoppel.

The House of Lords disagreed. Lord Hoffman distinguished between the contractual and the proprietary character of leases by saying that 'the term "lease" or "tenancy" describes a relationship between two parties who are designated landlord and tenant. It is not concerned with the question of whether the agreement creates an estate or

---

[1] This is the precise point and you need to make it in the opening paragraph.

[2] Remember not to give a general account of the facts but relate them to the issue mentioned in the first paragraph.

[3] This point is often missed. Although exam questions are often concerned with security of tenure you should point out that this case concerned liability to repair.

[4] This is the vital point. Make sure that you understand it as if you do not this will affect the rest of your answer and could lose you a lot of marks.

[5] This is the type of answer where you really do need to look at the views of the HL (or, now, the Supreme Court) and lower courts as the difference of view gives you material for your discussion.

other proprietary interest which may be binding upon third parties.' The nub of his reasoning is that it is the agreement between the parties which comes first and not the proprietary interest. Thus, as on the facts, the criteria for a lease laid down in **Street v Mountford** [1985] 2 All ER 289 HL were satisfied there was a lease.

[6] You could miss this out but that would be a pity as it was an important part of the discussion and you can demonstrate your knowledge of estoppel and gain extra marks.

Nor did Lord Hoffman agree that there could be no tenancy by estoppel,[6] although what is said in **Bruton** about the tenancy by estoppel is, strictly, *obiter dictum*. In the Court of Appeal Millett LJ said that the estoppel comes first; a tenancy by estoppel arises when the grantor purports to grant a lease but is unable to do so and the grantor is 'estopped' from denying his grant, thus giving rise to a tenancy by estoppel. However, Lord Hoffman said that what comes first is the tenancy and the parties are then estopped from denying any of the 'ordinary incidents or obligations of the tenancy on the ground that the landlord had no legal estate'. What he may mean, although this is not clear, is that the parties are estopped from denying that the lease is proprietary in character.

If Lord Hoffman's analysis is accepted, what are its consequences? The obvious one is that there will be two categories: leases which are legal estates, and leases which are not legal estates.[7] Looking at it from the other direction, contractual rights of occupation could fall into one of three categories:

[7] This is the point which you need to bring out in this answer. You can then develop it and earn extra marks by discussing the possible consequences of such a distinction.

(a) Proprietary leases giving an estate in land and enforceable against all third parties.

[8] This is a complex area and so it is vital to set out the different possibilities clearly as here.

(b) Contractual leases which do not confer an estate in land but do confer exclusive possession.

(c) Contractual licences which do not confer either an estate in land or exclusive possession.[8]

[9] You could at this point mention the status of contractual licences but at least you must be clear that as a general rule they do not bind third parties.

This may in turn lead to some contractual licences,[9] in category (c) being assimilated to category (b).

However, as a contractual lease does not give a proprietary interest it seems that:

[10] There is no need to mention these in detail: the point is that we do not know if they will apply.

(a) The formality requirements set out in the Law of Property Act 1925,[10] sections 52 and 54, and the Law of Property (Miscellaneous Provisions) Act 1989, section 2, will not apply as they apply only to interests in land and so contractual leases can be created informally.

(b) A contractual lease cannot be registrable under the LRA 2002 or count as an overriding interest under Schedules 1 and 3.

(c) Presumably, a contractual tenancy cannot be assigned by the tenant or the landlord,[11] for the ability to transfer leases flows from their proprietary status (see *Linden Gardens Trust Ltd v Lenesta Sludge Disposals Ltd* [1994] 1 AC 85 HL) and a contractual tenancy does not have this status.

[11] You should resist the temptation to set out the rules on assignment of leases here as we are just concerned with whether in principle a contractual licence can be treated in the same way as a lease.

(d) However, as with contractual licences, there will be the right to recover possession from a trespasser and equitable remedies may be available so that the lease may be enforceable against the grantor by specific performance or injunction (as in *Verrall v Great Yarmouth BC* [1981] QB 202 HC).

(e) What of the rule that a lease must be created for a term certain? Will this apply to contractual leases?

Lord Hoffman's attempt to create a new species of legal property right should be seen against the continuing concern over the lack of a proprietary status for certain types of contractual licences, especially residential ones.[12] Thus, the creation of a contractual tenancy might allow these licences to become contractual tenancies and so resolve a long-standing problem. However, before this happens, the practical problems of creating a new species of property right must be tackled first.

[12] You will gain many marks if you show that you can think across the whole spectrum of property law in this conclusion.

✓ Make your answer stand out

- Discuss the proprietary character of contractual licences.
- Demonstrate an ability to think across the spectrum of land law on the implications of the contractual tenancy.
- Read and refer to Bright (2000) Leases, Exclusive Possession and Estates. *LQR*, 116: 7.
- Read and refer to Lower (2010) The *Bruton* Tenancy. *Conveyancer*, 1: 38.

! Don't be tempted to . . .

- Spend too long on the facts of *Bruton*.
- Fail to bring out the differences in approach between the Court of Appeal and the House of Lords.
- Miss explaining the detailed implications of this case across land law.
- Fail to set this idea of a contractual tenancy in a wider context.

Question 3

'Principle and precedent dictate that it is beyond the power of the landlord and the tenant to create a term which is uncertain.' (Lord Templeman in *Prudential Assurance Co. Ltd* v *London Residuary Body* [1992] 2 AC 386)

Critically consider the rationale for this rule and its application in recent case law.

Answer plan

➜ State precisely what the rule means.

➜ Explain the historical rationale for the rule and refer to the 1925 property legislation.

➜ Look at the decisions in both *Prudential Assurance Co. Ltd* v *London Residuary Body* and *Mexfield Housing Co-operative Ltd* v *Berrisford*.

➜ Critically examine the present day reasons for the existence of this rule.

➜ Examine the possibility of changes in this rule.

Diagram plan

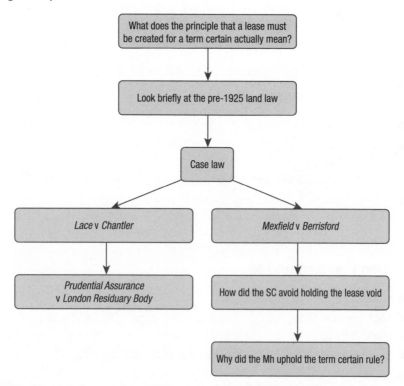

A printable version of this diagram plan is available from www.pearsoned.co.uk/lawexpressqa

Answer

There is a fundamental principle that to be valid a lease must be created for a term that is certain. Thus, the start date, the duration and the end date of the lease[1] must be ascertainable at the commencement of the lease. It is in fact possible for the parties to agree that the lease will commence on a future uncertain event such as when the property becomes vacant (**Brilliant v Michaels** [1945] 1 All ER 121 HC) but once that event has happened the lease must commence.

[1] An average answer would just say that the term must be certain, but in good answer you need to amplify this as shown.

The rule recently received detailed consideration in **Mexfield Housing Co-operative Ltd v Berrisford** [2011] UKSC 52, where the principle was reaffirmed, albeit with reluctance, but before we look at that decision we need to examine the rationale and background for this rule.[2]

[2] You could at this point plunge into a detailed account of the facts of *Mexfield*. Better to leave that for later and first earn those extra marks by showing evidence of research and setting the principle in its context.

Its origin is to be found in the pre-1925 property legislation.[3] As Lord Neuberger put it in **Mexfield**: 'There is much authority to support the proposition that, before the 1925 Act came into force, an agreement for an uncertain term was treated as a tenancy for the life of the tenant, determinable before the tenant's death according to its terms'. However, the principle that where the term was uncertain a lease for life was created seems to have been forgotten in the cases following the 1925 legislation.

[3] This paragraph shows attention to research detail and that you have an appreciation of the relevance of the 1925 legislation.

The operation of the term certain rule can be seen in **Lace v Chandler** [1944][4] KB 368 CA where a lease of a house for the duration of the war was held void. Many leases had been granted for the duration of the 1939–1945 war and following this case Parliament passed the Validation of War-Time Leases Act 1944 to validate them.

[4] It is usually better to mention the earlier cases and then lead up to the latest one.

In **Prudential Assurance Co. Ltd v London Residuary Body** (1992) a local authority purported to lease land until it was required for road widening. It was held that the lease was void but the tenant did have a periodic yearly tenancy by virtue of annual payment of rent. The House of Lords reached this decision with reluctance, Lord Browne-Wilkinson calling the outcome 'bizarre'.

The most recent decision on this area is **Mexfield Housing Co-operative Ltd v Berrisford** [2011] UKSC 52 where the claimant agreed to let a property to the defendant from month to month for a weekly rent. By clause 5, the defendant could end the agreement by giving one month's notice and by clause 6 the claimant could end the agreement only if e.g. the rent was in arrears for a certain time. The Supreme Court held that this was not a monthly periodic tenancy because of clauses 5 and 6.[5] It would have been void as of uncertain duration but the court held that it took effect as a lease for life and so was saved by the operation of section 149(6) LPA 1925 which converted leases for lives into leases for 90 years. Thus the court upheld the 'term certain' rule but managed to avoid its application in this case.

However, the solution of a lease for life will of course only work if there is a lease to an individual and not a company. As Lord Dyson pointed out in the Supreme Court in **Mexfield**, 'To treat an individual and a corporate entity differently in this respect can only be explained on historical grounds' which he felt was not 'a compelling justification for maintaining the justification today'.

If a court was unable to apply the reasoning in **Mexfield** to validate a lease, would that mean that there was no lease at all and so the 'tenant' was not a tenant at all but a mere licensee with no security of tenure?[6] Not necessarily. If as in the **Prudential Assurance** case the tenant was already paying rent then there could be a tenancy provided that the tenant has exclusive possession. The tenant can be considered a tenant at will.[7] The exact nature of tenancies at will has never been clear but there is no doubt that the tenant does not obtain an estate in the land and the tenancy can be ended at any time by the landlord. If so then if the tenant pays rent this will probably convert the tenancy into a periodic tenancy[8] as it will be clear that the parties intended a lease. Thus, as it will be a tenancy for a period not exceeding three years, then by section 54(2) of the LPA 1925 it can be valid even if not in writing.

Even so, the Supreme Court could have decided to change the law, so that it would be possible to create leases for an uncertain time. The main reason why it did not[9] was expressed by Lord Neuberger who gave the leading judgment in the Supreme Court and who said that, 'it does appear that for many centuries it has been regarded as fundamental to the concept of a term of years that it had a certain duration when it was created'. Furthermore Lord Neuberger referred to the not 'very attractive point' expressed by Lord Browne-Wilkinson in **Prudential Assurance Co. Ltd v London Residuary Body** that to change the law in this field 'might upset long established titles'. Lord Browne-Wilkinson also observed that, 'No one has been able to

---

[5] This is important as we shall see that in other cases the lease was saved by being regarded as a periodic tenancy.

[6] A good answer will start to ask questions such as this. In practice it would be no good just telling a client that their lease did not satisfy the 'term certain' rule. The obvious question would be: 'Yes – so ...?' Make sure that you always answer it!

[7] When you introduce a term such as this make sure that you explain it.

[8] There is an argument that periodic tenancies fall foul of the 'term certain' rule as they are leases of uncertain duration determinable by notice but in the Prudential Assurance case Lord Templeman said that such leases are saved from being uncertain as each party can determine the lease at the end of the period of the tenancy.

[9] Here you earn those extra marks by showing familiarity with the actual reasoning in Mexfield.

point to any useful purpose that it serves at the present day. If, by overruling the existing authorities, this House were able to change the law for the future only I would have urged your Lordships to do so.' This is the root of the problem: if the law was changed by the courts, then it would affect not just future leases but present ones,[10] and this disturbance to existing property rights was felt not to be justified. This may not be an ideal reason for leaving the law as it is but of course most leases are professionally drafted and the term certain rule is well known.

[10] Note that you are expressing your own views based on the material you have presented. This is exactly what the examiner wants to see.

[11] A mediocre conclusion would have baldly stated something like 'the certainty rule is old fashioned and should be abolished' which really gets us nowhere. Far better to include this research detail!

In view of this, is it likely that the 'certain term' rule will soon be changed? It seems unlikely.[11] Bright (2012) quotes a letter from the Law Commission to her stating that: 'the scale of the problem is unknown, particularly since the rule can be circumvented by careful drafting' and that 'investigation of the certainty rule is not a Government priority. Thus the Law Commission would not be including this as part of its Eleventh Programme of Law Reform. So for now it is for those drafting leases to ensure that their start, duration and end are certain.[12]

[12] A nice clear short conclusion like this always rounds off an answer well.

 Make your answer stand out

- Show a grasp of the basic principles of the pre-1925 property legislation.
- Demonstrate that you have read the judgments in *Mexfield* and not just a summary of the facts.
- Show a clear understanding of land law principles – basic idea of a lease, distinction between leases and licences etc.
- Come to conclusions of your own based on your analysis of what the courts have said.

! Don't be tempted to . . .

- Give lengthy accounts of the facts of the cases and fail to highlight the points of law.
- Just deal with the decision in *Mexfield* and not mention the other cases.
- Fail to look at the reasoning of the judges.
- Set out some quotations from the judgments but fail to discuss them and to set out your own analysis.

 Question 4

A contract for a lease is not as effective in conferring rights against all persons as a lease.
To what extent do you agree that the above statement represents the law as it stands at present?

Answer plan

→ Explain the formalities for the creation of legal and equitable leases.

→ Explain the availability of specific performance to enforce equitable leases.

→ Show how there are areas where rights are the same for both legal and equitable leases.

→ Explain the rules on the enforceability of legal and equitable leases against third parties.

→ Demonstrate the differences between legal and equitable leases: enforceability of
covenants and application of section 62, LPA 1925.

Diagram plan

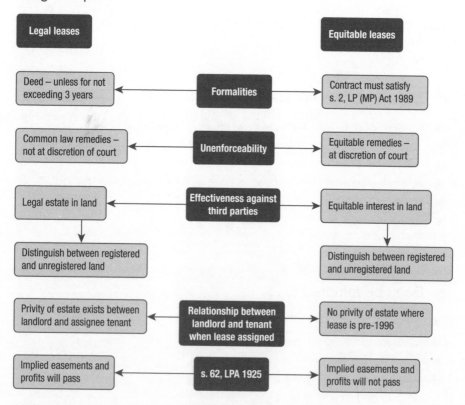

A printable version of this diagram plan is available from www.pearsoned.co.uk/lawexpressqa

Answer

I agree that this statement represents the present law. A contract for a lease is not as effective in all respects and against all persons as a lease. There are significant differences between the effectiveness of legal leases – which is what is meant in the question by 'leases' – and equitable leases, which are contracts for leases.[1]

A legal lease must be created by deed (s. 52(1), LPA 1925) unless it is for not less than three years, in which case it can be created without formalities provided that it complies with the requirements of section 54(1), LPA 1925: it is at the best rent obtainable, it is without a fine and it is in possession. Equitable leases can be created by agreement. The leading case on equitable leases today is[2] **Walsh v Lonsdale** (1882) 21 Ch D 9 where an agreement for a lease was held enforceable. Here an oral agreement for a seven-year lease was held binding on the grantor on the principle that 'equity looks on that as done which ought to be done'.[3] Since then section 2 of the Law of Property (Miscellaneous Provisions) Act 1989 has required all agreements for the sale or other disposition of an interest in land to be in writing, contain all terms agreed and be signed by the parties. The oral agreement in **Walsh v Lonsdale** would now create at most a periodic tenancy. Thus, the formal distinction between legal leases exceeding three years and equitable leases is reduced to the distinction between a deed and a written agreement.[4]

Thus, an equitable lease can in principle take effect as a lease against the landlord and be enforced against him whether it is made in law or in equity. However, an equitable lease is enforceable by equitable remedies, which are at the discretion of the court. So the court may, for example, refuse the grant of specific performance to enforce an equitable lease. In **Coatsworth v Johnson** (1886) 55 LJQB 220 HC, a tenant entered into possession under an agreement for a legal lease of farmland and so had an equitable lease. He claimed specific performance of the agreement for a lease but this was refused as he was in breach of the covenant to farm with good husbandry. The equitable lease could not be enforced and he was a mere tenant at will.

However, if an equitable lease is capable of being enforced by specific performance then, as Jessel MR said in **Walsh v Lonsdale**, '[the tenant] holds, therefore, under the same terms in equity as if a lease had been granted'. Thus the rights and duties of the parties under the lease will be the same. Another point of similarity is that by section 146(5)(a) of the LPA 1925 the provisions allowing a tenant to apply for relief from forfeiture apply to equitable leases and legal ones.[5]

[5] A point not often mentioned by students so make sure that you do!

[6] The question in effect asks two things and this picks up one of them: the relative effectiveness of legal and equitable leases in connection with their enforceability against 'all persons', i.e. third parties.

Nevertheless, as the question says, the equitable lease is not as effective against all persons[6] as a legal lease. An equitable lease only creates an equitable interest in land. When title to the land is unregistered then a legal lease is always binding on a purchaser of the freehold but an equitable lease is only binding on a purchaser for money or money's worth from the landlord if registered as an estate contract as a Class (iv) land charge (s. 4(6), Land Charges Act 1972). Where the title is registered, a legal lease for up to seven years is an overriding interest (Schedule 3, Paragraph 1 of the LRA 2002) and is binding on a purchaser without the need for registration. The fact that equitable leases are less effective than legal leases is shown by the situation where the holder of an equitable lease goes into possession and pays rent on a regular basis, such as monthly or yearly. They now have a legal periodic tenancy which would be an overriding interest.[7] Leases for longer than seven years require substantive registration (s. 27(2)(b), LRA 2002). Equitable leases should be protected by a notice on the register as estate contacts but if the tenant is in actual occupation then he may be protected by Schedule 3, Paragraph 2 of the LRA 2002 as being a person who has an equitable interest in the land and who is in actual occupation. The overall picture is that it is far more likely not that a tenant under an equitable lease will find that the lease is no binding on the purchaser of the freehold than the tenant under a legal lease.

[7] Here you are making a direct contrast between equitable leases and legal leases in the form of periodic tenancies. This type of clear explanation always brings extra marks.

The fact that a lease is only equitable can affect the relationship between the landlord and tenant when the lease is assigned. If privity of estate[8] exists between parties to a lease then the covenants in that lease can be enforced between them. Where there is a legal lease, there is privity of estate between the landlord and any assignee tenant and between any tenant and any assignee of the freehold reversion. Thus, leasehold covenants can be enforced between new parties to a legal lease. Privity of estate does not exist between parties to equitable leases (*Purchase* v *Lichfield Brewery*

[8] This area is dealt with later in more detail but here you do need to stress the term 'privity of estate' as this is the term on which this point hangs.

[1915] 1 KB 184 HC) although section 3(1) of the Landlord and Tenant (Covenants) Act 1995, which applies to leases granted on or after 1 January 1996[9] provides that all landlord and tenant covenants, except those which are personal, are enforceable between successors in title of the original parties. Thus, this particular distinction between legal and equitable leases only applies to leases granted before 1 January 1996.

Finally, the distinction between legal and equitable leases is important in connection with the implied grant of easements and profits under section 62 of the LPA 1925.[10] This provides that on a conveyance of land all rights appertaining to the land such as easements and profits[11] pass with the conveyance. As a result of **Wright v Macadam** [1949] 2 All ER 565 CA,[12] the conveyance may also elevate other rights to the status of easements such as, in this case, rights of storage. However, an agreement for a lease is not a conveyance within the statutory definition of a conveyance (s. 205(1)(ii), LPA 1925[13] and so an assignment of an equitable lease will not automatically carry with it the easements and profits that the assignor tenant will have enjoyed. Instead the easements will have to be spelt out in the assignment of the lease. Nor will it allow the creation of new easements or profits under the principle in **Wright v Macadam**.

Therefore, it can be seen that in all these ways a contract for a lease is not as effective in all respects and against all persons as a legal lease.[14]

[9] It is vital to stress that the position is different if the lease was granted on or after 1 January 1996. Only give enough detail here to illustrate the distinction between legal and equitable leases.

[10] You must show here just enough knowledge and understanding to illustrate this answer without going into too much detail.

[11] Students often forget that the rule also applies to profits.

[12] This is a separate point as *Wright* v *Macadam* is, in effect, an extension of the principle in section 62.

[13] This is the extra detail which brings extra marks: by stating the statutory authority you are lifting your answer to the level of a very good one.

[14] Note the reference back to the words of the question.

 Make your answer stand out

- Mention academic arguments, e.g. Gardner (1987) Equity, Estate Contracts and the Judicative Acts: *Walsh* v *Lonsdale* Revisited. *Oxford Journal of Legal Studies*, 7(1): 60 – on specific performance of equitable leases.

- Lord Browne-Wilkinson in *Tinsley* v *Milligan* [1994] AC 340 at 370–1 considered that now law and equity are fused there 'is one single law of property made up of legal and equitable interests'. What are the implications of this for this question?

- Likelihood that legal leases for three years or more will be overriding interests to bring them into line with the rule that only legal leases for three years or more require a deed.

> ## ! Don't be tempted to . . .
>
> ■ Go into detail about the types of lease – tenancies at will, leases for lives, etc.; just concentrate on looking at legal and equitable leases.
> ■ Discuss leases and licences – irrelevant.
> ■ Forget to check constantly that you are saying legal leases when you should and equitable leases when you should; it is all too easy to just say 'lease', in which case you will lose marks for inaccuracy.
> ■ Forget that, throughout, you are actually comparing legal and equitable leases and not writing about each of them in turn.
> ■ Give too much detail on section 62 of the LPA 1925: just enough to make your point in relation to the comparison between legal and equitable leases.

❓ Question 5

Earlier this year Barbara bought the freehold of 13 Mill Lane, Downtown from Eve. This has registered title and is divided into a downstairs office and an upstairs residential flat.

(a) The office is occupied by Fred under a ten-year lease contained in a deed at a monthly rent of £400. This provides that Fred is to use the premises solely as an office. Barbara has discovered that Fred is using the office as a betting shop and that he has demolished a wall at the side to enable customers to park their cars at the back.

(b) The flat is occupied by Tom under a two-year oral lease at a weekly rent of £350. Tom is complaining that he cannot sleep because of the constant revving up of motorbikes by Fred, who is a motorbike enthusiast, and he feels that the flat should have had adequate soundproofing installed. As a result, Tom has withheld the rent for the last two weeks.

Ignoring any question of security of tenure, advise Barbara whether the agreements made by Eve with Fred and Tom are binding on her and whether he can take steps to evict them.

Answer plan

→ Consider if the leases are legal or equitable.
→ Explain whether they bind Barbara.
→ Identify the covenants in the leases.
→ Analyse whether Barbara can sue on the covenants.
→ Explain the remedies of the landlord and relate them to the question.

Diagram plan

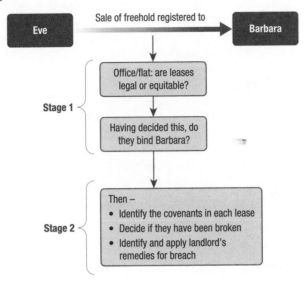

A printable version of this diagram plan is available from www.pearsoned.co.uk/lawexpressqa

Answer

(a) The first question is whether Fred's lease is legal or equitable and, as we are told that it is contained in a deed, it is legal as it complies with section 52(1) of the Law of Property Act (LPA) 1925 which requires a deed for the creation of a legal estate or interest in land. Title to the property appears to be already registered.[1] The lease to Fred is for ten years which by section 27(2)(b) of the Land Registration Act (LRA) 2002 requires substantive registration to bind Barbara. We are not told if it has been registered but, if not, Fred may have a legal monthly periodic tenancy based on payment of rent monthly. As this lease clearly does not exceed seven years and as this is not a case of first registration, it falls within Schedule 3, Paragraph 1 of the LRA 2002, which provides that legal leases not exceeding seven years are overriding interests, and thus it will bind Barbara even though it is not registered.

Fred is in breach of an express covenant in his lease to use the premises as an office as he is using them as a betting shop.

[1] It is always worthwhile checking if title is already registered or not and putting this in your answer. Make this a habit. This is relevant in this question because the rules on what is an overriding interest differ depending on whether it is a case of first or subsequent registration.

In addition he has demolished a wall. This is in breach of an implied covenant often known as not to commit waste. In ***Warren v Keen*** [1954] 1 QB 15 HC Denning LJ said that 'the tenant must take proper care of the place' and that the tenant must not damage the property wilfully or negligently. Clearly Fred is in breach of this.

The landlord, Barbara, may claim damages from Fred for breach of covenant and/or claim an injunction to restrain the breach. The injunction could be used to stop Fred using the premises as a betting shop. In addition, Barbara may claim to forfeit the lease but she can only do this if the lease contains a forfeiture clause.[2] If there is then Barbara must serve a notice on Fred under section 146 of the LPA 1925 which:[3]

(i)   specifies the breach;

(ii) requires it to be remedied if it is capable of remedy;

(iii) requires the tenant to pay compensation for the breach.

If the tenant fails to do (ii) and (iii) within a reasonable time, usually considered three months, the landlord may proceed to forfeit the lease.

The main issue is (ii) as in some cases the courts have held that breaches are incapable of some remedy, as where the breach has cast a stigma over the premises.

(b) Tom's lease is oral, but as it is for two years, section 54 of the LPA 1925 applies, which provides that leases not exceeding three years can be valid even though not by deed or in writing provided that three conditions set out in section 54(2) are satisfied.[4] These are that:

(i)   The lease takes effect in possession. This means that the lease must not be granted in advance of taking possession. We do not know if this is the case here.[5]

(ii) At the best rent. This means the best commercial rent. We are told that the rent is £350 a week. Is this the best rent?

(iii) Without a fine. A fine means a premium which is paid by the tenant and there is no evidence that this was paid.

We cannot tell, on the facts, if the lease was valid. If it was, then as this lease is for less than seven years, it will be an overriding

[2] You will lose marks if you do not state all the possible remedies which the landlord has, although you should look in more detail at forfeiture.

[3] Problem questions on leases normally expect you to discuss the landlord's remedy of forfeiture in detail. Do note that the procedure is different depending on whether the tenant's breach is of the covenant to pay rent or for other breach of covenant.

[4] Students often ignore these conditions and simply assume that section 54 applies as the lease does not exceed three years.

[5] The rule is strict: for section 54 to apply, the lease must take effect in possession. Exam questions do not always make it clear if this is so.

interest as in the case of Fred discussed earlier. However, if Tom has paid rent weekly he will have a weekly periodic tenancy which, as in the case of Fred, will be an overriding interest.

As the lease is oral, there can be no express terms but Tom might claim that the revving up of motorbikes by Fred is a breach of the implied covenant for quiet enjoyment. However, he will not succeed.[6] In **Southwark LBC v Mills** [2001] 1 AC 1 HL tenants sued their landlords as the activities of their neighbours were clearly audible and it was accepted that, although there was soundproofing, it was short of modern standards. The House of Lords approved the statement of Kekewich J in **Jenkins v Jackson** (1888) 40 Ch D 71 HC that quiet in the covenant for quiet enjoyment 'does not mean undisturbed by noise' and instead means that the tenant's actual possession will not be disturbed by the lessor or those acting under him. Furthermore, the court declined to imply a covenant that a landlord must install adequate soundproofing. Lord Hoffman pointed out that Parliament has dealt with the problems of substandard housing on numerous occasions but declined to impose a covenant requiring adequate soundproofing, and so it was not for the courts to do this.

[6] Do not assume that a covenant for quiet enjoyment means a covenant against excessive noise.

If Tom withholds the rent, he will be in breach of an implied covenant to pay rent and even if the landlord was in breach of covenant this would not justify a breach by Tom.[7]

[7] Do not make the mistake of saying that Tom is entitled to withhold rent as he thinks that the landlord is in breach. Two wrongs do not make a right!

The landlord's remedies for a breach of a covenant by the tenant to pay rent are to bring an action for arrears of rent and to claim forfeiture for non-payment of rent. If Barbara claims forfeiture, she must make a formal demand for rent unless, as is usually the case, the lease provides that this need not be done. Under section 212 of the Common Law Procedure Act 1852, if the landlord sues for possession and the tenant at any time before the trial pays into court all arrears of rent and costs, then all proceedings are stayed. Even if the tenant does not do this and judgment is given against him, he may apply for relief within six months after judgment and the court may grant relief on terms of payment of rent and costs and any other terms which it deems appropriate.

Make your answer stand out

■ Refer to the Law Commission Report (1996) *Landlord and Tenant: Responsibility for State and Condition of Property*, No. 238 on which covenants should be implied on a letting of property and especially para. 11.16.

■ Mention the Law Commission's proposals for reform of the law on forfeiture – see Law Commission Consultation Paper (2004) *Termination of Tenancies for Tenant Default*, No. 174.

■ Give a clear account of remedies, avoiding too much detail but relating the answer specifically to this question.

! Don't be tempted to . . .

■ Ignore the question of whether the leases are legal or equitable.

■ Ignore the fact that title to the land is registered.

■ Confuse the landlord's remedies for breach of covenant to pay rent with remedies for breaches of other covenants.

■ Assume that 'quiet enjoyment' means literally quiet.

❓ Question 6

In 2006, by a legal lease which was properly executed, Teresa granted Maggie a lease of a shop for 10 years. The lease makes the tenant liable for repairs but, although the shop was in disrepair when the lease was granted, Maggie has not made any repairs since taking it over. The lease also contains the following covenants:

(a) that the premises shall be used only as a high-class grocer;

(b) that the lease cannot be assigned without the landlord's consent;

(c) that at the end of the lease the tenant has the option to purchase the freehold;

(d) that the landlord may forfeit the lease in the event of a breach of covenant by the tenant.

In 2009 Teresa sold the freehold to Richard.

Maggie wishes to assign the lease to Fred but Richard objects on the ground that Fred runs a cut-price grocery shop elsewhere and he fears that Fred will run this shop in the same way.

Richard asks your advice on the following:

(a) What action should he take in respect of the breach of the repair covenant?

(b) Can he refuse a request by the tenant to purchase the freehold?

(c) Can he refuse consent to the proposed assignment of the lease and, if he does give consent, are there any conditions which he can impose?

Answer plan

→ Identify that this is a legal lease and also that it is a post-1996 lease and explain why this is significant.

→ Explain the position when freehold reversion is sold.

→ Consider the liability to repair.

→ Assignment of lease.

→ Conditions which may be imposed.

Diagram plan

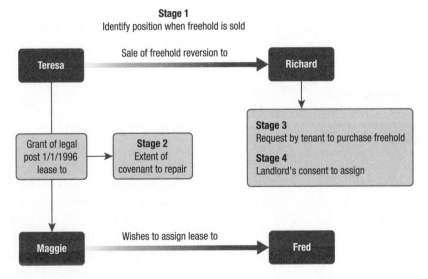

A printable version of this diagram plan is available from www.pearsoned.co.uk/lawexpressqa

[1] Always begin an answer to a problem question on covenants in leases with the two points in this paragraph.

Answer

The first points to note are that this is a legal lease and the date when it was granted.[1] Here it was granted in 2006 which means that the lease is governed by the Landlord and Tenant's (Covenants) Act 1995 which applies to all leases, both legal and equitable, granted on or after 1 January 1996.

The original landlord, Teresa, has sold the freehold reversion to Richard.[2] Under section 3(1) of the Landlord and Tenant (Covenants) Act (LT(C)A) 1995 the benefit of all landlord and tenant covenants passes on a sale of the freehold reversion. By section 2(1) of the Act the phrase 'landlord and tenant covenants' has a wider meaning than the 'touch and concern' test under the law applicable to pre-1996 leases and means that all covenants which affect the relationship of landlord and tenant pass, but not personal covenants. Clearly here all the covenants satisfy this test.

(a) Liability to repair the premises depends on the provisions in the lease. As Denning MR observed in *Warren v Keen* [1954] 1 QB 15 HC, 'Apart from express contract, a tenant owes no duty to a landlord to keep the premises in repair.' Here the lease makes the tenant liable for repairs but Maggie may object that they were in disrepair at the start of the lease and so she has no duty to make repairs. However, this argument will not succeed as in *Payne v Haine* (1847) 16 M & W 541 HC it was held that even if premises are in disrepair at the start of the lease the tenant must put them into repair at his own expense. The standard of repair is that of the reasonably minded owner after making allowance for the locality, character and age of the premises[3] (*Proudfoot v Hart* (1890) 25 QBD 42 HC). If the lease is assigned to Fred, he will be liable on the covenant as such a covenant is governed by section 3 of the LT(C)A 1995 which provides that on an assignment of a lease the burden of all landlord and tenant covenants will pass. The meaning of the phrase 'landlord and tenant covenants' was explained above and obviously includes a covenant to repair. As the lease contains a forfeiture clause if Fred does not make the repairs, Richard may bring forfeiture proceedings against him. Richard must, by section 146(1) of the LPA 1925, serve a notice specifying the breach, requiring it to be remedied and requiring the tenant to pay compensation.

(b) The question is whether the covenant giving the tenant the option to purchase the freehold binds Richard as a landlord and tenant covenant under section 3 of the LT(C)A 1995. Before the passage of this Act the test in *Spencer's Case* (1582) 5 Co Rep 16a applied[4] to all leases and this was whether the covenant 'touched and concerned the land'. If it did, then subsequent parties were bound. In **Woodall v Clifton** [1905] 2 Ch 257 HC it was held that this type of covenant did not 'touch and concern the land'. However, section 2(1) of the 1995 Act applies whether or not the covenant has reference to the subject matter of the lease and it is submitted that this will bind Richard and he will not be able to refuse a request from a tenant to purchase the freehold.

(c) The proposed assignment of the lease is governed by both the terms of the lease and also by statute.[5] The lease provides that the lease cannot be assigned without the landlord's consent. Under the Landlord and Tenant Act 1927, section 19(1A) (added by s. 22 of the LT(C)A 1995), the landlord and tenant of a non-residential lease, which this is, may agree in the lease what circumstances will justify the landlord in withholding consent. We are not told of any such circumstances and so we will assume that there are none.[6]

Section 19(1) of the Landlord and Tenant Act 1927 provides that in such a case the landlord cannot withhold consent unreasonably. In **International Drilling Fluids Ltd v Louisville Investments Ltd** [1986] All ER 321 CA it was held that the landlord is entitled to be protected from having the premises used or occupied in an undesirable way by an undesirable assignee, but consent to an assignment cannot be refused on grounds which have nothing to do with the relationship of landlord and tenant. So, a personal dislike would not be enough. In **Kened Ltd and Den Norske Bank Plc v Connie Investments Ltd** [1997] 1 EGLR 21 CA Millett LJ said that the essential question is, 'Has it been shown that no reasonable landlord would have withheld consent?'[7] However, where the landlord reasonably believes that a proposed assignment would lead to a breach of covenant in the lease this will be a valid reason for withholding consent. (See the House of Lords decision in **Ashworth Frazer Ltd v Gloucester City Council** [2001] UKHL 59 HL.) In this case the permitted use is a high-class grocer and we do not know that Fred intends to use the shop in breach of this. However, if Richard can prove that he will use it as a cut-price grocer in the same way as he appears to run his other shops then he is entitled to refuse consent. He also needs to remember that section 1(3) of the Landlord and Tenant Act 1988 provides that if the tenant asks for consent in writing, the landlord must give or refuse consent in writing and must do

[5] Always check what the lease says about assignment before you apply the statute.

[6] It will be the usual practice in an exam for there not to be any agreement between the landlord and the tenant setting out when consent can be withheld. This is so that you can discuss the general principles set out in the next paragraph.

[7] Obviously, the examiner will not expect you to recall long quotations but it will add to your marks if you recall straightforward ones such as these and apply them to the question.

this in a reasonable time, and that under section 1(6) it is for the landlord to prove that a refusal of consent was reasonable and that consent was given or withheld in a reasonable time.

Richard has also asked if there are any conditions which he can impose if he does give consent to the assignment of the lease. Under section 5(2) of the LT(C)A 1995 the tenant, on assigning the lease, is released from the tenant covenants but by section 16 the landlord may, as a condition of giving consent to an assignment, require the tenant to enter into an authorised guarantee agreement.[8] This means that the assignor tenant (Maggie) guarantees that the assignee tenant (Fred) will perform the covenants but this guarantee ends when the assignee tenant himself assigns the lease. At that point Richard, or whoever is now the landlord, can require them to enter into a similar covenant. In view of the continuing liability for failure to repair the premises, it would clearly be wise for Richard to insist on Maggie entering into an authorised guarantee agreement.

[8] If an exam question asks you about conditions which the landlord may impose on an assignment, you should mention this point.

✓ Make your answer stand out

■ Provide criticism of the old 'touch and concern' test for the running of covenants and how it was replaced by a wider test in the Landlord and Tenant (Covenants) Act 1995.

■ Mention the Law Commission's proposals for reform of the law on forfeiture – see Law Commission Consultation Paper (2004) *Termination of Tenancies for Tenant Default*, No. 174.

■ Clearly state the law on running of covenants where there is a freehold reversion.

■ Look in detail at the House of Lords' decision in *Ashworth Frazer Ltd* v *Gloucester City Council* (2001) UKHL 59.

! Don't be tempted to . . .

■ Forget that the Landlord and Tenant (Covenants) Act 1995 applies here.

■ Forget the different test for the running of covenants in the Landlord and Tenant (Covenants) Act 1995.

■ Forget that on an assignment of a post-1996 lease the landlord can require the tenant to enter into an authorised guarantee agreement.

7

Covenants affecting freehold land

How this topic may come up in exams

Exam questions in this area are traditionally regarded as difficult by students but the range of possible problem questions is considerably restricted and a clear plan for an answer carried through logically will pay tremendous dividends! Do not avoid this area but think of it as a challenge, as examiners, knowing the complexities of the law here, will readily reward students who make a really sound attempt. The proposals of the Law Commission for reform of the law in this area has given us an obvious, and not too difficult, area for essays and a useful point to mention at the end of problems.

■ Attack the question

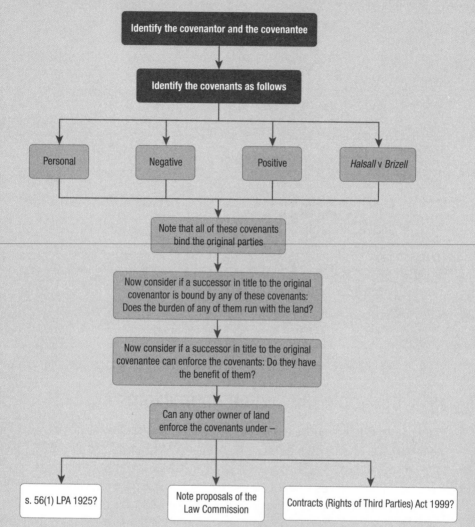

Identify the covenantor and the covenantee

Identify the covenants as follows

Personal

Negative

Positive

Halsall v *Brizell*

Note that all of these covenants bind the original parties

Now consider if a successor in title to the original covenantor is bound by any of these covenants: Does the burden of any of them run with the land?

Now consider if a successor in title to the original covenantee can enforce the covenants: Do they have the benefit of them?

Can any other owner of land enforce the covenants under –

s. 56(1) LPA 1925?

Note proposals of the Law Commission

Contracts (Rights of Third Parties) Act 1999?

A printable version of this diagram is available from www.pearsoned.co.uk/lawexpressqa

❓ Question 1

Arnold is the registered proprietor of 158 Seaview Road, a freehold property with registered title. In 2012 Arnold sold a plot to Barry. In his transfer, Barry covenanted as follows:

(a) Not to carry on any trade, business or profession on the land.

(b) To maintain all fences on his land which border on land retained by Arnold in good repair.

(c) Not to allow children to live at any house built on the land.

Barry subsequently built a house on his plot known as 'The Elms'.

Since then, Barry has sold his property to Deb. Now Deb has started a bed and breakfast business from her house, having obtained planning permission for the change of use, and she is refusing to repair a fence which blew down in a recent gale. She has six children who all live at The Elms.

Advise Arnold who wishes to take action to enforce the covenants.

How, if at all, would your answer differ if the recommendations of the Law Commission Report (2011) *Making Land Work: Easements, Covenants and Profits à Prendre* (LC 327) were implemented?

Diagram plan

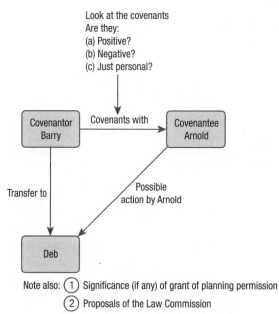

A printable version of this diagram plan is available from www.pearsoned.co.uk/lawexpressqa

Answer plan

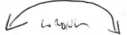

→ Identify the parties – Arnold is the covenantor and Barry is the covenantee.

→ Note that the question requires you to consider the running of the burden of the covenants.

→ Go through the covenants and decide which are positive, which are negative and which are merely personal.

→ Decide if Deb is liable on any of them in an action by Arnold.

→ Identify and apply the remedies available against Deb.

→ Apply the proposals of the Law Commission in its report (LC 327) to the situations.

Answer

[1] Right at the start of a question on restrictive covenants identify exactly who the parties to the covenant are.

[2] Point out that the covenantor's land has the burden of the covenant.

[3] In this short paragraph we have picked up a number of marks by clearly identifying the parties and the relevant terms. Questions on this area are not easy but if you lay a solid foundation like this you will gradually build up your marks.

[4] This is a straightforward and easily remembered point and should be placed near the start of any answer to a problem question.

In this question Barry, the covenantor, has entered into a number of covenants with Arnold, the covenantee.[1] Barry then sold the land with the burden[2] of the covenant to Deb. We are asked if Arnold can take action against Deb on the covenants.[3]

Barry as the original covenantor remains liable on the covenants and so Arnold can claim against him in the event of a breach by Deb.[4] This rule is not only one of common law but is also implied by section 79(1) of the Law of Property Act (LPA) 1925 which provides that a covenant relating to any land of the covenantor shall be deemed to be made 'on behalf of himself and his successors in title'. However, the rule in section 79(1) will not apply if the covenant provides that the liability of the original covenantor is to cease when he/she sells the land. Here we are not told if this is so. It is the universal practice, when land is sold, for the covenantor to take an indemnity covenant from the buyer so that if the covenantor, Barry, is sued for a breach committed by Deb, Deb will have to indemnify Barry for any damages which he has to pay.

The common law rule on covenants was established in **Austerberry v Oldham Corporation** (1885) 29 Ch D 750 where it was held that at common law covenants do not bind subsequent owners of land and this was followed in **Rhone v Stephens** [1994] 2 All ER 65. Thus at common law no action can be brought against Deb for breach of any of the covenants. However, it was held in **Tulk v Moxhay** (1848) 2 Ph 774 HC that in equity a covenant can bind subsequent owners on certain conditions. This rule was refined in subsequent cases so that it only applied to negative covenants. In **Haywood v Brunswick Permanent Benefit Building Society** (1881) 8 QBD 403 Brett LJ referred to covenants 'restricting the use of the land' and this is a good working definition of a negative covenant.[5] A rule of thumb is: does the covenant require the spending of money? If so, it is positive.

Here covenant (a) not to carry on any trade, business or profession on the land, is clearly negative and in principle can bind Deb under the principle in **Tulk v Moxhay**. Covenant (b), to maintain all fences on Deb's land which border on land retained by Arnold, is clearly positive and so cannot be enforced under **Tulk v Moxhay**.[6] The final covenant (c), not to allow children to live at any house built on the land, is subject to the rule that a covenant, in order to bind successors in title, must 'touch and concern' the land and this means that it must actually benefit the dominant land, in this case 158 Seaview Road,[7] and not be merely personal. In **Re Gadd's Land Transfer** [1966] Ch 56 HC Buckley J referred to 'something affecting either the value of the land or the method of its occupation or enjoyment' and it is submitted that a covenant not to allow children on the land does not come in this category and so will only bind Barry and not Deb.

Given that covenant (a) is negative it can then bind Deb provided that the following other conditions are satisfied:[8]

(a) The covenantee must own land for the benefit of which the covenant was entered into (**LCC v Allen** [1914] 3 KB 642). Here Arnold owns 158 Seaview Road, which adjoins Deb's land.

(b) The covenant must touch and concern the dominant land. It is clear that this covenant does satisfy the test mentioned above.

(c) It must be the common intention of the parties that the covenant shall run. Covenants made on or after 1 January 1926 are deemed to be made with subsequent parties (s. 79, LPA 1925).

(d) The covenantee must have notice of the covenant. As title to the land is registered, this means the covenant must be protected by a notice on the register of that title (s. 29, LRA 2002). If it is not, the covenant will not bind a purchaser.

Finally, the fact that Deb has obtained planning permission for the change of use to enable her to run a business from the house does

[5] A good way of improving your mark: an average answer would simply refer to 'negative' covenants but this answer goes one step further and looks more closely at what 'negative' means.

[6] Note that we have not said 'cannot be enforced' and left it at that as this covenant may be enforceable under other rules which it is better to look at later.

[7] This is often missed: the whole point of restrictive covenants is that they are interests in land which one piece of land (the dominant tenement) has over other land (the servient tenement) and so any covenant over the servient land must confer a benefit over the dominant land otherwise there is no connection between them.

[8] Do not assume that because the covenant is negative it is automatically binding.

[9] This point often appears in a question on covenants (and also on easements and profits where the answer is the same).

not affect the validity of the restrictive covenant.[9] (**Re Martin's Application** (1988) 57 P & CR 119 at 124.)

However, Deb may apply to the Upper Tribunal to modify or discharge this covenant under section 84 of the LPA 1925 and the fact that planning permission has been obtained may be a factor in persuading the Tribunal to grant the application.[10]

[10] Here is where you get the extra marks: it is not the actual existence of planning permission which is directly relevant but the fact that it can be used as evidence to discharge the covenant.

The only covenant which is binding on Deb is covenant (a), as a negative covenant. If she refuses to discontinue her use of the house as a bed and breakfast business then an action for damages may be brought and/or an injunction to restrain the continued use in the case of (b).[11]

[11] Make it a rule to always end an answer to a question on covenants with the remedies which are appropriate.

The proposals of the Law Commission on this area were set out as clause 2(1) of a draft bill[12] attached to the 2011 report on covenants. If they were implemented then the answers would be affected as the Law Commission has proposed that in future all obligations expressed as covenants will take effect as land obligations and will be capable of binding the land provided that:

[12] You could just quote the actual report but it is better to set out the words of the draft bill as you can then apply them to the question.

1 The covenantor owns an estate in land.

2 The obligation is capable of being imposed under clause 1. Clause 1 refers to obligations for the benefit of an estate in land and which touch and concern the land.

3 The benefit of the covenant touches and concerns land in which the covenantee has an estate.

4 The covenant is not expressed to be personal to either party.

[13] You may be tempted to say that clause 2(1) (4) above applies as it says that covenants will not bind as land obligations if they are expressed to be personal to either party. However, this will only apply where the covenant actually *says* that it is personal to the parties. In this case it is the *nature* of the covenant that makes it personal.

The effect would be that the distinction between positive and negative covenants would be abolished and clause 1(3) provides that land obligations include both negative and positive obligations and so both would be capable of binding third parties. Thus the answer on covenant (a) would be the same as the covenant is binding under the present law but whereas covenant (b) is not binding now as it is positive it would be binding under the Law Commission's bill as a land obligation. However, in both cases the benefit of the covenant would need to be protected by registration. However covenant (c) is a personal covenant and would not pass the test set out above as the benefit of the covenant would not touch and concern land in which the covenantee (Arnold) has an estate.[13]

✓ **Make your answer stand out**

- Give a clear structure to your answer first identifying the covenantor and covenantee, then identifying who has the benefit and who has the burden of the covenant.
- Read Cooke (2009) To Restate or Not to Restate? Old Wine, New Wineskins, Old Covenants, New Ideas. *Conveyancer* 448. This article, written by the Law Commissioner responsible for property law, is essential reading for a good mark as it gives her latest thinking on the Consultation Paper.
- Read also the article by Davis (1998) The Principle of Benefit and Burden. *CLJ*, 57(3): 522. This reviews this whole area.
- Although a grant of planning permission does not discharge a restrictive covenant, the implementation of that permission may alter the standard of what constitutes reasonable user (see Morritt LJ in *Watson* v *Croft Promo-Sport Ltd* [2009] EWCA Civ 15). Although this will probably not be the case in this answer, it is a point worth mentioning.

! **Don't be tempted to . . .**

- Rush in and start an answer before you have clearly identified the parties and the relevant terms.
- Fail to distinguish clearly between the four different covenants – the law, as is usual in these questions, is different for each.
- Explain what a personal covenant is.

❓ Question 2

Ted owned a large property, Firtrees, which did not have registered title. In 1980 he built a house, Oak Lodge, in the grounds of Firtrees and sold it to Laura. In 1981 he built a second house, Pinetrees, in the grounds of Firtrees and sold it to Roger. In 1982 he built a third house, Birches, in the grounds of Firtrees and sold it to Mark.

In 1984 Roger sold Pinetrees to Babs.

In each case the buyers from Ted entered into covenants which restricted their use of land, but which imposed different restrictions in each case. In the case of Roger the covenants which he entered into were:

(a) Not to allow the hedges surrounding Pinetrees to grow to more than 6 metres in height.

(b) Not to erect any building on Pinetrees that exceeds 10 metres in height.

Laura and Mark tell you that Babs has allowed the hedges to grow to at least 20 metres high and that she has told them that she is applying for planning permission to erect another storey on Pinetrees which will take its height to 20 metres.

Advise Ted, Laura and Mark on what action can be taken and against whom.

Answer plan

→ Identify the parties – Laura, Roger and Mark are all covenantors and Ted is the covenantee.

→ Note that the question requires you to consider the running of the burden of the covenants and also the benefit of it.

→ Go through the covenants and decide which are positive and which are negative.

→ Decide if Babs is liable on any of them.

→ Then consider separately if Ted, Laura and Mark can take action against Babs.

→ Finally, identify and apply the remedies available against Babs.

Diagram plan

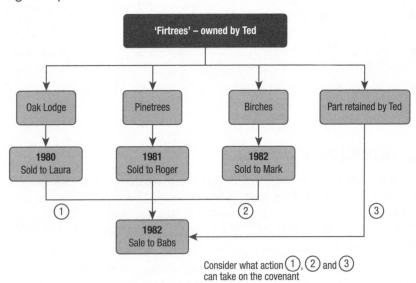

Consider what action ①, ② and ③ can take on the covenant

A printable version of this diagram plan is available from www.pearsoned.co.uk/lawexpressqa

Answer

In this question Laura, Roger and Mark have entered into covenants with Ted and so they are all covenantors. Ted is the covenantee. Roger then sold the land with the burden of the covenant to Babs. We are asked if Ted, Laura and Mark can take action against Babs on the covenants.[1]

There are different considerations to be borne in mind when considering the position of Laura and Mark but before we look at whether they can sue we need to decide if there has been any breach of the covenants and, if so, who might be liable.[2]

Roger as the original covenantor remains liable on the covenants and is potentially liable in the event of a breach by Babs.[3] This rule is not only one of common law but is also implied by section 79(1) of the LPA 1925 unless the covenant provides that the liability of the original covenantor is to cease when he/she sells the land. Here we are not told if this is so. It is the universal practice, when land is sold, for the covenantor to take an indemnity covenant from the buyer so that if the covenantor (Roger) is sued for a breach committed by Babs, Babs will have to indemnify Roger for any damages which he has to pay.

However, it is obviously better to claim against Babs as not only is she actually responsible for the breach, but also an injunction can be claimed against her as well as damages whereas only damages would be available against Roger.

The common law rule on covenants was established in ***Austerberry v Oldham Corporation*** (1885) 29 Ch D 750 where it was held that at common law covenants do not bind subsequent owners of land but in ***Tulk v Moxhay*** (1848) 1 H & Tw 105 it was held that in equity a covenant can bind subsequent owners on certain conditions. This rule was refined in subsequent cases so that it only applied to negative covenants. In ***Haywood v Brunswick Permanent Benefit Building Society*** (1881) 8 QBD 403 Brett LJ referred to covenants 'restricting the use of the land' and this is a good working definition of a negative covenant. A rule of thumb is: does the covenant require the spending of money? If so, it is positive. If it does not then it is

[1] Identify the parties and the relevant terms making sure that you identify who has the benefit of the covenant and who has the burden. The party with the benefit will be the claimant and the party with the burden will be the defendant.

[2] This question clearly involves questions on the running of the burden of the covenant (i.e. can third parties be sued on the covenant) *and* the running of the benefit of the covenant (i.e. can third parties sue for any breaches of the covenants). First deal with running of the burden as if there turns out to be no one who *can be* sued (i.e. the burden does not run) then there is no point is asking who *can* sue.

[3] This is a straightforward and easily remembered point and should be placed near the start of any answer to a problem question of this kind.

negative. Covenant (a) is positive even though it is actually phrased in negative terms as Babs will have to take positive action to prevent the hedges growing more then 6 metres in height. Thus it will not bind her and any action in respect of its breach will have to be taken against Roger. However, the covenant not to erect buildings that exceed more than 10 metres in height is negative and can bind Babs provided that the following other conditions are satisfied:

(a) The covenantee must own land for the benefit of which the covenant was entered into. (**LCC v Allen** [1914] 3 KB 642). Ted owns 'Firtrees'. There is, however, a question as to whether Laura and Mark are covenantees but this will be considered later.[4]

(b) The covenant must touch and concern the dominant land. This means that the covenant must actually benefit the land and it is clear that a covenant to keep buildings to a certain height will do so.

(c) It must be the common intention of the parties that the covenant shall run. Covenants made on or after 1 January 1926 are deemed to be made with subsequent parties (s. 79, LPA 1925).

(d) The covenantee must have notice of the covenant. As title to the land was unregistered at the time[5] and as the covenant was entered into on or after 1 January 1926, it must be registered as a Class D(ii) land charge, otherwise it will not bind a purchaser.

Ted can take action against Roger as they were the original parties to the covenant and he can also take action against Babs. The question is then whether Laura and Mark can claim the benefit of the covenants.[6] One way would be through a building scheme where all parties have entered into identical covenants and so create a kind of local law for a particular area. The conditions were laid down in **Elliston v Reacher** [1908] 2 Ch 374 but one element, that of mutuality, is lacking as each purchaser entered into different covenants[7] and this is a requirement (see **Emile Elias v Pine Groves** (1993) 66 P & CR 1.

Laura purchased Oak Lodge in 1980 before the sale of Pinetrees to Roger in 1981.[8] This is significant as it means that Laura cannot claim that when she bought Oak Lodge the benefit of the covenant entered into by Roger was annexed to Oak Lodge as at that time the covenants had not been imposed. Similarly it cannot be argued

[4] 'Park' this for now as if you deal with it at this point you will go completely off your present point which is whether ~~anyone~~ can sue Babs.

[5] When you come to this point in your answer do glance back at the question and check again if title was registered or unregistered.

[6] Make this point follow on from the previous one: the original parties can of course sue but whether successors in title can sue will depend on whether the benefit has passed to them.

[7] This point often arises in a question and you should watch for it.

[8] Watch for the scenario in this question where land with the burden of the covenant is sold after one piece of land (Oak Lodge here) and before the sale of another piece of land (Birches). The answer, as we see here, will be different in each case.

that the benefit of the covenants imposed on Pinetrees had been assigned to Oak Lodge. Laura cannot claim that the provisions of section 1 of the Contracts (Rights of Third Parties) Act 1999 apply here as the covenants were entered into before the Act came into force.[9] The only other possibility is the use of section 56(1) of the LPA 1925 which enables a party to 'take . . . the benefit of any condition, right of entry, covenant or agreement over or respecting land or other property, although he may not be named as a party to the convey-ance or other instrument'.[10] This will only apply where Laura was able to be a party to the covenant and identifiable and in existence at the date of the covenant (**White v Bijou Mansions** [1937] Ch 610). We would need to see the exact words of the covenant to decide if Laura was intended to be a party. If so, she can claim, if not, she cannot.

Mark is in a different position as he bought Birches after the sale of Pinetrees to Roger. He may claim that the benefit of Roger's cove-nant has been expressly assigned to the Birches or he may claim that the benefit of the covenant has been expressly annexed to his land as in **Rogers v Hosegood** [1900] 2 Ch 388[11] but again we would need to see the exact words of the conveyance to Mark.[12]

The final possibility, and the one most likely to be used by Mark, is to claim that the benefit of the covenant has passed to him by implied annexation under the principle in **Federated Homes v Mill Lodge Properties Ltd** [1980] 1 All ER 371.

If Babs is successfully sued the remedy sought[13] would probably be an injunction to restrain her from going ahead with the building.

[9] Watch for this point! If you do not you could waste time and thus marks on an explanation of the Act.

[10] Where you get a person in Laura's position then you need to think of two points: first the Contracts (Rights of Third Parties) Act 1999 and then section 56(l) of the LPA. Here the 1999 Act does not apply so we have had to turn to section 56(l).

[11] See that there are two possibilities: assignment or express annexation. We do not know if they will apply so the examiner will just expect you to mention them.

[12] Note how this question does not close off these possibilities as the examiner is hoping that you will earn marks by looking at them all.

[13] Never forget to mention remedies!

 Make your answer stand out

- Clear distinction in your answer between the question of who has the burden of the covenants and who has the benefit. It is absolutely crucial to get this right at the start.
- Distinguish between when section 56(1) of the LPA 1925 applies and when section 1 of the Contracts Rights of Third Parties Act 1999 applies.
- Read Stevens (2004) The Contracts (Rights of Third Parties) Act 1999. *LQR*, 120: 292 who argues that this Act does not in fact have a very wide application.
- Read the judgment of Neuberger J in *Amsprop Trading Ltd* v *Harris Distribution Ltd* [1997] 1 WLR 1025 on the circumstances in which section 56(1) of the LPA can apply.

> ! **Don't be tempted to . . .**
>
> - Assume that Ted, Laura and Mark all have the same rights to enforce the covenant. If they had, you would not have been asked to advise them separately.
> - Although the more difficult parts of the question deal with enforceability of covenants remember to deal with who can be liable first – i.e. has the burden passed?
> - Apply only section 1 of the Contracts (Rights of Third Parties) Act 1999 or section 56(1) of the LPA. Both need to be considered.

? Question 3

Ken is a large landowner who owns 25,000 acres used for mixed farming. The land, known as Kenshire, has registered title. A river runs through part of his land and there have often been floods in the winter. He has just completed an expensive drainage scheme which should prevent flooding in future but there will be a continuing cost from keeping the drains and banks in repair.

He intends to sell parts of this land to other farmers but he wishes to put covenants in each conveyance to:

(a) Oblige each farmer to contribute to the cost of the upkeep of the drains.

(b) Prevent each farmer from using the land sold to him in such a way that further flooding is caused.

In addition Ken wishes to impose extra covenants on particular areas of land sold.

Ken also wishes to be able to take action himself on the covenants in the event of a breach and he also wishes anyone who acquires his land in the future to be able to do so.

Advise Ken on how he can achieve these objectives.

Answer plan

→ Identify who is to be able to enforce the covenants and who the covenants are to be enforced against.

→ Explain the ways in which the benefit of the covenants can pass in equity.

→ Distinguish the passing of the benefit of the covenant at common law from that in equity.

→ Passing of the burden of the covenants – distinguish between covenants (a) and (b).

Diagram plan

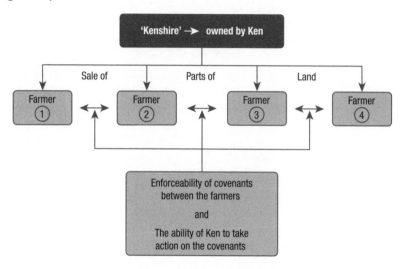

A printable version of this diagram plan is available from www.pearsoned.co.uk/lawexpressqa

Answer

This question is concerned with how Ken can make certain covenants which he intends to impose on sales of land binding on the buyers and also how to enable each buyer to sue any other buyer who is in breach of them. In addition he wishes to be able to enforce them.

[1] Make the identification of the covenantor and covenantee your first point.

Each farmer who buys a plot and enters into these covenants will be the covenantor and Ken, as the person with whom they enter the covenants, will be the covenantee.[1] There is no problem with Ken taking action against any farmer who breaches the covenant as they are both parties to it. However, problems could arise in cases when one farmer wishes to sue any other farmer under covenant (c) on the grounds that they have breached covenants (a) and/or (b).

[2] If they were not third parties and were instead parties to the contract there would be no problem with enforcement. Examiners are always impressed with answers which show a sure grasp of fundamentals as here.

When one farmer claims to sue another farmer the farmer who sues will be a third party to the original covenant made between Ken and that farmer.[2] In general a third party cannot sue on a covenant but as restrictive covenants are themselves interests in the land itself it is possible in some cases for third parties to sue and our objective must be to enable this to be so here.[3]

[3] We are not asked why something *cannot* be done but how it *can* be done and this must be the focus of your answer.

Where one farmer (X) who is not a party to the original covenant wishes to sue another farmer (Y) then X must show that the benefit of the covenant has passed to them. One clear way in which this can be done is by the existence of a building scheme which enables a common vendor, Ken here, to transfer the benefit of any covenant to every buyer of a plot so that a kind of 'local law' is created whereby all the parties have the same rights and obligations under the covenants and may enforce them against each other in equity. The requirements were laid down in **Elliston v Reacher** [1908] 2 Ch 374 but there cannot be a building scheme where different buyers are under different obligations (**White v Bijou Mansions** [1937] Ch 610). We are told that here extra covenants are to be imposed on different plots of land.[4] The practical answer is to impose the same covenants mentioned in the question on all the buyers, thus creating a building scheme, and then quite separately require particular buyers to enter into separate covenants as appropriate.

[4] This is a good example of where you need to mention a point as the examiner clearly expects you to and it could be relevant.

Another possibility is to expressly annex the benefit of the covenants to each plot of land when it is sold. Thus in **Rogers v Hosegood** [1900] 2 Ch 388 the benefit of a covenant was held to be expressly annexed to land where the covenant's wording was that 'the covenant may enure to the benefit of the vendors, their successors and assigns and others claiming under them to all or any of their lands adjoining': Compare these words with those in **Renals v Cowlishaw**[5] (1878) 9 Ch D 125 where the covenant had been made with the vendors 'their heirs, executors, administrators and assigns'. The crucial difference was that in **Rogers v Hosegood** the covenant mentioned the actual land to be benefited but in **Renals v Cowlishaw** it did not. The message is clear: Ken can achieve his object by expressly annexing the benefit of the covenants by using similar language to that in **Rogers v Hosegood**.

[5] *Renals* v *Cowlishaw* makes an excellent contrast with *Rogers* v *Hosegood* on express annexation. Set out the wording of the covenant in each and compare them.

[6] Where you get a question with the benefited land covering a very large area remember that you will need to consider if the covenant could benefit the whole area.

There is, however, a problem in that Kenshire covers 25,000 acres and the drainage scheme was designed to prevent flooding which had occurred on part of the land. It may be that some plots are a long way away from the river and so could not benefit from the drainage scheme. Will the covenants still apply to them?[6] The answer is again in the wording of the covenants which must state that they apply to 'each and every part of the land' as held in **Marquess of Zetland v Driver** [1939] Ch 1.

[7] Assignment of the benefit of covenants is now less important in view of the decision in *Federated Homes* which made implied annexation much easier. However, as we are advising a client in general it must be mentioned.

Even if this is not done it may be possible to argue that the benefit of the covenants has been annexed to the lands sold by implied annexation under the decision in **Federated Homes v Mill Lodge Properties Ltd** [1980] 1 All ER 371. This held that implied annexation is provided for by section 78(1) LPA 1925 which says that 'A covenant relating to the land of the covenantee shall be deemed to be made with the covenantee and his successors in title.' In **Federated Homes** itself the covenant said that it related to 'land of the covenantee' and in this case that will be Kenshire. So it is essential that the covenant makes this clear.

Another possibility is that instead of annexing the benefits of the covenants to the land sold, the benefit could be assigned.[7] This method was used, for example, in **Roake v Chadha** [1984] 1 WLR 40 but it does depend on the benefit of the covenant being expressly assigned each time the land is sold. Express annexation is more straightforward.

Anyone who buys Ken's own land from him in future will be a successor in title and will be able to sue any farmer who has bought their land from Ken and is in breach of the covenants. This is because at common law the benefit of a covenant can run to enable the successor in title of the original covenantee to sue the original covenantor.[8] (See **The Prior's Case** (1368) YB 42 Edw 3 and, for a modern illustration, **Smith and Snipes Hall Farm v River Douglas Catchment Board** [1949] 2 KB 500). However, the common law rule will not enable a successor in title of Ken to claim that the benefit has passed to them to enable them to claim against successors in title to the original covenantor.[9] In order to do this they must prove that the benefit has passed to them in equity and this can be done on proof that the benefit of the covenant has been annexed to them or has been assigned to them, both of which have been discussed above.

In addition we must decide if the burden has passed to successors in title of the original covenantors.[10] Although this is not directly raised by the question, we must mention this point to make the answer complete. Covenant (a) is positive and so is only binding on the original covenantor. Covenant (b) may be binding on successors in title under the principle in **Halsall v Brizell** [1957] 1 All ER 371 and could be said to be negative and so under the rule in **Tulk v Moxhay** (1848) 1 H and TW 105 will, in principle, bind subsequent parties provided that, it is registered against the burdened land.

[8] It is easy to get completely lost here so just remember this: if you get a question where Y is the original covenantee and has sold the land with the benefit of the covenant to X then X can sue on it provided that he/she is suing the original covenantor – the person who entered into the covenant with Y. However, the common law rule will not enable X to sue anyone who has subsequently acquired the land. To do this X must use the rules in equity. See the next note.

[9] This is very important and so do remember it otherwise you could go completely astray in the exam and lose lots of marks! If a person wishes to claim that the burden of the covenant runs in equity under the rule in *Tulk v Moxhay* then they must show that the benefit has passed to them in equity under the three rules mentioned above: by the existence of a building scheme, by annexation or by assignment.

[10] The question asks you about action being taken on the covenants but to make the answer complete you do need to briefly mention who can actually be sued which is what this final paragraph does.

Make your answer stand out

- Approach the question from the right angle: it is not asking you (as questions often do) to decide on the validity of existing covenants but to address the more practical issue of how covenants can be made binding on buyers of land and how to enable each buyer to sue any other buyer who is in breach of them.

- Deal with the issues of benefit and burden separately.

- Distinguish between the position at common law and in equity.

- Read *Crest Nicholson Residential (South) Ltd* v *McAllister* [2004] 1 WLR 2409 which considered the decision in *Federated Homes* v *Mill Lodge Properties*. Chadwick LJ held that statutory annexation under section 78(1) of the LPA could only occur if the covenant, or conveyances in which the covenant was contained, identified the land to be benefited either specifically or by implication. By contrast if you look at the wording in *Rogers* v *Hosegood* (see the answer above) where annexation was express, the actual land was not precisely identified. The result is that the rules seem tighter for implied annexation.

Don't be tempted to . . .

- Fail to set out the different issues right at the start.

- Distinguish between the different ways in which the benefit can run.

- Leave out one of the two methods of annexation.

- Confuse running of the benefit of the covenants in equity and at common law.

- Leave out a mention of when the burden can pass and distinguish between the different covenants.

Question 4

Critically consider the proposition that the present law on freehold covenants is unnecessarily complex and evaluate the proposals contained in the Law Commission Report (2011) *Making Land Work: Easements, Covenants and Profits à Prendre* (LC 327) for reform in this area.

Answer plan

→ Identify the main problems and give a brief historical background.

→ Explain the rule that positive covenants do not run with the land – how this has caused problems and then look in detail at how the Law Commission intends to deal with it.

→ Explore other areas, especially the proposals on the running of the benefit of covenants.

→ Mention the proposal of the Law Commission that covenants will be legal interests.

→ Conclusion – do restrictive covenants play any useful purpose in the law anyway?

Diagram plan

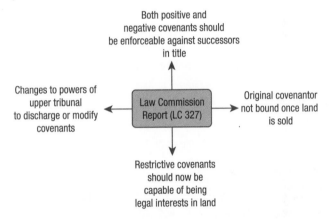

A printable version of this diagram plan is available from www.pearsoned.co.uk/lawexpressqa

[1] You should see from the question that you are asked two things and not one and so you need to make this clear in your introduction. This will at once impress your examiner and earn you extra marks. You could of course take the opposite view that the proposals will not achieve their desired result but there is general agreement that at least their implementation will improve the law.

Answer

The present law on freehold covenants is unnecessarily complex and I consider that the proposals of the Law Commission Report (2011) LC 327 will go a long way to both clarifying and modernising the law.[1]

There is no problem where the original covenantee wishes to claim against the original covenantor but problems certainly exist in two cases:

(a) Where it is sought to make a successor in title to the original covenantor liable on the basis that the burden of the covenant has passed to them.

(b) Where a successor in title to the original covenantee wishes to sue on the basis that the benefit of the covenants has passed to them.

The problem in (a) is that, whereas the burden of the covenant may pass to a successor in title if the covenant is negative, it will not if it is positive. The difficulties which this rule can give rise to can be seen in **Rhone v Stephens** [1994] 2 All ER 65[2] where the owner of a building, having divided it into two dwellings, sold one part, a cottage, and retained the other, the house. On the sale of the cottage he covenanted to maintain the roof that projected over the cottage. In fact the roof leaked and damaged the cottage. The present owners of the cottage, to whom the benefit of the covenant had been expressly assigned, sued the successors in title of the original covenantor but it was held that, as the covenant was positive, there could be no liability. If, for example, the covenant had been negative, such as not to run a business on the land, then there would have been liability.

In fact although the case which is the fountain head of the law here, **Tulk v Moxhay** (1848) 1 H and TW 105 actually concerned a negative covenant the court did not distinguish between positive and negative covenants and this development only came later in, for example, **Haywood v Brunswick Permanent Benefit Building Society** (1881) 8 QBD 403.

The failure of positive covenants to bind successors in title was described by the Law Commission (2008) in the Consultation Paper LC 186 (para. 7.39) as the 'greatest and clearest deficiency' in the law.[3] The Report which followed the Consultation Paper outlines (paras. 5.23–5.26) the ways in which positive covenants can be made to run with the land such as long leases, a right of entry annexed to an estate rentcharge, indemnity covenants and the 'benefit and burden' principle in **Halsall v Brizell** [1957][4] 3 All ER 371 but the Report concludes, rightly, that none of them are satisfactory as 'they can all be made to work but only indirectly, with unnecessary cost and risk' (para. 5.27).

The Report did not consider that the 'commonhold' method which was introduced by Part 1 of the Commonhold and Leasehold Reform Act 2002 was a solution[5] as it pointed out at para. 5.17 that it

[2] It often helps to 'anchor' your answer on a general point like this if you can give the facts of a case.

[3] This is the main issue raised by the question and you need to spend most of your answer on it.

[4] You should at least identify the ways in which positive covenants can be made to run in order to give a complete picture. If you have time you could explain how and why they are not satisfactory (e.g. the problems in identifying when the principle in *Halsall* v *Brizell* applies) but do not let this get you off the main point of the Law Commission's proposals.

[5] If you have time you could say more on this but the essential point is that it can apply as an alternative to leasehold. In fact you could do some research and show that the take up of commonhold has been very small.

applied where developers of freehold land wished to establish schemes of mutually enforceable covenants and is 'designed for truly interdependent developments such as flats, or business units that share facilities and physical structure'.

Thus the Law Commission has proposed that the law on positive covenants should be reformed (para. 5.63) and that they should be enforceable against successors in title as negative covenants are.[6]

[6] This was the main conclusion and so you should make this one of the central points of your answer.

However, this then brings with it the question of who can enforce those covenants especially as the law, by permitting the enforcement of covenants against successors in title, will be making the operation of covenants more burdensome.[7] To meet this point obligations are carefully defined (para. 6.38) and consist of:

[7] This is one of those essential connecting sentences which really add to your marks. Many students will only write about the positive covenants but there is much more to the Report than this.

1 A promise not to do something on the covenantor's land (these are the old negative covenants).

2 A promise to do something on one's own land or on a boundary structure.

3 A promise to make a reciprocal payment.

There is also a requirement that the benefit of the promise touches and concerns the land of the covenantee, and that the promise is not expressed to be personal. This would exclude, as now, personal covenants.

The Commission had noted in the Consultation Paper (para. 7.37) that the present rules as to the running of benefit and burden of restrictive covenants are a significant defect in the law because of their complexity. However, its Report points out (para. 6.45) that not all consultees agreed, and 'we accept that practitioners have learnt to live with the rules and to operate them efficiently'. Thus they will remain.[8]

[8] This is an important point: do not confine your answer to the proposed change in the law on positive covenants.

Underlying these changes is a more fundamental one. Restrictive covenants have always been equitable interests in land and the Report points out that 'These are generically different from easements and profits, because they cannot exist as legal interests in land.' It points out (para. 5.4) that the fundamental idea of a covenant is that it is a contractual right, and not a property right.[9] This contractual status is reflected in the fact that contractual liability between

[9] It is vital that you are clear on this as this point underlies much of the present law e.g. the fact that the covenantor remains liable on the covenant after he/she has parted with the land.

the original parties to a covenant persists despite changes in the ownership of the land; when the land is sold, the original covenantor remains liable. Nevertheless restrictive covenants have a hybrid status in that they can be made to bind a purchaser of land if they take effect as equitable interests.

The Commission proposes that all of this should be swept away and restrictive covenants should now be legal interests created by deed and added to the list of legal interests set out in section 1(2) (a) of the LPA 1925.[10] In addition they should only be capable of being created where title to the land is registered (para. 8.38).

[10] This is an important change which the examiner will expect you to mention.

Moreover clause 2(2) of the draft bill attached to the Report of the Law Commission specifically provides that promises in the form of restrictive covenants (e.g. not to build on land etc.) will take effect as land obligations and not covenants although the word covenant can still be used. They will run with the benefited land, and bind successors in title to the burdened land, because they are interests in land, but they will not bind the original covenantor. This means that the taking out of indemnity covenants so that the original covenantor will be indemnified against future breaches will not be necessary.

The Law Commission recommends that land obligations should be able to exist in equity, where, for example, the obligation was not created by deed but is in a written agreement which complies with the Law of Property (Miscellaneous Provisions) Act 1989 or is not registered. However, the Law Commission (para. 6.52) feels that there should be very few that remain equitable as generally land obligations will be contained in transfers of land and will become legal upon registration, in the same way as easements.

Finally, the powers for the Upper Tribunal to exercise its jurisdiction under section 84 of the LPA 1925 to discharge or modify covenants will be clarified and made more transparent.[11]

[11] Most students ignore this point but the jurisdiction under section 84 is important in practice.

Overall it is submitted that these proposals will bring clarity to an area where this has long been lacking and it is suggested that the draft bill implementing these proposals should be brought before Parliament as soon as possible.

✓ Make your answer stand out

- Look at how the law on restrictive covenants has developed in other jurisdictions – the Law Commission Report has many references, so follow one or two up!
- Read Cooke (2009) To Restate or Not to Restate? Old Wine, New Wineskins, Old Covenants, New Ideas. *Conveyancer* 448. This very readable article explains the Law Commission's proposals in depth. Note, though, that it is commenting on the consultation paper and not the final report.
- Look at Simpson (1986) *History of the Land Law* (2nd edn), especially at pp. 256–60 – this will give you some excellent background material on how and why the law of restrictive covenants developed.
- Do some research on how the jurisdiction of the Upper Tribunal (formerly the Lands Tribunal) exercises its jurisdiction under section 84 of the LPA 1925. How might this change and what will its effects be?

! Don't be tempted to . . .

- Just say what the law on restrictive covenants is: a merely descriptive answer to what is a specific question will earn you a very bad mark!
- Overlook one area at the expense of another: deal with problems in the law but not the Law Commission's proposals or vice versa.
- Do set the scene – do not plunge into an answer without first making sure that you have explained what the problems are.

🖎 Question 5

Critically consider the law on when a person who is not a party to a restrictive covenant can sue on that covenant.

Answer plan

→ Show where this point fits into the law on covenants.

→ Explain how section 56(1) of the LPA 1925 enables a third party to sue and mention what problems there are in the interpretation of this.

→ Reinforce this by distinguishing between two contrasting cases.

→ Now evaluate the effect of section 1 of the Contracts (Rights of Third Parties) Act 1999, indicating the problems in the interpretation of this.

→ Round off the answer by evaluating how the proposals in the Law Commission Report would change the law.

Diagram plan

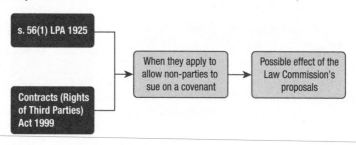

A printable version of this diagram plan is available from www.pearsoned.co.uk/lawexpressqa

[1] The word 'making' of the covenant is important and shows the examiner that you know exactly what you are talking about. When the covenant is made then successors in title of both the original covenantor and covenantee will be third parties but this is dealt with by the rules on the running of the benefit and burden of the covenant. A small point but one which will make your answer stand out.

[2] It really does help, especially in a complex area such as this, to set the scene with an example but do remember to refer to it as you go on.

[3] Here we are stating a very basic point but one which puts the question in its context of privity.

Answer

This question concerns the position of those who are third parties to the making of a covenant[1] and whether they can claim under it. For example, suppose that Ned covenants with John not to use Greenacres for business purposes but also enters with the same covenants with 'the owners of land adjacent to the land conveyed'. Amy is the owner of land adjoining and she wishes to enforce the covenant against Ned who has broken the covenant.[2]

The simple answer is that as Amy is a third party to the covenant then under the doctrine of privity of contract she cannot claim any rights under it nor be under any obligations under it.[3] This rule applied to deeds as well as contracts. However, Amy may be able to sue using section 56(I) of the Law of Property Act (LPA) 1925[4] which provides that: 'A person may take . . . the benefit of any condition, right of entry, covenant or agreement over or respecting land or other property, although he may not be named as a party to the conveyance or other instrument.'

The effect of this has never been entirely clear.[5] In **Beswick v Beswick** [1966] Ch 538 Denning MR gave it such a wide interpretation as to

completely abolish the doctrine of privity of contract. The majority of
the House of Lords [1968] AC 58 held that section 56 was inapplicable but this case did not concern real property but a promise to pay
money. The probability is then that section 56 allows a person in
some circumstances to take the benefit of a covenant to which they
are not a party but not in all cases, so that they cannot claim simply
by saying that it was made for their benefit. What are these cases?

4 This should be the next
point.

5 Now you start to earn some
extra marks as you are
showing that you are aware
of problems with this area.

The main point is that it must have been possible for that person to
have been a party. Thus in our example the fact that the covenant
was also made with 'the owners of land adjacent to the land conveyed' indicates that it was possible for Amy to have been a party.[6]
Suppose that instead the covenant was expressed to be made with
anyone who might at any future date become an owner of any land
adjoining? That person would not come within section 56(1) and
could not enforce the covenant because it would not necessarily
have been possible for them to have been a party. This is often
expressed by saying that the third party must have been in existence
and identifiable when the covenant was made.

6 This shows the advantage of
our example at the start as it
helps to make this point clear.

This can be seen by looking at two contrasting cases.[7] In *Re
Ecclesiastical Commissioners Conveyance* [1936] Ch 430 a
covenant was entered into with the covenantor to observe certain
restrictive covenants but in addition the covenantor covenanted to
observe the same covenants with the owners of land 'adjoining or
adjacent to' the land with the benefit of the covenant. It was held that
this covenant was enforceable by those who, at the date of the
conveyance of his land to the covenantor, did in fact own adjoining
or adjacent land. The point was that they were the present owners of
the land and as such they were in existence and identifiable when
the covenant was made.

7 Looking at a pair of cases
and contrasting them is
always an excellent way of
adding depth to your answer
and adding to your marks.

In *White v Bijou Mansions* [1937] Ch 610, X had bought land
which was part of an estate and he covenanted to use the land for
residential purposes only. Moreover, the covenantee agreed that any
future conveyance of any part of the estate would contain a similar
covenant. The question was whether a person who had bought land
on the estate later and entered into a similar covenant could be sued
by X. It was held that he could not; the crucial difference from that
case and *Re Ecclesiastical Commissioners Conveyance* was
that here the covenant was sought to be enforced against a future

[8] If you do use pairs of cases and contrast them then do make sure that you bring out the essential differences between them.

owner of land who may have been in existence when the first covenant was made but was not identifiable.[8]

Neuberger J in *Amsprop Trading Ltd v Harris Distribution Ltd* (1997) put it this way, 'The true aim of section 56 seems to be not to allow a third party to sue on a contract merely because it is for his benefit; the contract must purport to be made with him', i.e. does the covenantor actually promise the covenantee that owners of adjacent land will benefit?

[9] There are two main areas to consider in this answer: the first was section 56 (1) of the LPA 1925, but the examiner will also expect a discussion of section 1 of the Contracts (Rights of Third Parties) Act 1999. The point to get across is that they *appear* to cover the same ground and allow a third party to claim the benefit of a covenant but there are differences of detail. It is when you indicate these differences that you start to really earn high marks.

Under the Contracts (Rights of Third Parties) Act 1999,[9] section 1 a person who is not a party to a contract can take the benefit of a contractual term which purports to confer a benefit on him. Although this Act covers the whole of the law of contract, not just this area, here this Act and section 56(1) of the LPA overlap.

How far does section 1 apply to enforcement of contracts by non-parties? It is arguable that the Act only applies to contracts and not to deeds. Even if it applies to deeds then provided that the original covenant is valid it will permit the enforcement of covenants in wider circumstances than in the past. However, the essential condition is that the covenant purports to confer a benefit on the third party and this will have to be by express words. Provided that this is so then the third party may enforce it and it will not be necessary for the third party to have been in existence at the date of the covenant. Thus it is suggested that the decision in *White v Bijou Mansions* would have been different had this Act been in force at the time. In our example at the start of this answer the phrase 'the owners of land adjacent to the land conveyed' could then include not just present owners as under section 56(1) but also future owners.

It cannot be denied that this area of the law is complex and in conclusion it is worth noting that clause 3(1) of the draft bill attached to the Law Commission Report (2011) provides that the benefit of a covenant should pass to any person who is a successor in title of the original owner of the benefited estate or any part of it or who has an estate derived out of the benefited estate or any part of it.[10] This would, it is suggested, have the same effect as section 1 of the Contracts (Rights of Third Parties) Act 1999 but the language would be that of property law and not contract law. Presumably the 1999 Act would run alongside this provision, which itself might lead to confusion. There is yet more work to be done on this area of law.

[10] This is a really excellent way to round off an answer. You are seen to be up to date and you are also showing very clearly how the proposals in the Law Commission's Report would affect the present law.

Make your answer stand out

- Look in detail at the debate on what was decided in *Beswick* v *Beswick*: read the judgments of both the majority and the minority.
- Read the note on *Re Ecclesiastical Commissioner's Conveyance* at (1937) *Conveyancer* 74 and that on *White* v *Bijou Mansions* in (1938) *Conveyancer*, 2: 260.
- Read in detail exactly what the Contracts (Rights of Third Parties) Act 1999 says. A good place to start is MacMillan (2000) A Birthday Present for Lord Denning: The Contracts (Rights of Third Parties) Act 1999. *MLR*, 63(5): 721.
- Refer to the words of the draft bill attached to the Law Commission's report rather than to its recommendations: this will gain marks as, if the draft bill becomes law, then it is these words which will matter.

Don't be tempted to . . .

- Make sure that you concentrate on the precise issue: this is not a general question on covenants but only on the rights of third parties to enforce them.
- Only mention one area: remember that there are two areas of law which can apply in this situation.
- Forget to mention the proposals in the Law Commission Report.

www.pearsoned.co.uk/lawexpressqa

Go online to access more revision support including additional essay and problem questions with diagram plans, You be the marker questions, and download all diagrams from the book.

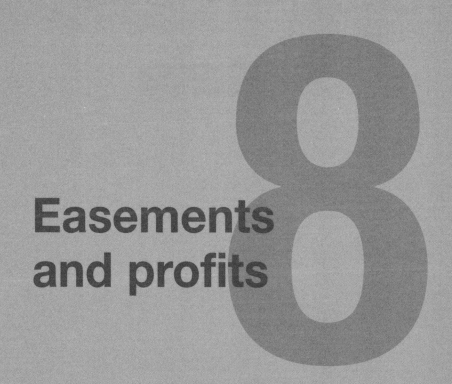

Easements and profits

How this topic may come up in exams

Problem questions on easements and profits tend to revolve around their characteristics and the methods of their creation together with prescription. Within this area there are two topics which need careful thought: whether there can be an easement of exclusive use, and the creation of easements by implication. Both are also likely subjects for essays as there have been recent cases on them and the law is not entirely settled. As with covenants, the proposals of the Law Commission for reform of the law in this area have given us an obvious topic too.

Attack the question

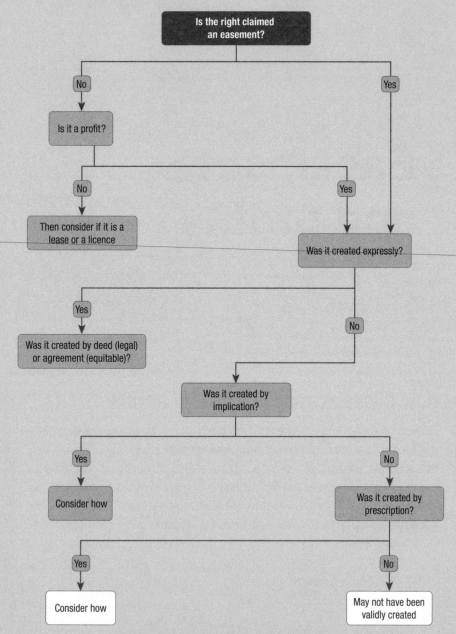

A printable version of this diagram is available from www.pearsoned.co.uk/lawexpressqa

❓ Question 1

Mary was the owner of Arbor Grange, a freehold property with registered title. The property includes a small cottage and an extensive wood.

In January 2012, Mary agreed in writing with her neighbour, Jean, that Jean could have a right of way along a driveway though the grounds of Arbor Grange, to provide a quicker access to a main road.

In March 2012, Mary sold the cottage to John. Before the sale, she had allowed him to move into the cottage and during that time she had allowed him to enter the wood to collect firewood and to store the firewood in a wood-store situated in the grounds of Arbor Grange, close to the cottage.

Mary has now sold Arbor Grange to Nick, who seeks your advice regarding the following claims:

(a) Jean claims a right of way across Arbor Grange.

(b) John claims the right to collect firewood and store it in the wood-store.

Advise Nick.

Diagram plan

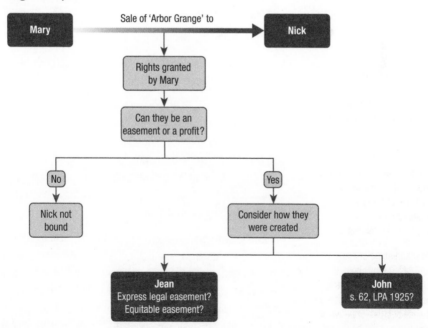

A printable version of this diagram plan is available from www.pearsoned.co.uk/lawexpressqa

Answer plan

→ Are the alleged rights capable of existing as easements and profits?

→ Are they legal easements/profits created by deed?

→ Are they equitable easements/profits created by written agreement?

→ Have they been created by implied grant?

→ Can they be enforced against Nick?

Answer

[1] It is vital that you address this issue in all problem questions on easements and profits although it may be that the answer is obvious in which case you need only mention the topic briefly.

The first question is whether the alleged rights are capable of existing as easements and profits?[1] In ***Re Ellenborough Park*** [1955] 3 All ER 667 it was held that to be valid as an easement the right must have the following characteristics:

(a) There must be a dominant and a servient tenement.

(b) The right must benefit the dominant land.

(c) The dominant and servient tenements must not be both owned and occupied by the same person.

(d) The right must be capable of being granted by deed.

[2] There is no need to plough through each characteristic here and apply it to the problem as there are clearly other issues which need to be discussed.

[3] Claims to an easement of storage often involve the possibility of exclusive possession and so you need to watch for this.

[4] This is the type of extra detail which really boosts your marks. The average student will simply mention an old case such as *Copeland* v *Greenhalf* and not be aware of recent developments.

Profits must also have the same characteristics except that there is no requirement of a dominant tenement.

The alleged rights do satisfy these characteristics.[2] A right of way is well established as an easement and the right to collect firewood is similarly well established as a profit. However, there is a problem with the claim for storage in the wood-store as a claim cannot be an easement if it offends the 'ouster principle'. This means that there cannot be an easement if the use amounts to exclusive possession or to a joint use of the servient land.[3]

In ***Copeland v Greenhalf*** [1952] 1 All ER 809 the claimant owned land on which the defendant had stored and repaired vehicles for 50 years. He claimed an easement by prescription. It was held that this was a claim to beneficial use of the land and so could not be an easement. Upjohn J described it as 'virtually a claim to possession of the servient tenement'. However, the law seems to be changing as in ***Moncrieff v Jamieson*** [2007] UKHL 42[4] Lord Scott in the

House of Lords proposed the test of whether the servient owner 'retains possession and, subject to the reasonable exercise of the right in question, control of the servient land'. The Law Commission Report LC 327 (2011) has proposed the abolition of the ouster principle and clause 24 of its proposed draft bill states that[5] 'use of land is not prevented from being of a kind which may be the subject of an easement by reason only of the fact that it prevents the person in possession of the land from making any reasonable use of it'. However, if the easement grants exclusive possession then it will not be valid.

[5] Try to make a note of where the Law Commission has put forward proposals for a change in the law so that you can slip it into your answer, as here. It is a sure way of boosting your marks.

Thus at least any right must be clearly defined and on the facts given we cannot say definitely if John has an easement of storage. If it is not an easement then it will only be a licence and so Nick will not be bound.

The next question is whether the alleged rights were validly created or acquired as easements or profits. We are told that Mary agreed in writing with Jean and this does not look as though the agreement was by deed. If an expressly created[6] easement or profit is to be legal then by section 52 of the Law of Property Act (LPA) 1925 it must be created by deed. Under section 1(2) of the Law of Property (Miscellaneous) Provisions Act 1989, to be a deed a document must be clear it is intended to be a deed, be signed and witnessed and be 'delivered'. If it is a deed then, as it was created after the provisions of the Land Registration Act (LRA) 2002 came into force, it must by section 27 of the LRA 2002 be registered, and if it is then it will bind Nick. If it is not then by section 29 it will not bind Nick. Jean cannot claim that she has an overriding interest under Schedule 3 Paragraph 2 of the LRA 2002 as her right of way does not amount to actual occupation.

[6] It is also possible to have easements which are legal created by implication under the rule in *Wheeldon* v *Burrows*, so if you had just said that 'to be legal an easement must be created by deed' this would not give a complete and accurate picture and you would lose marks.

As only the word 'writing' is mentioned, then it looks as though the document does not describe itself as a deed and so we must ask if it could be an equitable easement.[7] Under section 2 of the Law of Property (Miscellaneous) Provisions Act 1989 a contract for the sale or other disposition of land (which includes an equitable easement) must be in writing, contain all the agreed terms and be signed by each party. Again we cannot be sure if this is the case as, in particular, we do not know if the agreement contained all the terms. If it is a valid equitable easement then it must be protected by a notice to bind Nick (s. 29 LRA 2002).

[7] Do remember this point: the words 'in writing' are likely to indicate equitable easements, but you must explain why this is so: the requirement for a deed to describe itself as a deed.

[8] It is always worth considering the possibility of an easement of necessity where there is a claim to a right of way as here.

There is no evidence that Jean could claim an easement of necessity,[8] as the right of way was only to provide her with a quicker access to the main road and not the only means of access.

The rights claimed by John do not appear to have been granted either by deed or by a written agreement but there is the factor that they were granted to him before the cottage was sold to him and so they may be legal[9] profits and easements under the rule relating to implied grant under section 62 of the LPA 1925. This provides that a conveyance of the land shall be deemed to convey and shall operate to convey with the land all privileges, easements, rights appertaining or reputed to appertain to the land at the time of the conveyance. Thus if the right claimed was capable of existing as an easement or a profit prior to the sale by Mary to John then what were in effect potential easements and profits can now be actual ones and, as they are implied in the conveyance from Mary to John they will be legal also. This is the effect of *Wright v Macadam* [1949] 2 All ER 556 where the defendant let a flat to the claimant and gave her permission (i.e. a licence) to store coal in it. He later granted her a new tenancy. The grant of the tenancy was a conveyance under section 62(1) and, as a right to store coal was a right capable of being granted by law, the grant of the new tenancy had the effect of converting what was a licence into an easement. Incidentally, in *Wright v Macadam* it appears that the right of storage amounted to exclusive use but this may not help John as this was not part of the *ratio* of the decision.

[9] This is crucial. Always check for it in a problem question on easements: as the rights were granted before the sale, there is the possibility that the actual sale will convert them into actual easements. Stress too that in the case of easements and profits acquired under section 62 are legal interests in land.

If John has acquired these rights by implied grant then as legal easements they must be registered to bind Nick, as explained above in relation to Jean's claim. If not, then Nick will not be bound unless John can claim that they are overriding interests under Schedule 3 Paragraph 2 of the LRA 2002[10] on the basis that they belong to a person (John) who at the time of the disposition of Arbor Grange to Nick was a person in actual occupation. If so, then in order to escape from being bound by them Nick must show that either John did not disclose them when it would have been reasonable to do so or that they were not obvious on a reasonable inspection of the land. The actual storage must be obvious but it may be that John's right to enter the land is not.

[10] Do remember, if you get a problem question on implied easements, that these can be overriding interests and so will need to link your knowledge of this topic to that in Chapter 2 on registered land.

Make your answer stand out

- Note the comparison made in the Law Commission Report (2011) *Making Land Work: Easements, Covenants and Profits à Prendre* (LC 327) between exclusive possession in the law of leases and the ouster principle in the law of easements – see 3.193–3.204.
- Discussion of whether section 62 should still allow the creation of implied easements.
- Possibility that rights claimed by John may exist under *Wheeldon* v *Burrows* – unlikely but check why.
- Mention that John's right to enter the wood to collect firewood may be a licence coupled with a grant.

! **Don't be tempted to . . .**

- Spend too long on asking if the rights claimed satisfy the characteristics of easements laid down in *Ellenborough Park*.
- Miss the significance of the words 'Mary agreed in writing'.
- Miss the point that the rights claimed by John were granted to him before the actual sale of the cottage and so section 62 of the LPA can apply.
- Leave out a discussion of whether the easements and profits acquired under section 62 of the LPA are overriding interests.

? Question 2

John has owned Red Farm for a number of years, together with Blackacre which adjoins it. In 2012 he sold Red Farm to Mike but retained Blackacre. When John transferred Red Farm to Mike the transfer did not mention any easements or other rights.

Mike asks your advice on the following:

(a) Fred, who owns nearby Green Farm claims that he has the right to graze his cattle on a field which is part of Red Farm, as the owners of Green Farm have done this 'for centuries'. However, Mike knows that during the outbreak of foot and mouth disease in 2001 Fred's herd was destroyed and so he could not have exercised this right then, although Fred does now have a herd.

(b) The only direct access from the road to Red Farm is on a track which is unsuitable for motor vehicles. Mike knows that John always used another route across Blackacre to reach Red Farm and Mike wishes to know if he has now acquired the right to use it.

(c) Sam has had a licence, granted annually for the last 30 years, to use a path across a field on Red Farm. Sam has now written to Mike saying that as he has had the licence for so long it is now 'his for good'.

Answer plan

→ Consider if there is a claim to a profit by prescription.

→ What about an easement of necessity?

→ Consider the law on acquisition of easements by implication under *Wheeldon* v *Burrows* and whether this could be applicable here.

→ Similarly, consider the possible relevance of a claim to an easement by implication under section 62 of the LPA 1925.

→ Claim to a right of way: conditions for a claim to an easement by prescription.

Diagram plan

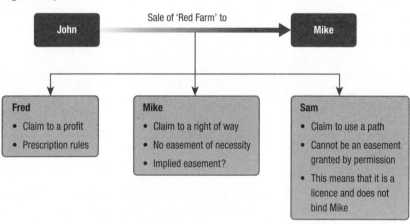

A printable version of this diagram plan is available from www.pearsoned.co.uk/lawexpressqa

Answer

(a) Fred's claim is to a profit as grazing is taking something from the land. It is obviously not based on any written evidence and so the profit cannot be either an express legal profit or an equitable profit. He claims that the owners of Green Farm have a grazed cattle on Blackacre 'for centuries'[1] and this must be a claim arising by prescription. Under section 2 of the Prescription Act 1832 a claim to a profit by prescription requires 30 years' continuous use, but where the easement was exercised with the oral agreement of the servient owner, it is 60 years.[2] There is no evidence of any oral permission so the period is 30 years but by section 4 Prescription Act 1832 the period must be 'next before' the action and this is obviously not the case here as there was an interruption in 2001.[3] The next possibility is a claim to prescription at common law which requires use since 'time immemorial' which technically means since 1189. In practice use since 1189 will be presumed, provided that the profit has been exercised for as long as anyone can remember and could have been exercised in 1189.[4] Use 1189 since will depend on proving that the farms were in different ownership since 1189, as otherwise there could not be a dominant and a servient tenement and it is very unlikely that it will be possible to do this.

The final hope is to use the doctrine of the lost modern grant[5] which involves the court making two assumptions: that there was originally a grant of the right and that it has now been lost. In **Dalton v Angus** (1881) 6 App Cas 740 it was held that a grant will be assumed if there has been 20 years' continuous use and that the grantor was not legally incompetent to make the grant. There is 20 years' use, and the rule in section 4 of the Prescription Act 1832 requiring that the period must be next before action does not apply here. The grantor would be the owner of Red Farm and there is no evidence that they were not competent to make the grant. Thus it seems likely that Fred will have a valid claim to a profit by prescription. The Law Commission Report[6] (2011) LC 327 proposed that the present rules law on acquisition of easements by prescription should be abolished and replaced by one single method of acquisition by prescription with a proposed period of 20 years (para. 3.123).

(b) This is a claim to a right of way which can, of course, exist as a valid easement. The problem is that there is no evidence that it has been expressly created, either by deed, which would make it legal, or in writing, which would make it equitable.

---

[1] Language like this must mean a possible claim by long use (prescription).

[2] Do make a note of these two periods.

[3] This is a familiar point in exam questions. The effect is that there cannot be a successful claim under the Prescription Act 1832 and so you then need to consider other possibilities.

[4] The message is not to get worried about the actual date of 1189.

[5] This will usually be the last possibility you examine.

[6] This reference will increase your marks as although a detailed knowledge of the Law Commission's proposals is not required, (so resist the temptation to describe them in detail) good students do keep up to date!

Nor can Mike claim an easement of necessity as there is an alternative route to his land. If there had been no alternative access, Mike's claim might have succeeded, and the fact that he needs access in order to use motor vehicles would not prevent a claim, as an easement allows access for any purpose which is essential to maintain the enjoyment of the land.

However, Mike will have a claim to an easement under the rule in **Wheeldon v Burrows** (1879) 12 Ch D 31 which provides that on a grant of land, the grantee (e.g. the buyer) will acquire, by implication, all easements which: are continuous and apparent and have been and are at the time of the grant used by the grantor for the benefit of the land. This rule applies where land has one owner who then sells off part, and the effect is that if before the sale the owner enjoyed a quasi-easement over part of his land that will become an actual easement by implied grant on the sale. Here part of John's land[7] (Red Farm) enjoyed a quasi-easement over other land which he owned (Blackacre) and so when Mike bought Blackacre this quasi-easement could become[8] an actual easement. The next question is whether the exercise of the right of way was continuous and apparent.[9] There is no need for the road to be a made road so long as it is apparent, as in **Hansford v Jago** [1921] 1 Ch 322 where a strip of land marked with rough tracks was within the rule in **Wheeldon v Burrows**. The use is obviously continuous as we are told that John always used this route to reach Red Farm. Thus Mike can claim an easement which, as it is implied into the grant to him by John of Blackacre will be a legal easement.

In addition Mike may be able to claim an implied easement under the operation of section 62 of the LPA 1925[10] which provides that a conveyance of the land shall be deemed to convey and shall operate to convey with the land all privileges, easements, etc. appertaining or reputed to appertain to the land at the time of the conveyance. The general view expressed in **Sovmots Investments Ltd v Environment Secretary** [1977] 2 All ER 385 is that 'diversity of occupation' is needed for section 62 to apply, i.e. it is necessary for each piece of land to be occupied by different people. This would exclude section 62

[7] A small point but important: it is not John personally who enjoys the easement. Instead his *land* enjoys it.

[8] You should say 'could' not 'would' as we have not yet established if the conditions for this rule to apply have been satisfied.

[9] When you have decided that *Wheeldon* v *Burrows* could apply you should then move on to this next point.

[10] This is exactly the kind of thinking which lifts an answer from an average 2.2 to a good 2.1.

here as before the sale Red Farm and Blackacre were occupied by the same person. This has now been doubted in **P & S Platt Ltd v Crouch** [2003] EWCA Civ 1110 but this decision is open to the serious objection that rights cannot be apparent if they are exercised by an owner over his/her own land and the decision in **Sovmots Investments Ltd v Environment Secretary**, which is one of the House of Lords, was not cited to the Court of Appeal in **Platt**. It is worth mentioning that the Law Commission Report (2011) LC 327 has proposed (para. 3.64) that easements should no longer be capable of creation by implication under section 62 of the LPA 1925 although section 62 itself would remain.

(c) Sam will not have a claim to an easement here as although he has exercised the right of way for 30 years, which would satisfy the prescription period of 20 years under section 2 of the Prescription Act 1832, provided that it was continuous, he is exercising it under a licence. One of the conditions for claiming an easement by prescription is that the use shall not be by permission and here it is. In addition licences are not binding on third parties (**King v David Allen** [1916] 2 AC 54) and so a licence granted by a predecessor in title will not bind Mike. In **London Tara Hotel Ltd v Kensington Close Hotel Ltd** [2011] EWCA Civ 1356 a claim to an easement also failed, as use was by licence.[11]

[11] The facts of this case were actually more complex than in the problem but a good answer would recognise that there is no need to go into detail. What is important is to recognise that the essential point of the case is the same as the facts of the problem.

✓ **Make your answer stand out**

- Clear explanation of the different methods of prescription in (a).
- Recognition in (b) that the situation could involve the application of section 62 of the LPA 1925 as well as *Wheeldon* v *Burrows*.
- Reference to the Law Commission Report (2011) *Making Land Work: Easements, Covenants and Profits a Prendre* (LC 327). Look both at the proposals it contains and at its account of the law. Law Commission consultation papers and reports set out the law remarkably clearly and can add to your knowledge – and your marks.
- Read and refer to Bridge (2009) Prescriptive Easements: Capacity to Grant. *CLJ*, 68(1): 40.

> ## ! Don't be tempted to . . .
>
> - Forget in (a) to investigate all three methods of prescription.
> - Spend long on deciding if the rights are actually easements and profits: they obviously are except in (c).
> - In (b) miss that, although you need to mention easements of necessity, in fact this does not apply and so you need to investigate other areas.
> - Just mention the actual Rule in *Wheeldon* v *Burrows*, but also mention the conditions for it to apply.

📝 Question 3

Consider the situations where easements may be created in the absence of an express grant together with proposals for reform in this area.

Diagram plan

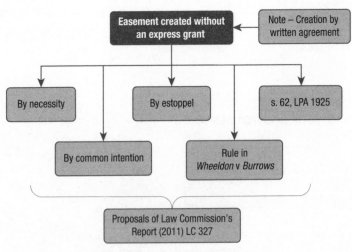

A printable version of this diagram plan is available from www.pearsoned.co.uk/lawexpressqa

Answer plan

→ Start by looking at easements of necessity.

→ Move on to easements implied by common intention and by estoppel.

→ Explain acquisition of easements under *Wheeldon* v *Burrows* in more detail.

→ Equally explain how section 62 LPA 1925 can enable an easement to be acquired.

→ Conclude by evaluating the effect of the Law Commission proposals in this area.

Answer

This question deals with the way in which easements can be created in the absence of an express grant. Where there is an express grant a legal easement is created, but here we are looking at ways in which, despite the absence of a grant, easements can be created by some form of implication. Easements can also be created by written agreement in which case they are equitable[1] but here we are dealing only with creation of easements by implication. They all have the common feature that, although created by implication, the easement is then implied into the grant and so technically these end up as express easements.

[1] This question is clearly about implied easements as the reference to 'the absence of an express grant' shows. However, it could theoretically also involve equitable easements as these are created in the absence of an express grant and so best to make it clear at the start that you will not be dealing with them.

The methods of creation will first be examined and then proposals for reform in what is a complex area.

The first example is easements by necessity e.g. access to land-locked land. A good recent case is *Adealon International Corp. Proprietary Ltd* v *Merton LBC* [2007] EWCA Civ 362 where land only had access to a road to the north over land owned by another, and access to a road to the south could only be obtained by a grant of planning permission. The court held that an easement of necessity would not be granted as there was a realistic possibility of access to the land in future.

In *Wong* v *Beaumont Property Trust Ltd* [1965] 1 QB 173 CA basement premises were leased as a restaurant. Public health regulations could, unknown to the parties, only be complied with by installing a new ventilation duct through the premises above which were retained by the landlord. It was held that the tenant was entitled to have an easement to maintain and construct the duct.

[2] An average answer would simply say that this case is an example of an easement by estoppel but a good answer would identify that the exact *ratio* is somewhat obscure and that a possible explanation is an easement by estoppel.

A possible example of an easement by estoppel[2] is ***Ives Investments Ltd v High*** [1967] 2 QB 379 where the defendant agreed with the claimant's predecessor in title that foundations of the claimant's flats might remain on the defendant's land. In return the defendant, whose access to his house was affected by the building of the flats, could gain access to his garage by crossing the claimant's land. Although the decision was partly on the benefit and burden principle in ***Halsall v Brizell*** [1957] Ch 169 it could also be argued that the right of access is an example of an easement by estoppel arising through expense by the defendant in resurfacing the access road in reliance on the promise that he would have the right of access.

In ***Wheeldon v Burrows*** (1879) 12 Ch D 31 it was held that an easement can be acquired by implied grant. The principle is that on a grant of land, the grantee (e.g. the buyer) will acquire, by implication, all easements which:

(a)   are continuous and apparent;

(b)   have been and are at the time of the grant used by the grantor for the benefit of the land.

[3] Always use an example where you need to convey exactly what a somewhat complex point really means. If you do it will make sure that the examiner understands the points you are making.

As an example, suppose that John owns Blackacre and Whiteacre but then sells Whiteacre to Sue. Access to the main road from Whiteacre is along a path which crosses Blackacre. Sue will acquire an implied easement of a right of way across Blackacre under this rule.[3] The effect of the Rule in ***Wheeldon v Burrows*** is that what was a quasi-easement before the sale, as of course a person cannot have an easement over land which they own, becomes an actual easement on sale.

[4] Often students are confused and imagine that the principle in *Wright* v *Macadam* represents the main use of section 62. This is not so: explain how section 62 of the LPA works first as we have done here and then mention this case.

The final method of creation of easements by implication is under section 62 of the Law of Property Act (LPA) 1925 which provides that a conveyance of the land shall be deemed to convey and shall operate to convey with the land all privileges, easements, rights appertaining or reputed to appertain to the land at the time of conveyance. This provision is not itself controversial: it merely provides that on a conveyance of land certain rights that it has (e.g. easements and profits) are automatically also conveyed. What is controversial is the use which has been made of it to create easements where none seemed to exist before.[4] In ***Wright v Macadam*** [1949] 2 All ER 565 the defendant let a flat to the claimant and gave her permission (i.e. a licence) to store coal in it. He later granted her a new tenancy. It was held that the grant of the tenancy was a conveyance under section 62(1) and, as a right to store coal was a right capable of being granted by law, the grant of the new tenancy had the effect of converting what was a licence into an easement.

In ***Sovmots Investments Ltd v Environment Secretary*** [1977] 2 All ER 385 it was considered that 'diversity of occupation is needed for section 62 to apply, i.e. it is necessary for each piece of land to be occupied by different people. This was doubted in ***P & S Platt Ltd v Crouch*** [2003] EWCA Civ 1110 where an easement was implied under section 62 even though the land had been owned by the same person.[5] If the principle in this case is accepted then the scope of ***Wheeldon v Burrows*** would be greatly reduced, but ***Platt*** is open to the serious objection that rights cannot be apparent if they are exercised by an owner over his/her own land as there is no need for a right as such to be able to do this.

[5] There is no space to give the actual decision in *Platt* so confine yourself to the principle.

If an easement by implication is established then as it is implied in the actual grant of the easement it will be legal[6] unless the easement was implied in a written agreement when it will be equitable.

[6] There are many consequences from the fact that easements acquired by implication are legal so make a habit of pointing this out.

There is no doubt that the law on the acquisition of easements by implication is complex and, in particular, the relationship between ***Wheeldon v Burrows*** and section 62 of the LPA is unclear. For example it cannot be right that a claim to an implied easement can succeed under section 62 of the LPA 1925 but not under ***Wheeldon v Burrows***.

The Law Commission asked whether the law on acquisition of easements by implication should be recast into statutory form. It regards section 62 as a 'trap for the unwary' as the parties may not know how it works, or even that it will apply and so they will not take it into account when negotiating the transfer. Moreover there are uncertainties over its precise scope and its relationship with ***Wheeldon v Burrows***, as mentioned above.

[7] As always, reference to relevant Law Commission reports and consultation papers is the kind of detail which lifts your answer from the average to the good or very good!

The Law Commission Report (2011) LC 327 proposed that easements should no longer be capable of creation by implication under section 62(1) of the LPA 1925.[7] Section 62 itself would remain but the ***Wright v Macadam*** principle which was engrafted onto it would not. It recommended that the methods of creation of easements by necessity, common intention and under ***Wheeldon v Burrows*** should be abolished and replaced by a single statutory principle that easements will be implied where they are necessary for the reasonable use of the land (para. 3.45) bearing in mind five factors[8] e.g. the use of the land at the time of the grant; the potential interference caused to the servient land by the use of the easement or inconvenience to the servient owner. Profits could not be created in this way.

[8] It would be excellent to include all five factors but, as here, you may not have time. So show the examiner that you know how many there are and select some significant factors to mention.

Although some areas of the law on acquisition of easements by implication perform a useful function, such as easements by necessity, others should be restricted in scope or abolished.

✓ **Make your answer stand out**

- Discussion of the decision in *Platt*.
- Further explanation of the Law Commission Report (2011) *Making Land Work: Easements, Covenants and Profits a Prendre* (LC 327).
- Contrast *Wheeldon* v *Burrows* with section 62 of the LPA 1925.
- Mention the views of Mummery LJ in the Court of Appeal in *Adealon International Corp. Proprietary Ltd* v *Merton LBC* who observed that the principle of an easement of necessity was not a free-standing rule of public policy but one of implication in all the circumstances. What counted against the claimant was that he had owned the land to the north and could have stipulated for an easement over that land when he sold it.

! **Don't be tempted to . . .**

- Avoid the section at the end on proposals for reform.
- Make sure that you contrast *Wheeldon* v *Burrows* with section 62 of the LPA and do not just describe them in a mechanical way.
- Omit to mention all the ways in which easements can be created by implication.

 Question 4

Critically consider the place of the ouster principle in the law of easements especially in the light of claims to an easement of car parking and the proposals in the Law Commission Report (2011) *Making Land Work: Easements, Covenants and Profits à Prendre* (LC 327).

Answer plan

→ Explain what the idea of an ouster clause is in relation to easements.
→ Outline the history of ouster clauses.
→ Analyse their application to claimed easements of car parking.
→ Consider the problems which exist in ascertaining exactly what the present law is.
→ Consideration of the proposals of the Law Commission.

Diagram plan

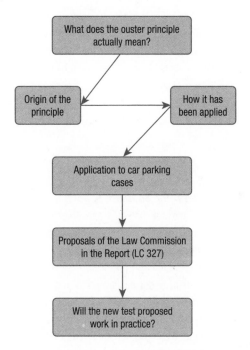

A printable version of this diagram plan is available from www.pearsoned.co.uk/lawexpressqa

Answer

The principle that an easement cannot give the grantee exclusive use of the servient land (known as the ouster principle) is based on the need to distinguish easements from freehold and leasehold estates in land, which give the holder the right to exclusive possession, as distinct from use, of the land. A lesser right such as an easement cannot therefore allow the holder the right to in effect treat the land as his own but only to exercise certain rights over it such as a right of way. It is also important to distinguish an easement from a licence which, although not an estate in land, nevertheless gives the licensee rights over the whole land which is licensed.[1] The Law Commission in its report was clear that a grant of exclusive possession of land could not be an easement although of course it could be a lease or licence. The problem is with ouster clauses, which can give exclusive use.

This origin of the ouster principle is probably the decision in *Dyce v Hay* (1852) 1 Macq 305 and its application is seen in *Copeland v Greenhalf* [1952] 1 All ER 809 where the claimant owned land on which the defendant had stored and repaired vehicles for 50 years. He claimed an easement by prescription. It was held that this was a claim to beneficial use of the land and so could not be an easement. Upjohn J described it as 'virtually a claim to possession of the servient tenement (ST) if necessary to the exclusion of the owner'.

However, the exact extent of the ouster principle is uncertain and it has not always been consistently applied by the courts.[2] In *Attorney General for Southern Nigeria* v *John Holt & Co Ltd* (1915) a right to store materials and other goods on the servient land was held to be an easement and in *Wright* v *Macadam* the claim to storage of coal in a shed appeared to be a claim to an exclusive right to store, although the claim proceeded on the basis of an implied easement under section 62 of the LPA 1925. The ouster principle was not applied in *Miller* v *Emcer Products Ltd* [1956][3] Ch 304 to a claim to the use of a lavatory, as the court made the sensible point that all easements involve the exclusion of the dominant owner to some degree as when a right of way over a path is exercised at that moment no one else can literally occupy that part of the path.

In *London and Blenheim Ltd* v *Ladbrooke Retail Parks Ltd* [1994] 1 WLR 31 Judge Baker proposed a test of degree, 'A small coal shed is one thing. The exclusive use of a large part of the alleged servient tenement is another'.[4]

The question is now the extent to which these principles have been applied in car parking cases. The existence of an easement of car

---

[1] You should mention licences separately although they do not of course give an interest in land. This is because in many cases, such as rights of storage, if a right cannot be an easement it will have to take effect as a licence.

[2] This is the theme of the essay and so needs to be mentioned clearly near the start.

[3] An answer on areas where the principles in the case law has not been consistent does need a clear review of the cases where you recognise that it is not possible to find a consistent theme in the judgments.

[4] It is obviously impossible to recall long quotes but try to keep short and sharp ones like this in mind.

parking was recognised for the first time in **Newman v Jones** (1982) (unreported) where Megarry VC said, 'I feel no hesitation in holding that a right for a landowner to park a car anywhere in a defined area is capable of existing as an easement'. What, though, is the position where a right to park in a defined space is claimed? In **London and Blenheim Estates Ltd v Ladbrooke Retail Parks Ltd** the right was to park cars on any available space in the car park and, although the claim failed on other grounds, it was held that this was capable of being an easement.

[5] This is the leading modern English authority on car parking and must be mentioned in an answer on car parking and ouster clauses.

In **Batchelor v Marlow** [2001] EWCA Civ 1051,[5] A claimed a right to park up to six cars between 9.30am and 6pm on land owned by B. A claimed an easement as B still had 120 hours a week to use the land as he wished. The court applied the ouster principle and held that B had no reasonable use for the land for parking as he could not park on it when parking spaces were most needed and so the claim failed. As the court put it 'His right (i.e. the right of the dominant owner) is curtailed altogether for intermittent periods during the week'. One issue was whether there should be a different test where the right was claimed by express grant from where it was claimed by prescription.[6] There is some merit in this, as obviously there would then be a stricter test where prescription was claimed as where there was an express grant the owner of the ST would have expressly agreed to it. However, the Court of Appeal disagreed.

[6] This is an example of the extra research detail which improves your marks.

[7] Do emphasise that this is a Scottish decision as Scottish law in this area is slightly different.

In **Moncrieff v Jamieson** [2007] UKHL 42 the House of Lords held that Scottish law[7] recognised that there could be a servitude (easement) of parking. Here the property when sold had no direct vehicular access and so the seller granted the buyer the right of access across his land and a right to park to unload. The issue was whether there was an extra right to park for longer periods. It was held that an easement would be implied but there was a difference of view over the test to be applied. The view of Lord Scott probably represents that of the majority[8] and he said that it was sufficient if the owner of the ST retained possession and control of the land. In effect the ouster point is sidestepped.

[8] It is always difficult to state the *ratio* of a case where there have been a number of judgments (or speeches in this case) which say slightly different things. This is why I have been tentative and said that his view 'probably' represents that of the majority.

[9] If you can find a quote which can give you a neat conclusion then this is ideal!

Haley (2008)[9] suggests that the law should recognise that, in appropriate circumstances, there can be a right to park provided that the claimant is not asserting permanent and exclusive rights in relation to the entirety of the ST and this may be as far we can get to a general principle.

The Law Commission Report (2011) LC 327 has proposed the abolition of the ouster principle and clause 24 of its proposed draft bill states that 'Use of land is not prevented from being of a kind which may be the subject of an easement by reason only of the fact that it prevents the person in possession of the land from making any reasonable use of it'. However, if the easement grants exclusive possession then it will not be valid. The effect of these proposals would be, as the Law Commission recognises, to reverse the decisions in **Copeland v Greenhalf** and **Batchelor v Marlow**. However, the Commission feels that it is important to bring more certainty to the area of easements of car parking especially in view of the practical importance of this right. It points out that recent Land Registry data suggests that over 7,500 exclusive rights to park were created in 2009/2010.[10]

[10] You can easily find this kind of research detail in documents such as Law Commission reports. If used in the right place it can really add value to your answer.

The problem is going to be drawing a distinction in practice between an easement that attempts to give exclusive possession, which will not be valid, and one that stops short of exclusive possession, even if it deprives the owner of all reasonable use of the land, which will be valid. Will this lead to too many fine distinctions being drawn?

✓ Make your answer stand out

- Show a clear understanding of the basic principles of the law on leases and licences as well as easements.
- Research *Wright* v *Macadam* – where does this answer say that there 'appeared' to be an exclusive right of storage?
- Refer and research articles on car parking and ouster clauses such as Hill-Smith (2007) Rights of Parking and the Ouster Principle after *Batchelor* v *Marlow*. *Conveyancer* 223–34; Junior (2008) Warning – Parking Problems Ahead (*Moncrieff* v *Jamieson* applied). *SLT*, 1: 1–2; and Haley (2008) Easements, Exclusionary Use and Elusive Principles: The Right to Park. *Conveyancer* 244.
- Investigate the reasons for and against having different tests for an easement of car parking depending on whether the claim is based on express grant or prescription.

Don't be tempted to . . .

- Just go through the cases and not investigate the principles on ouster clauses and car parking.
- Consider only the most recent cases.
- Try to come to a definite conclusion as in fact the law here is not in a settled state.
- Omit dealing with the ouster principle in general as well as discussing car parking.

Question 5

'The categories of servitudes and easements must alter and expand with the changes that take place in the circumstances of mankind.' (Lord St Leonards LC in *Dyce* v *Hay* (1852) 1 Macq 305)

Consider this statement especially in the light of modern cases involving the possible creation of new easements.

Diagram plan

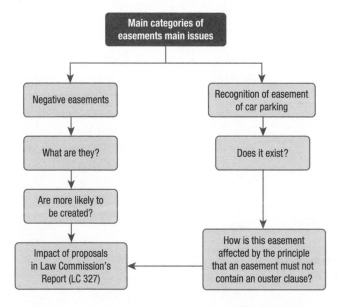

A printable version of this diagram plan is available from www.pearsoned.co.uk/lawexpressqa

Answer plan

→ Consider briefly what the question is about.

→ Make the distinction between positive and negative easements clear.

→ Problems with negative easements and possible solutions.

→ Application of the law to car parking.

→ Conclusion – will the law recognise new easements?

Answer

In general, the categories of easements are well known and well settled. Familiar examples are rights of way, light, support and a right to have a fence maintained by a joint owner.[1] The question is whether these categories are closed or whether new categories can be created. One issue is whether new negative easements can be created. A negative easement exists where the owner of the servient tenement (ST) has no actual obligations but is restricted in the use of the land. It has been felt that negative easements should not be created as they did not actually relate to anything done on the actual land, unlike a positive easement (such as a right of way) which involves a landowner going onto or making use of something in or on a neighbour's land.[2] (See Littledale J in *More v Rawson* (1824) 3 B & C 332 at 340.)

However, in fact negative easements have been created as, for instance, the right to receive support[3] (*Dalton v Angus & Co* (1881) 6 App Cas 740) and a right to receive air, water or light in defined channels (see *Colls v Home and Colonial Stores Ltd* [1904] AC 179). The emphasis is on the word 'defined channels' as is seen in *Webb v Bird* (1861) 10 CBNS 268 where a claim by the owner of a windmill against a neighbour who had built a house which stopped the flow of air to his windmill was rejected as the claim was to a general undefined flow of air.

However, the categories of negative easements are unlikely to be extended[4] to include, for example, the right not to have television reception interfered with.[5] In *Phipps v Pears* [1964] 2 All ER 35, for example, there was a claim to an easement to protection of one house from rain and frost by another house. This would mean that

[1] As this answer progresses we will come to areas where there is some doubt about what the law is. This is why it is important to begin by explaining where the law *is* settled.

[2] As much of this discussion concerns negative easements you need to be clear on the distinction between negative and positive easements.

[3] This needs to be your first point.

[4] This follows from the previous point.

[5] A simple example helps to make the idea clear.

the other house could not be demolished. The claim was rejected. The problem is that if new negative easements are created then this imposes further restrictions on the right of the owner of the ST to use his property. As Denning MR put it in **Phipps v Pears**, 'if we were to stop a man pulling down his house, we would put a brake on desirable improvement'. In **Hunter v Canary Wharf Ltd** [1997] AC 655 Lord Hope said that as negative easements 'represent an anomaly in the law because they restrict the owner's freedom, the law takes care not to extend them beyond the categories which are well known to the law'.

The Law Commission Report (2011) LC 327 recommended that, for the future, attempts to create negative easements expressly will give rise to land obligations if the requirements of clause 1 of the draft bill are met, but existing negative easements will remain. The reason for this change is that the rights capable of being created by a Land Obligation would be much greater than those covered by the present restrictive covenants and in particular it would be possible for a positive covenant to take effect as a Land Obligation. For example, it might be possible to create a positive obligation of the kind which was claimed in **Phipps v Pears** (above) but which would take effect as a Land Obligation.

The other area where there is the question of a new easement being recognised is car parking rights. It seems clear that there can be a easement of car parking as this was recognised for the first time in **Newman v Jones** (1962) (unreported) where Megarry VC said that 'I feel no hesitation in holding that a right for a landowner to park a car anywhere in a defined area is capable of existing as an easement'.

The question is not if there is such an easement but how the exercise of it affects the principle that an easement must not give the owner of the dominant tenement exclusive use of the ST.[6] In **London and Blenheim Estates Ltd v Ladbrooke Retail Parks Ltd** [1994] 1 WLR 31 the right was to park cars on any available space in the car park and, although the claim failed on other grounds it was held that this was capable of being an easement.

[6] This is a crucial sentence as it links the question of car parking easements with a general issue on the law of easements.

In **Batchelor v Marlow** [2001] EWCA Civ 1051 A claimed a right to park up to six cars between 9.30am and 6pm on land owned by B.

A claimed an easement as B still had 120 hours a week to use the land as he wished. The court applied the ouster principle and held that B had no reasonable use for the land for parking as he could not park on it when parking spaces were most needed and so the claim failed. As the court put it, his right (i.e. the right of the dominant owner) is curtailed altogether for intermittent periods during the week. One issue was whether there should be a different test where the right was claimed by express grant from where it was claimed by prescription,[7] but the Court of Appeal held that there was not.

In ***Moncrieff* v *Jamieson*** [2007] UKHL 42 the House of Lords held that Scottish law[8] recognised that there could be servitude (easement) of parking. Here the property when sold had no direct vehicular access and so the seller granted the buyer the right of access across his land and a right to park to unload. The issue was whether there was an extra right to park for longer periods. It was held that an easement would be implied but there was a difference of view over the test to be applied. The view of Lord Scott probably represents that of the majority and he said that it was sufficient if the owner of the ST retained possession and control of the land. In effect the ouster point is sidestepped.

The Law Commission Report (2011) LC 327 recommends in its draft bill (clause 24) that use of land 'should not prevented from being of a kind which may be the subject of an easement by reason only of the fact that it prevents the person in possession of the land from making any reasonable use of it'. This would have the effect of reversing the effect of ***Batchelor* v *Marlow***. (See paras. 3.188–3.205.)

In conclusion, the law does still have the capacity to recognise new easements but, as with easements of car parking,[9] these are positive easements where at least the servient owner knows that the right is actually being exercised and so, where a claim by prescription is being acquired, the owner can take action to prevent this. It is much less likely that new negative easements will be recognised.

[7] This point will gain marks as it shows that you have actually read the details of the case and not just the bare facts.

[8] It is important to emphasise that this is a Scottish decision as the law in Scotland differs from English law and any decisions on Scottish law are only of persuasive authority.

[9] You do need a conclusion which tries to propose some ideas on what the law should be.

Make your answer stand out

■ See Dawson and Dunn (1998) Negative Easements – A Crumb of Analysis. *Legal Studies*, 18: 510.

■ See the Law Commission Report (2011) *Making Land Work: Easements, Covenants and Profits a Prendre* (LC 327).

■ See the Scottish Law Commission (1998) discussion paper *Real Burdens*, No. 106.

■ See if you can find other examples of the law recognising new easements.

! **Don't be tempted to . . .**

■ Begin with a long account of the characteristics of easements as laid down in *Re Ellenborough Park*.

■ Give a descriptive account of the law on what can be an easement.

■ Confuse what a negative easement is – make your terms clear.

www.pearsoned.co.uk/lawexpressqa

 Go online to access more revision support including additional essay and problem questions with diagram plans, You be the marker questions, and download all diagrams from the book.

Mortgages

How this topic may come up in exams

Problem questions on the terms of a mortgage are generally considered good prospects to obtain marks although you need to remember that the law is not always clear cut and you may well not be able to come to a definite conclusion. In addition, you can expect problems on priority of mortgages, which can be more difficult, and applications by the mortgagee for a sale. There is also a possibility of a question with an angle on undue influence.

Essays can focus on mortgage conditions and on the law on remedies of the mortgagee.

All in all, not a difficult area with the possible exception of priorities and so a 'must' for revision!

Attack the question

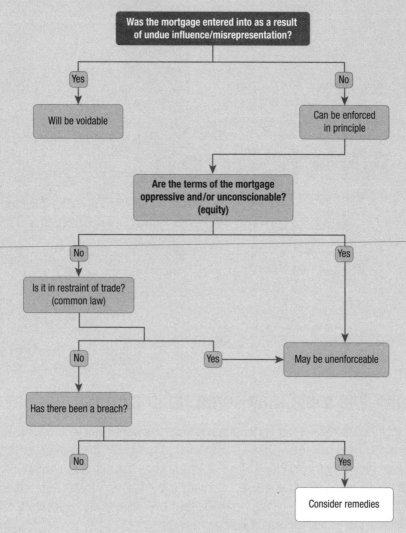

A printable version of this diagram is available from www.pearsoned.co.uk/lawexpressqa

 Question 1

In *Jones* v *Morgan* [2002] 1 ELGR 125 Phillips MR said that 'the doctrine of a clog on the equity of redemption. . . . is an appendix to our law which no longer serves any useful purpose'. Do you agree?

Answer plan

→ Set the scene by looking at the historical basis of equitable intervention.

→ Explain the principle that there must be no clog on the equity of redemption.

→ Analyse the application of this principle in the cases.

→ Explain the principle that a mortgage cannot contain a provision allowing the mortgagor an option to purchase the property.

→ Law Commission Report.

Diagram plan

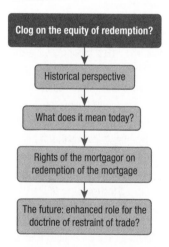

A printable version of this diagram plan is available from www.pearsoned.co.uk/lawexpressqa

[1] You do need to mention equity in general at the start and set the scene as to what the nature of equity is. It is impossible to understand how the present law of mortgages works without understanding the crucial part played by equity in its development.

Answer

The question refers to the doctrine of a clog on the equity of redemption and we need to begin by noting the part played by equity[1] in developing the law on mortgages. Mortgages were traditionally entered into when someone needed a loan as they were in debt and so they might be persuaded into entering a mortgage on terms which were very onerous. Thus equity aimed to protect them and proceeded on the basis that the terms of the mortgage were likely to be dictated by the mortgagee.

[2] Stress the changing character of mortgages over the years.

Today[2] mortgages are usually made because a person wishes to buy or lease a house rather than because he is in debt and is desperate for a loan on virtually any terms. However, it is still true that the terms of the mortgage are dictated by the mortgagee as lenders usually require borrowers to enter into mortgages on standard terms and there is no room for individual negotiation. For example, a potential borrower would not normally be able to negotiate his own interest rate.

In particular, equity still insists on the principle of the equity of redemption, which means that the mortgagor still has the right to redeem the mortgage even though the redemption date has passed provided that he pays all sums owing.[3] This flows from a fundamental equitable principle expressed by Lord Davey in **Noakes v Rice** [1902] AC 24 HL, 'Once a mortgage, always a mortgage'. He then explained that this means that the mortgagee must not make any stipulation which will prevent a mortgagor who has paid back the sums owing 'from getting back the mortgaged property in the condition in which he parted with it'. If there are any terms in the mortgage which prevent this happening, these are known as clogs on the equity of redemption, and historically equity viewed these as objectionable. One example is where the mortgagee is obliged to buy goods from the mortgagor or sell them to him for a period which continues after the mortgage has ended. (See **Krelinger v New Patagonia Meat and Cold Storage Co Ltd** [1914] AC 25 HL.)

[3] At this point make sure that you have clearly explained what the equity of redemption is.

[4] Equitable doctrines are often very old and it will add to your marks if you are able to go back to the source of them!

The doctrine[4] that there must be no clog on the equity of redemption has its origin in early equity cases such as **Jennings v Ward** (1705) 2 Vern 520 CA where Trevor MR said that 'a man shall not have interest for his money on a mortgage, and a collateral advantage besides for the loan of it'. Thus, when the mortgage is repaid, there shall be no 'clog' on it. However, this absolute principle has long gone and in a celebrated passage in **Krelinger v New Patagonia Meat and Cold Storage Co Ltd** [1914] AC 25, Lord Mersey described the doctrine as an 'unruly dog, which, if not securely chained to its kennel, is apt to wander into places where it ought not to be'. How far is the dog under control?

To answer this we must look at the two main applications of the principle that there must be no 'clog'. First, the principle that, on redemption, the mortgagor is free from all the conditions of the mortgage. In fact, the courts have not always applied this principle entirely consistently.

In *Bradley* **v** *Carritt* [1903] AC 253 HL the defendant mortgaged shares in a tea company to a tea broker and agreed to use his 'best endeavours' to ensure that the broker had the sale of the company's teas and that if teas were sold elsewhere the defendant would pay the broker the amount of commission he would have earned. This was held void as after redemption of the mortgage the shares would be of no value to the defendant as on sale he would be liable for any loss of commission. However, in *Biggs* **v** *Hoddinott* [1898] 2 Ch 307 HC a hotel was mortgaged and the mortgagee agreed that during the term of the mortgage he would only sell beer brewed by the mortgagor. This was held valid, one reason being that the tie was to end on redemption of the mortgage.

In *Krelinger* **v** *New Patagonia Meat and Cold Storage Co Ltd* [1914] AC 25 a firm of woolbrokers lent money on a mortgage which could be repaid at any time in the next five years. The mortgagor also agreed to give the mortgagee first refusal on all their sheepskins and to pay commission on any sold to a third party. This agreement was to last for the full five years. This collateral agreement was upheld on the basis that the agreement to give first refusal was, in fact, a separate agreement[5] from the mortgage and so was not a clog on the right to redeem. In fact, there have been few reported cases on this area since Krelinger which may indicate that the law is now in a satisfactory state.

[5] This is the vital point about Krelinger.

The second application of the 'clog' principle is that the mortgagor should be able to actually redeem the mortgaged property when the mortgage ends and this has been held to conflict with a stipulation that the mortgagor has the right to purchase the mortgaged property when the term of the mortgage ends.[6] In *Samuel Jarrah Timber* **v** *Wood Paving Corporation Ltd* [1904] AC 323 the House of Lords applied this principle with reluctance, so that an option to purchase was held void. Lord Halsbury LC regretted that what he called a 'perfectly fair bargain' to purchase the property was void as it was linked to a mortgage. The consequences of this rule were avoided in

[6] In an essay on the equity of redemption do remember that it affects various ways in which the law has developed.

[7] Even though this report is now dated it is the last word so far on this subject from the Law Commission and so needs to be quoted.

[8] In essay questions always try to end with some positive ideas of your own based on your research on how the law should develop.

[9] The facts of this case are an excellent illustration of how the courts seek to control unconscionable bargains.

[10] A mention of the law on restraint of trade will, of course, boost your marks and you might also include a reference to the doctrines of undue influence and economic duress. The point is that if the idea of a clog on the equity of redemption is abolished then we need some means of protecting mortgagors from exploitation. Or do we?

Reeve v *Lisle* [1902] AC 461 HL where the option to purchase was contained in a separate agreement but the doctrine was applied, with reluctance, by the Court of Appeal in *Jones* v *Morgan* [2002] 1 ELGR 125.

The Law Commission Report (1991) No. 204 on land mortgages[7] recommended the abolition of the equitable jurisdiction dealing with clogs on the equity of redemption. The government said that, due to lack of support for the proposals, they would not be implemented.

It is suggested that the doctrine that there must be no clog on the equity of redemption has, as Lord Phillips suggests, outlived its usefulness but its abolition should not mean the end of equity's jurisdiction in the area of mortgages. Instead renewed emphasis should be placed on the fundamental principle of equity[8] that there must be no unfair or unconscionable collateral advantage for the mortgagee as illustrated, for example, by *Cityland and Property (Holdings) Ltd* v *Dabrah* [1968] Ch 166 HC.[9] This jurisdiction does not exist where the terms of the mortgage are unreasonable but where the transaction is not merely 'hard or improvident' but 'overreaching and oppressive' (*Alec Lobb (Garages) Ltd* v *Total Oil Ltd* [1985] 1 WLR 87 HC). Meanwhile, there is no reason why the common law doctrine of restraint of trade[10] cannot play its part as advocated by Diplock LJ in *Esso Petroleum Ltd* v *Harper's Garage (Stourport) Ltd* [1968] AC 269 HL: 'I am not persuaded that mortgages of land are condemned today to linger in a judicial cul de sac built by the Courts of Chancery before the Judicature Acts from which the robust doctrines of the common law are excluded.'

This is surely the way forward.

✓ Make your answer stand out

- Read Thompson (2001) Do We Really Need Clogs? *Conveyancer* 502. This will add depth to your answer on this aspect.
- Consider how the equitable doctrine of unconscionability might play a part – read the decision in *Jones* v *Morgan* (2002).
- Set the scene clearly by emphasising the nature of equity and equitable intervention.
- Read *Warmborough Ltd* v *Garmite Ltd* [2003] EWCA Civ 1544 – interesting remarks by Jonathan Parker LJ on the clog on the equity of redemption.

> ! **Don't be tempted to . . .**
>
> - Just go through the cases without explaining that they are examples of equitable intervention.
> - Omit to give your essay a structure by building your account of the cases round the two separate areas where the 'clog' principle has been applied.
> - Fail to point out that the cases themselves show inconsistencies in approach and show how this is so.
> - Fail to adopt a critical approach – see the penultimate paragraph.
> - Fail to contrast the cases and bring out differences in approach by the courts.

? Question 2

In 2005 Frank purchased a 21-year legal lease of a petrol station. He mortgaged the premises to Wells Co., a petrol company, in order to finance the purchase. The mortgage deed included the following covenants by Frank:

(a) Only to sell petrol and oil supplied by Wells Co. for a period of 30 years from the commencement of the mortgage.

(b) To pay the principal and interest over a period of 20 years and if he wishes to redeem the mortgage before the expiration of 20 years then to pay a sum equal to 5 years' interest to Wells Co.

Frank has now been approached by Drills Ltd, another petrol company, that is keen to buy the lease from Frank and, pending the purchase, to supply him with petrol and oil. Advise Frank on whether and to what extent the above covenants are binding.

Answer plan

→ Explanation of fundamental equitable principles: idea of a clog on the equity of redemption and that equity will only intervene if the terms of the mortgage are oppressive.

→ Application of these principles to situation (a): changing attitude of the courts. Is the collateral agreement enforceable?

→ Possibility of doctrine of restraint of trade applying here?

→ Application of these principles to situation (b): equity's attitude to penalties on early redemption.

Diagram plan

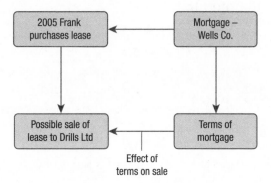

A printable version of this diagram plan is available from www.pearsoned.co.uk/lawexpressqa

Answer

[1] Do emphasise at the start of a problem on mortgages that it is equity which has laid down the fundamental principles.

[2] It is vital to stress the limits of the intervention of equity.

[3] Make sure that you explain exactly what this term means.

(a) A mortgagor owns the equity of redemption and a fundamental principle of equity[1] is that there must be no unfair or unconscionable collateral advantage for the mortgagee. In **_Alec Lobb (Garages) Ltd_ v _Total Oil Ltd_** [1985] 1 WLR 87 HC it was held that for equity to intervene the transaction must not be merely 'hard or improvident' but 'overreaching and oppressive'.[2] A collateral advantage[3] is where, in addition to the return of the loan with interest, the mortgagor obtains an additional advantage and this is an example as Frank is bound to not only repay the mortgage but also to only sell petrol and oil supplied by the mortgagee for a period of 30 years which is 5 years longer than the mortgage term of 25 years. The principle is that this kind of stipulation operates as a 'clog on the equity of redemption' because even after redemption the mortgagor would not recover his property as it was before the mortgage, as it would still be bound by a tie to the mortgagee.

[4] This paragraph deals with three cases all of which have slightly different decisions on the facts. Make sure that you bring this out.

In **_Biggs_ v _Hoddinott_** [1898] 2 Ch 307 HC[4] the mortgagor agreed to sell only beer brewed by the mortgagee for 5 years, but this collateral advantage ceased on redemption of the mortgage and was upheld. In **_Noakes & Co. Ltd_ v _Rice_** [1902] AC 24 HC the tenant of a public house mortgaged a lease which had more than 26 years to run and agreed that, during this time, he would not sell any malt liquor other than provided by the mortgagors. Moreover, this term would continue even though the mortgage was redeemed earlier and it was held void. The leading case is now **Krelinger v New Patagonia Meat and Cold Storage Co Ltd** [1914] AC 25 HL where a firm of woolbrokers lent money on a mortgage which could be repaid at any time in the next 5 years. The mortgagor also agreed to give the mortgagee first refusal on all their sheepskins and to pay commission on any sold to a third party. This agreement was to last for the full 5 years. This collateral agreement was upheld on the basis that the agreement to give first refusal was in fact a separate agreement from the mortgage and so was not a clog on the right to redeem.

The requirement to only sell petrol and oil supplied by Wells Co. for a period of 30 years from the commencement of the mortgage lasts for 5 years after the mortgage has expired and it appears to be in the actual mortgage itself and so the principle in **Noakes v Rice** does not apply. The only question is whether it can be argued that, in fact, this is a separate agreement from the mortgage. If so, it can be enforced. If not, it cannot. It is suggested that on the facts it looks like part of the actual mortgage and so is unenforceable although this is a tentative conclusion as we lack all the information.[5]

Another possibility is that this term might be struck down at common law as being in unreasonable restraint of trade[6] as in **Esso Petroleum v Harper's Garage (Stourport) Ltd** [1968] AC 269 HL where a tie requiring a petrol station to only sell a particular brand of petrol for 5 years was upheld but one for 21 years was not. Note that the test here is unreasonableness and not unconscionability.

(b) The provision that, if Frank wishes to redeem the mortgage before the expiration of 25 years, he must pay a sum equal to 5 years' interest to Wells Co. involves the possible application of the equitable principle that where postponement of the right to redeem is delayed to such an extent that the equity of redemption is valueless then the mortgagor may be allowed to redeem earlier. Equity does not automatically strike down clauses preventing or hindering early redemption as in **Knightsbridge Estates Trust Ltd v Byrne** [1939] Ch 441 CA[7] where a mortgage for a term of 40 years could not be redeemed earlier.

[5] We must apply the law to the question but we cannot, on the facts, come to a definite conclusion. Remember that very definite conclusions are often a sign of weakness not strength!

[6] This mention of another possibility will certainly gain you extra marks. Also point out that here we are dealing with common law principles and so different considerations will apply. In particular, the emphasis will be on whether a stipulation is unreasonable and not whether it is unconscionable.

[7] This is a useful case to start with in answers on this area, but if a lease is involved you need to then mention *Fairclough*.

However, here the parties were both commercial organisations experienced in these matters and the length of the term suited them both. Here Frank appears to be an individual dealing with what is, presumably, a large oil company. There is the additional factor that Frank has a lease for 21 years[8] and there is a penalty against redemption earlier than 20 years. In *Fairclough v Swan Brewery Co. Ltd* [1912] AC 565 PC the mortgagor was the tenant of a brewery which had a lease with 17 and a half years to run. A mortgage prevented redemption until six weeks before the end of the lease and this was held to be void as, by the time the mortgage was ended, the mortgagor recovered nothing of value. Nevertheless, the courts today may decide that if there was no evidence of oppression and as the agreement was a commercial one it should not be set aside on the principle mentioned earlier in *Alec Lobb (Garages) Ltd v Total Oil Ltd* that for equity to intervene the transaction must not be merely 'hard or improvident' but 'overreaching and oppressive'.[9]

[9] Note the emphasis on fundamental principles.

In this case there is a period of one year between the redemption date of the mortgage and the end of the lease but there is the additional factor not present in *Fairclough* that Frank must pay a sum equal to 5 years' interest to Wells Co. if he wishes to redeem early. This could be viewed as a penalty for early redemption and so amount to a clog on the equity of redemption and so be void. However, the courts today will look at the substance of the transaction and we need to ask if there was any bargain whereby in return for paying this extra sum there was a lower rate of interest, for example, in the early years of the mortgage. If not, then it is possible that, unless there is any reason why the payment of such a large sum can be justified, it is likely that it will be struck down as oppressive.

✓ Make your answer stand out

- Stress fundamental equitable principles.
- Consider the difficult decision in *Santley* v *Wilde* [1899] 2 Ch 474 CA which appears to conflict with *Fairclough* v *Swan Brewery*.
- Mention the doctrine of restraint of trade.
- Show how slightly different facts led to different decisions.

! Don't be tempted to . . .

- Come to conclusions which are too definite.
- Fail to pick up the different decisions in this area – there are subtle distinctions between the cases.
- Miss the fundamental principles.
- Mention only one case per point: e.g. *Krelinger*.

Question 3

Critically consider the statement that the remedies currently available to a mortgagee need to be reformed to make them accord with the economic realities of the twenty-first century.

Answer plan

→ Introduction: why this topic is important.

→ Consider the following remedies of the mortgagee: action for debt, possession and sale, foreclosure.

→ In the case of each remedy make sure to state the essential statutory points clearly and any leading cases.

→ Evaluate the effect of the HRA and the *Horsham* case.

Diagram plan

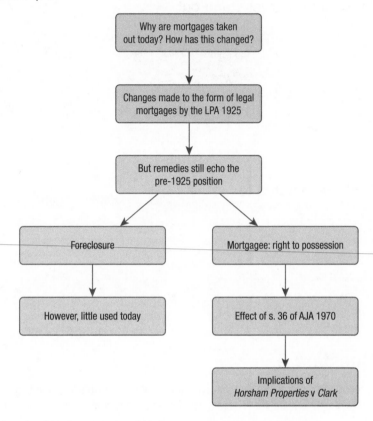

A printable version of this diagram plan is available from www.pearsoned.co.uk/lawexpressqa

[1] You need to make the point at the start that the problem is that the law has not moved on. However, do resist the temptation to give an account of the history of mortgages.

[2] This gets the answer on the right lines at the start. You have avoided the temptation of taking the easier (but wrong) route of just listing the remedies and instead you are engaging with the issue raised by the question.

Answer

The reasons why mortgages are taken out have changed over the years but the form of a mortgage, and with it the remedies available to a mortgagee against a mortgagor, are rooted in history.[1] Mortgages were traditionally taken out to secure an existing debt but today they are usually entered into because a person wishes to buy or lease a house or flat. However, the law of mortgages still contains echoes of the principle that applied before the Law of Property Act (LPA) 1925.[2] This was that a first legal mortgagee of a freehold[3] over the mortgaged property obtained a legal fee simple on creation of the mortgage. This is no longer the case, and the mortgagee's security is now a legal charge by deed over the mortgaged property, but the consequences of the mortgagee's holding of the fee simple remain.

The remedy traditionally available to the mortgagee was foreclosure. Where the mortgagee obtained the fee simple, this was logical. The courts declared that the mortgagor had lost the right to redeem the mortgage and so the mortgagee was left with the fee simple. Even though the form of mortgages has changed, this remedy of foreclosure still exists and, if it is used, the mortgaged property is vested in the mortgagee and the mortgagor has no rights to any surplus resulting from any sale. The drastic nature of foreclosure is mitigated to some extent by the rule that a court order is needed for a foreclosure and the courts can reopen a foreclosure order where, for instance, there is a marked difference between the value of the property and the amount lent. The result is that foreclosure has fallen into disuse. In ***Palk and Another* v *Mortgage Services Funding Plc*** [1993] 2 WLR 415 Nicolls VC observed that, 'So far as I am aware, foreclosure actions are almost unheard of today and have been so for many years. Mortgagees prefer to exercise other remedies. They usually appoint a receiver or exercise their powers of sale.' The question is then whether this remedy should still exist.[4]

The fact that mortgagees had the legal fee simple meant that the mortgagee was entitled to possession at any time after the creation of the mortgage and this right is now, by section 87(1) of the LPA 1925, given to the legal chargee. Thus Harman J observed in ***Four Maids Ltd* v *Dudley Marshall Properties*** [1957] Ch 317 that the right to possession arose 'before the ink was dry on the mortgage'[5] unless there was provision to the contrary in the mortgage deed and in ***Ropaigealach* v *Barclays Bank*** [2000] QB 263 Clarke LJ observed that 'I suspect that many mortgagors would be astonished to discover that a bank which had lent them money to buy a property for them to live in could take possession of it the next day'.

Unlike the foreclosure remedy, this right does have current practical implications as it means that the mortgagee has the fundamental right to go into possession of the property without a court order[6] (***Ropaigealach* v *Barclays Bank*** [2000]). However, a mortgagee would normally only go into possession without a court order if the property was unoccupied as section 6(1) of the Criminal Law Act 1977 makes it an offence for any person without lawful authority to use or threaten violence to enter premises if he knows that there is someone there who opposes his entry.

If a court order is sought then by section 36 of the Administration of Justice Act (AJA) 1970 the court may, if it appears that the mortgagor will, within a reasonable period, be able to pay sums due under the mortgage, or remedy the breach of any other default arising under it:

(i)   adjourn the proceedings; or

(ii)   on giving an order for possession, to stay or suspend execution of it or postpone the date for delivery of possession.

However, section 36 applies only where the property consists of or includes a dwelling house.[7]

The rule was that any arrears should be paid off in two years but in **Cheltenham & Gloucester BS v Norgan**[8] [1996] 1 WLR 343 it was held that the remaining term of the mortgage should be the starting point and a number of relevant considerations were set out to assist courts in deciding what is a reasonable period to allow for repayment, such as how much the borrower can afford to pay, are there any temporary difficulties in making repayments and how long these may last and the reason why arrears have accumulated.

Horsham Properties Group Ltd v Clark [2008] EWHC 2327[9] shows the significance of the mortgagee's right to possession and the limitations of section 36 of the AJA 1970. Under section 101 of the LPA 1925[10] a mortgagee has the power to sell the mortgaged property when the mortgage money has become due (s. 101(1)(i)) or, by section 101(1)(iii), to appoint a receiver of the income from the property, which they did in this case. If the mortgagee had sought possession in pursuance of a sale under section 101(1)(i), then section 36 of the AJA would have applied. However, they appointed a receiver who then sold the mortgaged property by auction to Horsham Properties. Horsham's legal title to the property overreached that of the occupiers, the mortgagors, who were now simply trespassers. Instead Horsham could rely on the mortgagee's right to possession with the result that the mortgagors lost their home without a court order.

The mortgagor's claim that this result violated their right to the peaceful enjoyment of their possessions guaranteed by Article 1 of

[7] An important point to note if you get a problem question on this area. Note that section 36 will apply where a part of the property is used as a house and part for other purposes e.g. shop. See also section 39(2).

[8] Although this area is governed by statute law, there are important cases on the interpretation of the statutory provisions. Make sure that you know the main ones. You could construct an interesting answer by looking at the extent to which case law has attempted to move the balance more to the interests of the mortgagees.

[9] Up to this point the answer has described statute law and its interpretation by the courts. Here your answer takes off as it were and starts to earn you the marks for a really good pass. This is an important recent case which also involves the ECHR.

[10] Although not directly relevant here, you should remember that whereas section 101 sets out when the mortgagee's power of sale arises, it is section 103 which sets out when that power is actually exercisable.

the First Protocol to the European Convention on Human Rights, as incorporated into UK law by the Human Rights Act 1998, was rejected as the loss of their home had occurred without any state intervention, and so Article 1 was not engaged.

[11] This is the kind of research detail which really adds to your marks.

This result was widely felt to be unsatisfactory and a private members' bill, the Home Repossession (Protection) Bill, was introduced.[11] This would have amended section 101 of the LPA 1925 by ensuring that a mortgagee of a dwelling house could not exercise the power of sale without first obtaining an order of the court, and the court would be given substantially the same powers as those found currently in section 36 of the AJA 1970. However, it did not become law.

[12] As you read this paragraph, note how the central themes of this essay have been summarised and then right at the end the actual words of the question are brought in.

It seems clear that[12] the continuing presence of the archaic remedy of foreclosure, the right of the mortgagee to take possession at any time and the failure of the law to provide that there should always be a court order when possession is sought show that the quotation is justified and that the law of mortgages needs to be reformed to make it accord with the economic realities of the twenty-first century.

✓ Make your answer stand out

- Keep the idea of a critical approach in mind when looking at each remedy and beware of the temptation to just describe it.
- See Greer (2009) *Horsham Properties Group Ltd* v *Clark*: Possession – Mortgagee's Right or Discretionary Remedy? *Conveyancer* 516–24. Material from this extra discussion of the case will add value to your answer.
- Read also Wood (2009) *Horsham Properties Group Ltd* v *Clark*: A Year On. *Coventry Law Journal*, 14(2): 31–6.
- Research into current levels of mortgage repossessions.

! Don't be tempted to . . .

- Just describe the remedies.
- Fail to mention case law.
- Explain how the remedies relate to each other.
- Miss the last point on the ECHR.

❓ Question 4

In 1993 Tony purchased a house, 'Southmead', for £200,000 of which £175,000 was provided by a loan from the Hanbury Building Society. Title to the property was unregistered. This loan was secured by a properly executed charge by way of legal mortgage over the property. The building society retained the title deeds as security for the charge.

In 1994 Tony created a charge over the property in favour of the Shark Building Society to secure his overdraft which then stood at £20,000. The charge also secured any other monies 'which the bank, in its absolute discretion, might advance'. This charge was protected by a Class C (i) land charge.

By 1995 the value of the property had increased to £250,000 and Tony borrowed £40,000 from the Friendly Building Society to finance some extensions to the property. This was also secured by a charge over the property.

In 1996 Tony borrowed a further £10,000 from the Nice Building Society, secured by a charge over the property, to fund the installation of double glazing.

In all of the above cases, the charges were properly executed legal charges.

In 1997 the Shark Building Society made a further loan to Tony of £3,000.

The Friendly Building Society and the Nice Building Society did not protect their charges by registration at the time but the Friendly Building Society did protect its mortgage by registration as a Class C (i) land charge in January 1998.

Tony is now bankrupt. His overdraft stands at £30,000 and all of the loans are still outstanding. The house has decreased in value and is unlikely to realise more than £230,000 when sold after paying the costs of sale.

Explain the order in which the mortgagees will be paid if 'Southmead' is sold by one of the mortgagees.

How would your answer differ if title to the house was registered and the mortgages were registered at the time of their creation?

Answer plan

➡ Identify that title to the property is unregistered and that all the mortgages are legal.

➡ Distinguish between the rules applicable to protection of first mortgages from those applicable to second and subsequent mortgages and apply these rules.

➡ Identify the situation where tacking of subsequent mortgages may be possible and apply the relevant rules.

➡ Identify the situation where there are two possible rules governing priority of a mortgage and apply the rules.

➡ State and explain the rules on priority of mortgages in registered land.

Diagram plan

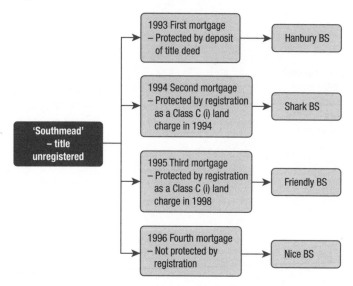

A printable version of this diagram plan is available from www.pearsoned.co.uk/lawexpressqa

Answer

Title to the house is unregistered and so the rules on priority of mortgages in unregistered land will apply. It is worth pointing out that if any of the mortgages had been created on or after 1 April 1998 this would have triggered registration of the property.[1] All of the mortgages are legal and are properly executed.[2]

The first mortgage was taken out in 1993 for £175,000 in favour of the Hanbury Building Society. A legal mortgage is not registrable as a land charge and instead priority is secured by the retention of the title deeds.[3] As the Hanbury Building Society has done this, it will have priority over all other mortgagees and will be able to exercise its remedies as a mortgagee.[4] This means that it will probably take possession of 'Southmead' and sell it to recover its loan of £175,000. As the value of the property is £230,000 this means that, after the Building Society has deducted the costs which it has incurred in the sale, there will not be enough left to satisfy the claims of the other mortgagees.[5]

[1] Although this is strictly a side issue it does deserve a mention as it shows the examiner that you were aware of this point.

[2] The rules on priority would differ if the mortgages were equitable and so you need to check for this.

[3] This point is often forgotten by students.

[4] You do not need to discuss remedies in detail but it will add to your marks if you state the remedies briefly.

[5] Make a calculation at the start of the amounts owing against the value of the property.

The charge over the property created in favour of the Shark Building Society was protected by a Class C (i) land charge at the time of its creation and so it will be next in priority. This is because by section 198(1) of the Law of Property Act 1925 registration constitutes actual notice of the charge to a purchaser and thus subsequent purchasers will take subject to this charge.[6] It is only what are termed 'puisne' mortgages, which are second or subsequent mortgages such as this one, which can be registered as first mortgages and, as we have seen, are protected by the retention of the title deeds by the mortgagee.

In 1997 the Shark Building Society made a further loan to Tony of £3,000 and the question is whether this can rank in priority to the charge created in 1994 even though it was not protected by a Class C (i) land charge. The charge taken by the Shark Building Society also secures any other monies 'which the bank, in its absolute discretion, might advance'.[7] The question is whether this clause allows the Building Society to 'tack' further advances onto this charge so that they also have the same priority as the actual charge. Tacking is dealt with by section 94 of the Law of Property Act (LPA) 1925 which provides that a prior mortgagee (the Shark Building Society in this case) shall have a right to make further advances to rank in priority to subsequent mortgages:

(a) if an arrangement has been made to that effect with the subsequent mortgagees; or

(b) if he had no notice of such subsequent mortgages at the time when the further advance was made by him; or

(c) whether or not he had such notice as aforesaid, where the mortgage imposes an obligation on him to make such further advances.

In this case, there is no evidence of any arrangement with subsequent mortgagees under (a) and there is no reason why the subsequent lenders in this case should agree to the Shark Building Society having priority over their loan. Nor does (c) apply as the wording of the charge does not impose an obligation on the Shark Building Society to make further advances as it expressly states that it has an 'absolute discretion to do so'. Thus, (b) applies and the Shark Building Society can tack further advances onto the loan of 1994 until they have notice of any subsequent mortgages.

[6] This is a very good example of how to gain extra marks. You could have stopped at the end of the first sentence and this would have been correct but we have continued and given the statutory authority for what we have said and its implications.

[7] When you see this wording, check further down the question to see if there have been further advances.

The problem is that the subsequent mortgages to the Friendly Building Society in 1995 and the Nice Building Society in 1996 were not protected by registration as Class C (i) land charges and, as we saw above, section 198(1) of the LPA provides that registration as a land charge constitutes actual notice of that charge. The Friendly Building Society did protect its loan by a charge in 1998 but the loan of £3,000 to Tony which the Shark Building Society wishes to tack was made in 1997. The conclusion must be that it can do so and that this loan will have priority over the two subsequent mortgages.

The final question is that of priority between the Friendly Building Society and the Nice Building Society. The mortgage to the Friendly Building Society was taken out in 1995 and that to the Nice Building Society in 1996. Neither was protected by registration at the time but, as we have seen, the Friendly Building Society eventually protected its charge by registration in 1998. By section 4(5) of the Land Charges Act 1972, priority between charges which should have been registered as Class C (i) charges, which both of these are, are void against a purchaser for money or money's worth and by section 205(1) (xxi) of the LPA 1925 a purchaser includes a mortgagee.[8] Thus as the charge to the Friendly Building Society had not been registered at the time of the mortgage to the Nice Building Society the charge of the Friendly Building Society will be void against that of the Nice Building Society and the Nice Building Society will have priority.

However, this point is not certain and there is a view that the provisions of section 97 of the LPA 1925 mean that priority of mortgages shall rank in order of the date of their creation. In this case, as the mortgage to the Friendly Building Society was created first, it will have priority.[9]

It has never been decided with certainty which of these alternatives is correct[10] but one powerful argument in favour of the application of section 97 of the LPA is that it was included in the LPA specifically to deal with this point and if it does not apply then it is completely redundant. On the other hand, section 4(5) of the Land Charges Act 1972 applies to other interests in land.

If the title to 'Southmead' was registered and all of the mortgages were registered at the time of their creation, priority would be governed by this time and they would rank in priority accordingly (s. 48, Land Registration Act (LRA) 2002). Thus, the order would be

[8] This is another example of a small point of extra detail which will increase your marks.

[9] You should watch for this point in any question on priorities between mortgages in unregistered land as it is a very familiar one. The basic scenario is the one here: Mortgage A was created first but, when Mortgage B was created, Mortgage B had not been registered. The application of section 4(5) of the Land Charges Act gives a different result to that if section 97 of the LPA is applied. The point is quite simple but you need to be clear on it.

[10] The worst thing which you could do would be to come down definitely in favour of one alternative or the other.

the mortgages granted to the Hanbury Building Society, the Shark Building Society, the Friendly Building Society and the Nice Building Society. The ability of the mortgagee to tack the mortgage is governed by section 49 of the LRA 2002, which has the same conditions as in section 94 of the LPA 1925 but it also adds another which is that where the parties have agreed a limit up to which further advances can be made, then tacking can take place up to that limit. This has not happened here.

 Make your answer stand out

- Consider in more detail the controversy over whether the order of priority between unregistered mortgages should in fact be governed by section 97 of the LPA 1925 and not section 4(5) of the Land Charges Act. Another view is that the Land Charges Act 1925, the predecessor of the Land Charges Act 1972, was actually passed before the LPA 1925 and so it should prevail where there is a conflict, as here.
- Another argument in this debate is that the actual wording of section 97 of the LPA is that a mortgage 'shall rank according to its date of registration as a land charge pursuant to the Land Charges Act 1972'. Thus, section 97 only provides machinery for the operation of the Land Charges Act and so it is the Land Charges Act which should prevail.

Don't be tempted to . . .

- Overlook that title to the land is unregistered.
- Overlook the question at the end which asks what the position would be if the title was registered.
- Think that the mortgages should simply rank in priority according to the date of their creation and ignore the need to register second or subsequent mortgages as land charges.
- Fail to apply to the question all the possible cases when tacking of a mortgage can be allowed.

Question 5

'Unless the creditor who is put on inquiry takes reasonable steps to satisfy himself that the wife's agreement to stand surety has been properly obtained, the creditor will have constructive notice of the wife's rights.' (Lord Browne-Wilkinson in *Barclays Bank Plc* v *O'Brien* [1994] 1 AC 180)

Consider why the courts felt it necessary to state this principle and the ways in which it has been applied in subsequent cases.

Answer plan

→ Give some background by considering the social reasons behind this principle.

→ Explain the actual *ratio* of *Barclays Bank* v *O'Brien* clearly.

→ Critically consider the interpretation and development of the principle in *O'Brien* in later cases, especially *Royal Bank of Scotland* v *Etridge*.

→ Conclude by looking at possible future developments.

Diagram plan

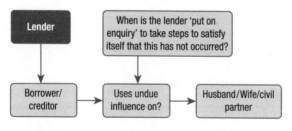

A printable version of this diagram plan is available from www.pearsoned.co.uk/lawexpressqa

Answer

[1] It is important to note that the law does not only apply in the husband and wife situation but this seemed to be its starting point. The courts initially referred to cases where a husband unduly influenced his wife but you should point out that it could equally well be the other way round.

This quotation from the speech of Lord Browne-Wilkinson in ***Barclays Bank Plc*** v ***O'Brien*** [1994] 1 AC 180 HL deals with the situation where one party is asked to stand surety for the debts of another and, in particular, where a wife is asked to stand surety for the debts of her husband.[1] The law has developed since ***O'Brien*** although the fundamental principle remains and this essay will explain the fundamental principle and assess the developments. There is a typical scenario where the husband has a business which needs more capital. His main asset is the home which he owns with his wife. He persuades his wife by undue influence to agree to execute a document which mortgages the home in return for a loan. The wife in this case in effect stands surety for his agreement to repay the loan.

The issue here is not undue influence itself. In this discussion it will be assumed that this has occurred. Instead it is the extent to which the creditor is affected by it.[2] The problem is that the creditor in whose favour the mortgage deed was signed, typically a financial institution, will have no knowledge of any undue influence. Suppose that the husband defaults on the loan and the creditor begins possession proceedings. The wife may say that her agreement was procured by the undue influence of her husband but the creditor may reply that that is a matter between her and her husband. It is the task of the courts to make some causal link between the wife and the creditor.

As Lord Browne-Wilkinson pointed out, the large number of cases of this type coming before the courts reflects changes in social attitudes and the distribution of wealth which has recently occurred.[3] Wealth is now more widely spread and a high proportion of privately owned wealth is invested in the matrimonial home. In addition the majority of matrimonial homes are now in the joint names of both spouses. Therefore, in order to raise finance for the business enterprises of one or other of the spouses, the jointly owned home has become a main source of security. The provision of such security requires the consent of both spouses.

Scott LJ in the Court of Appeal found that there were two previous lines of authority.[4] One was the agency theory: that the rights of the creditor bank could only be adversely affected by the wrongful acts of the principal debtor, the husband, in procuring the surety's liability if the principal debtor was acting as the agent of the creditor in procuring the surety to join, or the creditor had knowledge of the relevant facts (see **Kings North Trust v Bell** [1986] 1 WLR 119). The other theory considered that equity affords special protection to a protected class of surety, such as those where the relationship between the debtor and the surety is such that influence by the debtor over the surety and reliance by the surety on the debtor are natural features of the relationship.

Lord Browne-Wilkinson pointed out that only the second theory would give protection to the wife. He invoked the doctrine of notice[5] in

[2] There is no reason why you cannot give an account of the law on undue influence but I suggest that if you explore the main issues in this question you will not have time for it! It is also worth bearing in mind that the principles in *O'Brien* can also apply where there has been misrepresentation.

[3] Beware of saying too much on the general social background to the law as you can easily write a sociology essay! But it is vital to explain why this area of the law has become important.

[4] Many students will go straight to the HL decision but discerning students (you?) when discussing a major case will also look at what was said in the CA.

[5] You could do some research and mention that this is not exactly notice as it is understood in cases involving the priority of equitable rights on a transfer of property.

determining the enforceability of securities by third party creditors in situations such as these and outlined circumstances in which a third party creditor will be 'put on enquiry'. When these circumstances arise, the creditor will be fixed with constructive notice of the undue influence. However, use of the doctrine of notice has been criticised on the ground that notice has traditionally referred to notice of a prior right but here it refers to the possibility of a right existing in the future, in this case a right to set the transaction aside for undue influence.[6]

[6] It is vital to point out that the idea of notice in these cases is now not accepted. See Thompson (2003), especially pages 130–2.

In *Royal Bank of Scotland v Etridge* (No. 2) [2002] 2 AC 773 HL Lord Nichols used the analysis of a tripartite transaction between creditor, debtor and surety. However, he retained the central notion that in certain cases a creditor can be put on enquiry and a transaction entered into as a result of undue influence may be set aside unless the creditor takes certain steps.

When, then, is a creditor 'put on enquiry'? Lord Nichols said that this would be where a husband or wife stands surety for the debts of the other or where they cohabit or even where there is no cohabitation as in *Massey v Midland Bank Plc* [1995] 1 All ER 929 CA. Miss Massey, who signed the form, never cohabited with Mr Potts, but Steyn LJ pointed out that she had a stable sexual and emotional relationship with him over many years, and they had two children. Thus he was clear that the *O'Brien* principle applied to her. Since the Civil Partnership Act 2004 the categories will also include civil partners. If, however, a loan is advanced to the parties jointly, the creditor is not put on enquiry as in *CIBC Mortgages v Pitt* [1994] 1 AC 200 HL.

The House of Lords in *Etridge* then clarified the steps which the creditor should reasonably be expected to take in satisfying itself that the security has been properly obtained:

(a) The lender must contact the surety and request that they nominate a solicitor.

(b) The surety must reply, nominating a solicitor.

(c) The lender must, with the consent of the surety, disclose to the solicitor all relevant information – both the debtor's financial position and the details of the proposed loan.

(d) The solicitor must advise the surety in a face-to-face meeting at which the debtor is not present. The advice must cover an explanation of the documentation, the risks to the surety in signing and emphasise that the surety must decide whether to proceed.

(e) The solicitor must, if satisfied that the surety wishes to proceed, send written confirmation to the lender that the solicitor has explained the nature of the documents and their implications for the surety.

[7] It is important to deal with the applications of these principles.

Other issues remained to be clarified.[7] The first is whether the creditor is responsible for the advice given. Lord Nicholls was clear that this was not so. He observed that the solicitor is not the agent of the creditor and that, 'In the ordinary case, therefore, deficiencies in the advice given are a matter between the wife and her solicitor.' A difficult area is where advice is given by a solicitor who also acts for the company on whose behalf the loan was sought, as in **Banco Exterior Internacional v Mann** [1995] 1 All ER 936. Here it was held to be sufficient that the mortgagee had been shown a certificate that independent advice had been given. What, however, if the creditor actually knew that, despite the certificate, no advice had been given? There are still questions in this area which have not been settled.

✓ Make your answer stand out

- Give a clear explanation of the *O'Brien* principle.
- Mention earlier attempts by the courts to provide protection for wives etc.
- Consider Andrews (2002) Undue Influence – Where's the Disadvantage? *Conveyancer* 456. This looks at the decision in *Etridge*.
- Consider Houghton and Livesey (2001) Mortgage Conditions: Old Law for a New Century?, in Cooke (ed.) *Modern Studies in Property Law*.
- Consider Thompson (2003) Mortgages and Undue Influence, in E. Cooke (ed.) *Modern Studies in Property Law*, Vol. 2. This gives a clear account of the law and of how it has developed, which many textbooks do not do.

! Don't be tempted to . . .

- Just describe the law.
- Spend a great deal of time on undue influence itself.
- Avoid explaining the link between the decision in *O'Brien* and that in *Etridge*.
- Disregard the conditions laid down in *Etridge* for the creditor to observe.

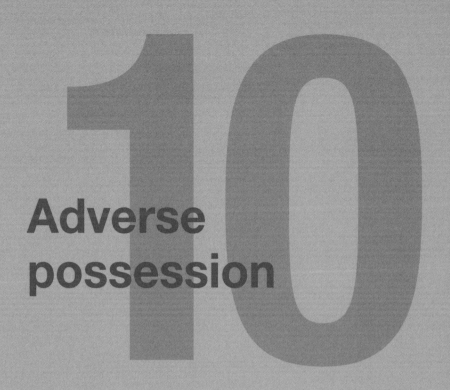

Adverse possession

How this topic may come up in exams

This area is popular with examiners as it contains material for detailed problem questions and also a number of topics for essays. Problems are likely to focus initially on the basic requirements for adverse possession but then they can cover a variety of topics such as earmarked land, leaseholds, the mechanics of acquiring title by this method and the impact of the ECHR.

Essays may focus on whether it should be possible to acquire title by adverse possession at all and perhaps on the social aspect with an angle on urban squatting and homelessness.

In summary, an excellent area for all students and especially good to score those vital extra marks on!

■ Attack the question

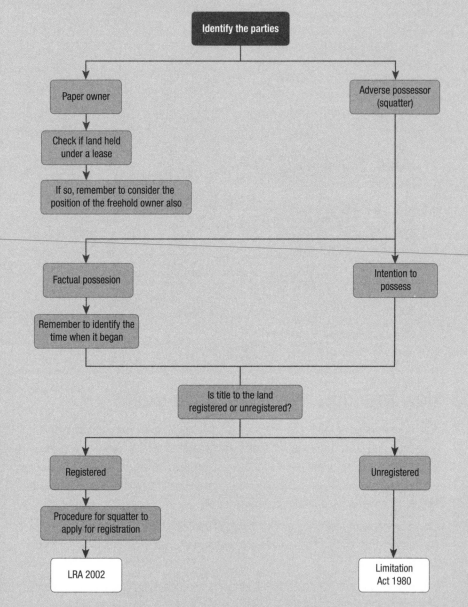

```
                        ┌──────────────────────┐
                        │  Identify the parties │
                        └──────────────────────┘
```

Paper owner

Check if land held under a lease

If so, remember to consider the position of the freehold owner also

Adverse possessor (squatter)

Factual possesion

Remember to identify the time when it began

Intention to possess

Is title to the land registered or unregistered?

Registered

Procedure for squatter to apply for registration

LRA 2002

Unregistered

Limitation Act 1980

A printable version of this diagram is available from www.pearsoned.co.uk/lawexpressqa

❓ Question 1

Peter allowed Lucy and her daughter Kate to occupy a cottage on his farm while she worked for him. When Lucy's employment ended in 1998, Peter said that Lucy and Kate could stay until they had found somewhere else to live. In 1999 Lucy died but Kate remained in the cottage and Peter said that this was 'all right by me' but that Kate must vacate the premises by 31 December 1999.

After that time, Peter sent several letters asking Kate to vacate the cottage. However, Kate decided to stay and started to improve her accommodation although she told a friend, Anne, that 'if Peter comes and tells me to go then I will have to'. She installed a telephone, fitted a new front door and built fences around the garden.

Peter became unwell and so he did not take steps to remove Kate from the cottage. In 2006 he sold the farm, including the cottage, to John.

John wrote to Kate and said that she must leave. However, Kate replied that she had been there so long and spent so much money on improvements, that it would be wrong for her to leave especially as she was in poor health but that if John wanted her to pay for the use of the cottage then she would 'think about it'. John decided to do nothing for the time being, although he was aware that Kate was continuing to spend money on improvements.

It is 2011 and John seeks your advice as to the present position regarding any claim Kate may have for adverse possession and as to the procedures which would apply to any application for registration under the Land Registration Act 2002.

Diagram plan

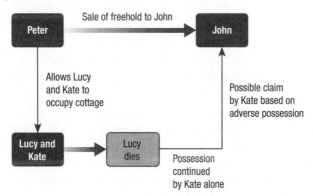

A printable version of this diagram plan is available from www.pearsoned.co.uk/lawexpressqa

Answer plan

→ Note that title is registered – calculate the period of adverse possession required and by whom: when did adverse possession actually begin?

→ Consider if there was factual possession.

→ Continue by considering whether there was the intention to possess.

→ Explain the position on the sale of the freehold to John.

→ Explain the procedure under the LRA 2002 for the squatter to be registered.

Answer

[1] This is an excellent way to start: you have set the answer in the context of who has to prove what.

[2] You will need to apply the relevant procedures in the LRA to the question only when you have decided that there has been adverse possession for the requisite period. Why not draw a diagram and a timeline before you start on a problem question on adverse possession?

[3] This is an important point – do watch in each question for when the period of adverse possession began. If the adverse possessor of registered land had completed 12 years before the LRA 2002 came into force on 13 October 2003 (i.e. if Kate's adverse possession began on 1 January 1991 or earlier) then if title was registered she would be entitled to be registered and the safeguards for the registered proprietor would not apply (Sched. 12, Para. 18(1), LRA 2002).

Although there is no statutory definition of adverse possession, its essence is possession of land which is inconsistent with the title of the true owner and which amounts to a denial of that title. In **Powell v McFarlane** (1977) 38 P & CR 452 HC it was emphasised that there is a presumption that the owner of the land with the paper title is in possession and so in any action based on adverse possession the burden of proof is on the squatter[1] to prove both:

(a) factual possession (*corpus possessionis*);

(b) intent to possess (*animus possidendi*).

These will be examined in detail later but at the outset it is vital to note that as title to the land is registered then under the Land Registration Act (LRA) 2002 the period of adverse possession needed is a minimum of 10 years.[2] It should be noted that the scheme under the LRA applies even though the period of adverse possession began before the LRA came into force on 13 October 2003[3] (see Sched. 6, Para. 1(1)). We are told that Lucy originally occupied the cottage while she worked for Peter and that even after her employment ended in 1998 Peter allowed her to stay until they had found somewhere else. Clearly, at these times Lucy did not have the intent to possess as she was there by the permission of the owner and so her possession was not inconsistent with Peter's title. Thus, in **J.A. Pye Ltd v Graham** [2002] 3 All ER 865 HL it was accepted that the period when the claimant held under a licence did not count towards the period of adverse possession. Thus, when Lucy died in 1999 she was not in adverse possession and the question is whether Kate, who continued in possession, can establish this.

Peter told Kate that she must vacate the cottage by 31 December 1999 but Kate remained in possession after then. It is clear that Peter wanted her to leave as he sent several letters asking Kate to go and so there can be no argument of any implied licence[4] after that date.

The question is now whether the acts done by Kate amount to factual possession. She installed a telephone, fitted a new front door and built fences around the garden. In **Powell v McFarlane** Slade J held that the adverse possessor must show that he has dealt with the land as an occupying owner. This is demonstrated by exercising control over the land and, as Slade J pointed out, clear evidence of this is 'the locking or blocking of the only means of access'. Thus, in **Williams v Usherwood** (1983) 45 P & CR 235 HC[5] the Court of Appeal held that the enclosing of land by a fence, together with parking three cars and paving a driveway with decorative paving stones, the fitting of the door and building of fences, is conclusive evidence of factual possession and it is suggested that in particular Kate's fitting of the door and building of fences around the garden is enough.

Intent to possess means the intention to exclude the whole world and the acts done showing factual possession together with her failure to reply to the letters which Peter sent asking Kate to vacate the cottage amount to this. The fact that Kate told Anne that 'if Peter comes and tells me to go then I will have to' does not show the lack of intent to possess as it is merely an acknowledgement by her of Peter's ownership and, as the House of Lords held in **J.A. Pye Ltd v Graham**, what is required is not the intention by Lucy to own but to possess.

It is submitted that as this is now 2011 Kate will have the requisite 10 years' factual possession and the intention to possess and that she will be able to apply to be registered as owner of the cottage.

The fact that Peter became unwell and so did not take steps to remove her does not affect her claim as any illness of Peter's could only be relevant if it amounted to a mental disability which meant that he was unable to make decisions on an actual application by Kate to be registered as proprietor (Sched. 6, Para. 8(2) LRA 2002).

John bought the cottage from Peter in 2006 and so, as he is a purchaser[6] under section 29 and section 30 of the LRA 2002 and this is a case where the title to the land is already registered,[7] he is bound by interests which fall under Schedule 3 of the LRA 2002. These include the interest[8] of a person in actual occupation as Kate is. However, John will not be bound if the interest is not within his actual knowledge at the time of the disposition nor could it have been discovered on a reasonable inspection of the land (Sched. 3 Para. 2). However, as Kate was living in the cottage John clearly should have discovered her occupation and so will be bound by it.

It is for Kate to apply for registration and, on receipt of the application, the Registrar must give notice of it to John as the registered proprietor (RP) and to a number of others including the owner of any registered charge over the property. If John does not respond within 65 working days, Kate is entitled to be registered as owner of the estate. John may serve a counter-notice which means that the matter is dealt with under Schedule 6, Paragraph 5 and, unless Kate can establish that she comes within one of three special circumstances, John has two years from the date of the rejection of Kate's application to commence proceedings for possession.

[9] There is no point in mentioning the others as they clearly do not apply so do not waste time on setting them out!

[10] The examiner is not looking for a long discussion of estoppel but just a sentence which captures its essence especially as estoppel does not seem to apply.

[11] If you have time certainly mention the details of the decision but at the very least set out the essence of what it says as it is the most recent leading case.

The only one[9] of these relevant to this situation is Schedule 6, Paragraph 5(2): that it would be unconscionable because of an equity by estoppel for the registered proprietor to seek to dispossess the applicant. The question in estoppel cases is whether a party has reasonably relied on an assurance by the other as that person's conduct[10] (see **Thorner v Major** [2009] UKHL 18 HL)[11] and here, although Kate may claim that she has spent money on improvements and John was aware of this, there is no evidence of any assurance by John, and so it is submitted that estoppel would not apply.

✓ Make your answer stand out

- Include a further discussion of what constitutes factual possession and whether this is so here: a possible case to look at is *Purbrick* v *Hackney LBC* [2003] EWHC 1871.
- Make a brief mention at the end that an argument that the law on adverse possession infringes the HRA would not succeed and why – *Pye (J.A.) (Oxford) Ltd* v *UK* (2005) ECHR 921 and *Ofulue* v *Bossert* [2008] EWCA Civ 7.
- Refer to the possibility that even though a claim to be registered on the basis of an estoppel under Paragraph 5(2) of Schedule 6 of the LRA does not succeed, this may not bar a separate application on the basis of estoppel – point is uncertain.
- Refer to Law Commission Report (2001) *Land Registration for the 21st Century: A Conveyancing Revolution*, No. 271, para. 14.42, on the circumstances in which the Law Commission thought that estoppel could apply.

! Don't be tempted to . . .

- Deal with the mechanics of acquiring title under the LRA 2002 before you have decided if there is adverse possession.
- Confuse the position of Kate with that of Lucy – treat them separately.
- Assume that Kate has factual possession – she almost certainly does, but state and apply the law!
- Overlook the position on the sale to John – do not assume that he is automatically bound or that he is not bound at all! Instead leave yourself time to mention Schedule 3, Paragraph 2, LRA 2002.
- Overlook the estoppel point. It may not succeed but, on the facts, it should be mentioned.

? Question 2

For many years, Fred had used a field, Blackacre, under annual grazing licences, granted by Mike, the registered leasehold proprietor of the field. Mike held a 99-year lease and the freehold title is held by Robbie.

In 1998 Fred wrote to Mike to request the renewal of the licence. He also asked if he might use the land more extensively than before. Fred received no reply. In the meantime, he did indeed use the field more extensively and he also replaced some of the boundary fences and the old gate.

In addition Fred owned another field, Whiteacre, which adjoins the land of Mike. When he bought Whiteacre in 2000 the seller, Teresa, told him that there had been a previous boundary dispute between her and Mike but that, as Teresa had heard nothing from Mike for some time, Teresa assumed that Mike was 'happy with the situation'.

It is now 2013.

(a) Fred wishes to make an application under the Land Registration Act 2002 to be registered as leasehold owner of Blackacre.

(b) Mike has put boundary posts on Whiteacre but Fred says that some of the land they enclose belongs to him.

How, if at all, would your answer differ if title to the land was unregistered?

Answer plan

→ Identify the parties and their legal status – freeholder, leaseholder and licensee.

→ When did adverse possession begin?

→ Decide if there is both factual possession and an intention to possess on the part of Fred.

→ Consider the relevance or not of the possibility that the land may be intended for another use in future.

→ Explain the procedure on an application under the LRA 2002.

→ Explain how Robbie as the freeholder would be affected by a successful application by Fred.

→ Explain the position if title unregistered.

Diagram plan

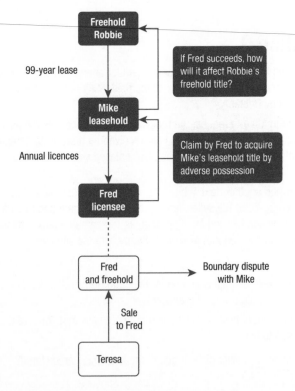

A printable version of this diagram plan is available from www.pearsoned.co.uk/lawexpressqa

Answer

[1] If you get a question on
adverse possession involving
a lease you should first
consider if the claim will
succeed against the
leaseholder. The rules are
the same as if the claim was
to the freehold. Only if you
consider that the claim might
succeed need you go on to
look at the effect on the
freeholder.

[2] Never forget to mention
these two points!

[3] Note the difference from the
period where title is
unregistered.

[4] You need to identify very
clearly exactly how long a
period of adverse possession
is required and how much
there is in the situation.

(a) Fred is making a claim to be registered as the leasehold proprietor of a field where at present Mike is the leaseholder under a 99-year lease and the freehold title is held by Robbie. We shall first consider Fred's claim against Mike's leasehold title and then, if Fred does succeed against Mike, the effect which this will have on Robbie as the freeholder. The position if title to land is unregistered will be dealt with later.[1]

In **Powell v McFarlane** (1977) 38 P & CR 452 it was emphasised that there is a presumption that the owner of the land with the paper title is in possession and so in any action based on adverse possession the burden of proof is on the squatter to prove both:

(a) Factual possession (*corpus possessionis*)

(b) Intent to possess (*animus possidendi*).[2]

As title to the land is registered then under the Land Registration Act (LRA) 2002 the period of adverse possession needed is a minimum of 10 years.[3]

Originally Fred held the field under annual grazing licences and so no question of adverse possession can arise as he did not have the intent to possess as he was there by the permission of the owner and so his possession was not inconsistent with Mike's title. (**J.A. Pye Ltd v Graham** [2002] 3 All ER 865). So any period of adverse possession will begin in 1998 when Fred's licence expired.

In **Powell v McFarlane** Slade J held that factual possession is shown by the adverse possessor dealing with the land as an occupying owner in exercising control over the land and he pointed out that clear evidence of this is 'the locking or blocking of the only means of access'. Here factual possession by Fred is demonstrated by using the field more extensively and replacing some of the boundary fences and the old gate.

Fred can apply for registration after 10 years' possession and here he has 13.[4] The Registrar must give notice of the application to Mike as the registered leasehold proprietor and Robbie as the registered freehold proprietor. Both can respond within 65 working days by serving a counter-notice and so, unless Fred can establish that he comes within one of three special circumstances set out in Paragraph 5(2) of the LRA 2002, none of which apply,[5] Mike has two years from the date of Fred's application to commence proceedings for possession.

[5] There is no point in saying any more than this especially as you will have seen that in part (b) you will need to deal with this issue in more detail.

If title to the land is unregistered then under section 15(1) of the Limitation Act 1980 the period of adverse possession is 12 years and Fred has achieved this.[6] The requirements of factual possession and intention to possess are the same as for registered land and so Fred will then need to make an application to be registered as owner of the field. However, there are no provisions for Mike or Robbie to object and so Fred is likely to become the registered owner.

[6] It is easy to forget that if title is unregistered the period is different – this is a basic point and you will lose marks if you get it wrong!

Assuming that Fred does succeed in his claim he will be registered as the new proprietor of the leasehold estate[7] (Sched. 6 Para. 1 LRA 2002). Thus Robbie's freehold title is not affected by Fred's registration as the new leaseholder. Fred becomes, by operation of the LRA, an assignee of the lease and is bound by all the covenants and any other obligations in it (Sched. 6 Para. 9(2) LRA 2002). If Fred wishes to succeed to the freehold, he will have to wait until Mike's lease has expired and then, assuming that Robbie or his successor in title takes no action to either grant a new lease or evict him, he can then begin a new period of adverse possession against the freehold title.

[7] This is a vital point as the rest of this paragraph follows from it. Also the position is different if title is unregistered.

The position is different if title is unregistered. Here there is no statutory assignment of the lease to Fred although Fred is entitled to possession for the remainder of the term of the lease. Thus Mike will remain liable on the lease (**St Marylebone Property Co. Ltd v Fairweather** [1963] AC 510) and there is no privity of estate between Robbie and Fred. Thus they cannot claim directly against each other. Of course it may well be that Mike does not pay rent to Robbie as he is no longer in possession and if so Robbie will be able to take action against him for, for example, forfeiture of the lease and this will end Fred's rights.[8] Moreover if Fred breaches any of the covenants in the lease Robbie may take action, not against him but against Mike, and so the lease may be forfeited. Moreover as Mike is not a tenant he cannot apply for relief from forfeiture.

[8] This section is a good example of the interrelationship between different areas of land law and why you should not leave out topics when revising. If you had left out leaseholds you could not have said all this!

Robbie may be unhappy that Fred is now in possession of the land and the rent may be small and Mike may still be paying it so that Robbie will be unable at the moment to take action to forfeit the lease. In *St Marylebone Property Co. Ltd v Fairweather* (1963) it was held that the tenant might surrender the lease to the freeholder who then has an immediate right to possession[9] and so a surrender by Mike to Robbie would allow Robbie to seek possession against Fred who would, because Mike had surrendered the lease, be a trespasser. However, it is not clear what the dispossessed tenant has to surrender: in *St Marylebone Property Co. Ltd v Fairweather* the House of Lords distinguished between the tenant's title to the leasehold estate, which the squatter had defeated, and his estate in the land which he still held and which he could therefore surrender, but this seems a very fine distinction.[10]

(b) This is a boundary dispute between Fred and Mike and Fred could apply to be registered as leasehold owner under Paragraph 5(4) of Schedule 6 of the LRA 2002. This requires that, for at least 10 years of the period of adverse possession ending on the date of the application, the applicant (or any predecessor in title) reasonably believed that the land to which the application relates belonged to him. Under section 98 of the Land Registration Act the date for deciding the question of reasonable belief is the day preceding the start of the proceedings. If so, then the applicant can apply to be registered at once. Here Fred's belief dates from 2000, i.e. 13 years ago. In *Zarb v Parry* [2011] EWCA 1306[11] it was held that the owners' belief that the land belonged to them was still reasonable as, although they knew that there had been a boundary dispute when they bought the property, they thought that it had been resolved. Fred could argue that Teresa's words that Mike was 'happy with the situation' made his belief reasonable. In *IAM Group Plc v Chowdrey* [2012] EWCA Civ 505 it was held that it might be reasonable in these cases to make enquiries of your solicitors when you buy the land to see if there had been a boundary dispute and here Mike could argue, in response to Fred's claim, that Fred should have checked when he bought the land. If title was unregistered then Fred would simply be able to acquire title on the basis of 12 years' possession.

[9] Remember that this point is only relevant where title to the land is unregistered and the question involves adverse possession of a lease.

[10] This decision is controversial and so you will add marks if you say this and explain why it is controversial.

[11] This area of the law is starting to generate case law and extra marks have been gained by an awareness of it.

Make your answer stand out

- Read the decision in *J.A. Pye Ltd* v *Graham* in detail especially on the issue of the licence held by the adverse possessor.
- Criticism of the decision in *St Marylebone Property Co. Ltd* v *Fairweather* by Professor H.W.R. Wade in (1962) Landlord, Tenant and Squatter. *LQR* 78 at 559: 'It infringes fundamental principles to allow a man to cure his own bad title by transferring it to another.'
- Mention that in *Chung Ping Kwan* v *Lam Islands Development Co. Ltd* [1997] AC 38 the Privy Council did not take the opportunity to comment on the decision in *St Marylebone Property Co. Ltd* v *Fairweather*.
- Explain that in *Pye (J.A.) (Oxford) Ltd* v *UK* (2005) ECHR 921 it was held that the unregistered land system was ECHR compliant, so explain why the new system under the LRA 2002 with its safeguards for the owner will also be compliant.

! Don't be tempted to . . .

- Forget the end of the question: remember to also deal with the position where title is unregistered.
- Omit to deal with whether there has been adverse possession before you discuss the position of Fred as against Mike, the leaseholder.
- Forget that adverse possession against the leaseholder does not affect the title of the freeholder.
- Omit in (a) to set out the relationship between Fred as the new tenant and Robbie, the freeholder.

Question 3

Critically consider the statement that 'the law relating to adverse possession has been changed fundamentally by the Land Registration Act 2002'. (Cooke (2003) *The New Law of Land Registration*)

Answer plan

→ Explain what adverse possession means.

→ Consider how the law was changed by the LRA 2002.

➜ Contrast this with the position where title to land is unregistered.

➜ Look at areas where position was not altered by the LRA 2002.

➜ Summing up – refer back to the question: evaluate if the LRA made a fundamental change in the law or only the procedure for actually acquiring title.

Diagram plan

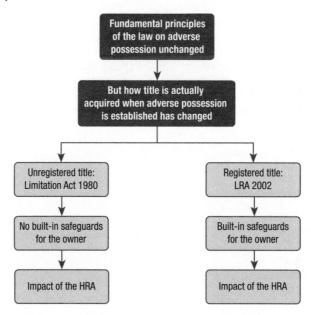

A printable version of this diagram plan is available from www.pearsoned.co.uk/lawexpressqa

Answer

¹ A fundamental point but always worth remembering: start with a basic definition which will save you time later.

² Do make it clear that the old law still applies to unregistered land.

The essence of adverse possession is that a person (the claimant, also popularly known as the squatter) by possession of land acquires title to it from the previous owner, who is known in this context as the registered or 'paper' owner.¹ The LRA 2002 made substantial changes to the law which, as we shall see, have made it substantially more difficult to acquire title by this method. Before the new regime was introduced by the LRA 2002 the basic rules were the same for both registered and unregistered titles and now these rules still apply where title to land is unregistered. Therefore, a comparison between them is still of practical importance.²

[3] This is important and you will lose marks if you rush in and explain the differences before clearing the ground and explaining the similarities.

[4] The Law Commission Report (2001) No. 271 is an excellent source of material so put in quotes from it which assist your argument.

[5] This is a good example of what you should always search out for before the exam to boost your marks: a sound practical example which involves some research. It is guaranteed to impress the examiner.

[6] Take each point separately and contrast the two systems.

[7] Superficially, the law seems to have tilted in favour of squatters as the period is now only 10 years, but the actual mechanics of gaining title have actually tilted the law very much the other way.

[8] This is a fundamental point and is the crucial change made to the law by the LRA 2002 and so you must stress it.

[9] You could, at this point and if you have time, give an example of how this could be so by looking at the law of estoppel and the decision in the recent important case of *Thorner* v *Major* [2009] UKHL 18. See the Law Commission Report (2001) No. 271, Para. 4.40).

However, the basic requirements of claiming title by adverse possession, factual possession of the land with the intention to exclude others, apply in all cases.[3] The differences arise mainly when the adverse possessor has satisfied these requirements and actually wishes to make good his or her claim to the land. The fundamental point is that, as the Law Commission Consultation Paper (1998) No. 254 points out: 'Where title is registered, the basis of title is primarily registration then possession' (para. 10.11).[4] It is, of course, the opposite for unregistered land.

Where title to land is unregistered section 15(1) of the Limitation Act 1980 provides that the adverse possessor has to have 12 years of adverse possession. The paper owner's title is extinguished at once (s. 17 Limitation Act 1980) and the squatter has a new title. Thus, where the paper owner has taken no interest in the land and may not even know that it is theirs, they will lose title with no warning. A good example is *Ellis* v *Lambeth LBC* (1999) 32 HLR 596 CA where the council did not notice that the squatter was in occupation for more than 14 years and it lost title when the squatter claimed title.[5]

In contrast[6] under the LRA there are considerable safeguards for the registered owner (see Schedule 6 of the LRA 2002 where the detailed rules are set out). Here the squatter can apply to be registered after 10 years, unlike 12 years for unregistered land. However, this apparent shortening of the time required is deceptive.[7] If neither the registered proprietor nor anyone else served with notice, such as a chargee, objects to the application by serving a counter-notice then the squatter is entitled to be registered. However, the objection is simply a veto as it does not have to be justified[8] and, thus, there is no reason for a registered proprietor to lose title provided that he receives the application.

If the paper owner exercises this veto, he has two years in which to evict the squatter unless one of three situations set out in Paragraph 5 of Schedule 6 of the LRA 2002 applies. If so, the squatter is entitled to be registered after 10 years. These are:

(a) Where it would be unconscionable because of an equity by estoppel[9] for the registered proprietor (the paper owner) to seek to dispossess the squatter. This could be where an owner has allowed the squatter to build on land through a mistaken belief that the squatter is really the owner of it.

(b) Where there is a claim by a person with an independent right to registration, e.g. where the squatter is entitled to the land under the will or intestacy of the previous owner.

(c) Where the squatter already owns adjoining land and reasonably believes that the disputed land also belongs to him. This is intended to deal with cases where the boundary on the register does not match that on the ground.

Of the three cases above, the first two are in a sense unnecessary as there is already a right to be registered as owner which does not depend on 10 years' adverse possession.[10] It is the third case which will give rise to claims.

When the squatter is registered then it will be as the new registered proprietor of the estate against which he adversely possessed[11] (Sched. 6, Para. 9) and he takes subject to all existing legal and equitable rights in the land except registered charges[12] (Sched. 6, Paras. 9(2) and 9(3)). This is why a registered chargee is entitled to be served with notice of an application so that it can object.

Where the adverse possessor possesses against a leasehold title, the squatter only acquires the leasehold and not the freehold. If the claim succeeds, the adverse possessor will be registered as the new proprietor of the leasehold estate[13] (Sched. 6, Para. 1, LRA 2002) and he will become, by operation of the LRA, an assignee of the lease and is bound by all the covenants and any other obligations in it (Sched. 6, Para. 9(2), LRA 2002).

If title is unregistered, there is no statutory assignment of the lease to the squatter although he is entitled to possession for the remainder of the term of the lease. Thus, the disposed leaseholder will remain liable on the lease (*St Marylebone Property Co. Ltd v Fairweather* [1963] AC 510 HL). It was also held in this case that the tenant might surrender the lease to the freeholder who then has an immediate right to possession. This will not apply where title is registered.

Finally, is the law on adverse possession under either the registered or unregistered system in breach of the ECHR?[14] Article 1 of the First Protocol says that 'No one shall be deprived of the peaceful

[10] In effect, the first two were included to tidy up the law by providing a mechanism for registration in these cases.

[11] This is another fundamental point which the examiner will expect you to stress.

[12] This point is often missed by students so a mention of it will gain a mark or two!

[13] Note the link with the basic point: where title is registered then the previous title is not extinguished as in unregistered title but the squatter succeeds to it. Emphasise this as it will show the examiner that you are clear on the basic point.

[14] Although the Court of Appeal has held in *Ofulue v Bossert* that UK adverse possession law does comply with the ECHR, an examiner would expect you to discuss this point in view of the extensive discussion of it in case law and academic articles.

enjoyment of his possessions except in the public interest and subject to the conditions provided for by law and the general principles of international law'. In *Pye (J.A.) (Oxford) Ltd v UK* (2008) 46 EHRR 1083 the Grand Chamber of the ECtHR held that UK law does not infringe the ECHR and found that adverse possession was a justified control of use of land rather than a deprivation of possession and this was within the margin of appreciation. In *Ofulue v Bossert*

[15] It is important to include this decision as well as that of the ECtHR mentioned above as *Ofulue v Bossert* is, of course, that of the UK courts.

[2008] EWCA Civ 7 the Court of Appeal[15] held that this decision establishes that UK law complies with the ECHR. This decision was on the position where title was unregistered and it is even more likely that the law in the LRA 2002 where title is registered will be compliant with the ECHR with its safeguards for the paper owner.

[16] You do not need a long conclusion but do emphasise these two points as it rounds the answer off nicely.

In conclusion, the law on actually acquiring title by adverse possession has indeed changed fundamentally as a result of the LRA 2002 but the law on what is actually meant by adverse possession is very largely unaltered.[16]

 Make your answer stand out

- Look into the Law Commission's Consultation Paper (1998) *Land Registration for the Twenty-First Century*, No. 254, paras. 10.4–10.78. Do not be daunted – there are only 33 pages on adverse possession! This was a consultative document and so you should search for it under 'Reports'.

- Look at the law of estoppel and the decision in the recent important case of *Thorner v Major* [2009] UKHL 18. See the Law Commission Report (2001) *Land Registration for the Twenty-First Century: A Conveyancing Revolution*, No. 271, para. 4.40).

- Follow this with research into the actual Law Commission Report (2001) No. 271, part X1V. In particular, note the discussion at para. 14.69 of the decision in *Central London Estates Ltd v Kato Kaguku Co Ltd* [1998] 4 All ER 948 where the land is leasehold and how this decision influenced the final report.

- Mention the criticisms of *St Marylebone Property Co. Ltd v Fairweather* in Wade (1962) Landlord, Tenant and Squatter. *LQR*, 78: 541. For an excellent analysis of the law on adverse possession, see Cooke (1994) Adverse Possession – Some Problems of Title in Registered Land. *Legal Studies*, 14: 1.

- Look further at the discussion on whether the law on adverse possession is ECHR-compliant – see e.g. Kerridge and Brierley (2007) Adverse Possession, Human Rights and Land Registration: And They All Lived Happily Ever After. *Conveyancer* 552.

Don't be tempted to . . .

- Spend ages at the start just explaining what the general law of adverse possession is – the whole point is that this is generally the same whether title is registered or unregistered. Why not just say this?
- Set out the rules for both registered and unregistered land without comparing them.
- Ignore the difference between the registered and unregistered systems in cases where there is adverse possession against a leaseholder. This is one of the most significant differences between them.

🖎 Question 4

In *J.A. Pye Ltd v Graham* [2002] 3 All ER 865 Lord Browne-Wilkinson said that in cases of adverse possession the 'necessary intent is an intent to possess not to own and an intention to exclude the paper owner only so far as is reasonably practicable'.

Evaluate this statement in the context of the present law of adverse possession.

Answer plan

→ Explain exactly what Lord Browne-Wilkinson meant in the quotation.

→ Evaluate the significance of the squatter only needing to show an intention to possess.

→ Consider the implied licence theory – how it evolved and was applied in the cases.

→ Explain that the implied licence theory is no longer good law.

→ Mention the attempt to resurrect this theory in *Beaulane Properties* v *Palmer* and explain why it did not succeed.

Diagram plan

A printable version of this diagram plan is available from **www.pearsoned.co.uk/lawexpressqa**

Answer

This statement of Lord Browne-Wilkinson in **J.A. Pye Ltd v Graham** [2002] 3 All ER 865 was intended to banish from the law of adverse possession what he called the 'heretical and wrong' view that the intentions of the owner of the land are relevant and to emphasise that it is the intention of the adverse possessor which counts. Furthermore the adverse possessor does not have to intend to own the land but only to possess it.[1]

The fact that the adverse possessor (usually referred to as the squatter) does not have to intend to own the land is, in a way, a statement of the obvious as in many if not most cases the squatters are squatting on land which they know is not theirs. In other cases, the squatter may at first honestly believe that it is his, as in the case of a boundary dispute, and in others the squatter may not have any intention at all except to occupy land which no one else happens to be occupying.

This is shown by the decision in **J.A. Pye Ltd v Graham** itself where the squatter had held the land under a licence agreement which was not renewed, and so at this point his possession became adverse.[2] Clearly, he did not intend to own the land at that time as he knew that it belonged to the licensor. Similarly, in **Williams v Jones** [2002][3] EWCA Civ 1097 CA a tenant successfully claimed adverse possession after he continued to possess the land after rent had neither been paid nor sought for many years. The point was that it was the tenant's continued possession which counted. However, the requirement of possession adverse to the paper owner was emphasised in **Clowes Developments (UK) Ltd v Walters** [2005] EWHC 669 HC where permission was under a licence originally granted to another member of the family and then continued. Thus, as there was no possession as such, the claim to title by adverse possession failed.

Lord Browne-Wilkinson's emphasis on the intention of the adverse possessor also means the exclusion of the 'implied licence' theory[4] that the claimant is assumed to have been given an implied licence to use the land because his actions were not inconsistent with an intended use by the owner. The effect of this was that if the possessor's actions *were* inconsistent with the owner's intended use then there could be no adverse possession and this made the success of a claim to adverse possession dependent on the intentions of the owner. Thus, in **Leigh v Jack** (1879) 5 Ex D 264 HC it was held[5] that where possession did not affect plans which the paper owner had for the future use of the land, the possessor could not begin to acquire adverse possession (i.e. the period of years required would not begin to run) until his use did conflict with those plans. Thus, where land was vacant but was earmarked for future use, an adverse possessor who occupied it could not be in adverse possession until either the owner abandoned his plans or the claimant did acts which made those plans impossible. In **Wallis's Cayton Bay Holiday Camp Ltd v Shell Mex and BP Ltd** [1974][6] 3 All ER 575 CA the defendant owned land in the middle of a field in which it intended to erect a garage. The rest of the field belonged to Wallis who, for over 12 years, also farmed the defendant's land. The defendant then abandoned plans to erect a garage because a proposed road was not going to be built. It was held that Wallis had not acquired title by adverse possession because time could only run from when the defendant abandoned its plans for the road. In effect, whether there was adverse possession was held to depend on the owner's state of mind.

This rule was rejected by the CA in **Buckinghamshire CC v Moran** [1989] 2 All ER 225.[7] A strip of land had been reserved by the council for a road diversion for many years, although nothing separated the strip from the adjoining house that the claimant had bought in 1971. He padlocked the only access to the strip and exercised complete control of it until 1985 when the council sued to recover it. It was held that he had demonstrated an intention to possess the plot that overrode the council's future intended use of it. The Court of Appeal held that the issue was the intention of the adverse possessor and not that of the paper owner. Here the possessor was well aware of the future intentions of the council but that was not the point. However, Slade LJ did accept that in some circumstances knowledge of the paper owner's future intentions for the use of the land may be relevant, e.g. if it indicates that the possessor does not intend to use the land so as to interfere with the paper owner's future intended use of the land, there will not be the requisite intention.

[5] It is important that you look back at what the law was here as the point of Lord Browne-Wilkinson's remarks was that the law had been wrong and it was right to change it.

[6] You are earning extra marks by mentioning this case as well as *Leigh* v *Jack*.

[7] This case follows from *Wallis* v *Shell Mex* as it shows the change in attitude.

[8] This case brings the story up to date. You should by now have gained crucial marks by mentioning the four main cases on this point. In addition you should stress the general point made by Lord Browne-Wilkinson that there is only a requirement to exclude the paper owner as far as is reasonably practicable. This then leads you on to earn marks by explaining that in some cases it may be that the existence of an intended use for the land by the paper owner may prevent adverse possession. You are thinking ahead about where the law might develop and this will earn you marks.

[9] This is another example of a case which is no longer good law but as this is an essay question which asks you how the law has developed you need to mention it.

This was confirmed by Lord Browne-Wilkinson in *J.A. Pye Ltd* v *Graham* [2002] 3 All ER 865 by emphasising that only an intention to 'exclude the paper owner only as far as is reasonably practicable' is needed. Thus, provided that the owner is excluded in order for the squatter to establish factual possession, that will be enough. He did observe, however, that where the adverse possessor is aware of some special purpose for which the owner needs the land, and the use made by the adverse possessor does not conflict with that use, then that may 'provide some support' for a finding that the adverse possessor did not intend to possess but only had an intention to occupy until it was required by the paper owner. Thus, the door is left open for such a claim as in *Wallis's Cayton Bay Holiday Camp Ltd* v *Shell Mex and BP Ltd* but on the basis of the adverse possessor's intention and not any presumed intent by the owner.[8]

It should be added that in *Beaulane Properties* v *Palmer* [2005] HRLR 19 the High Court sought to reintroduce the implied licence idea in order to make the relevant legislation, section 75 of the Land Registration Act 1925, compliant with the Human Rights Act.[9] It did this by holding that, as the squatter's action in that case was not inconsistent with any use or intended use of the land by the owner, his possession of it was not adverse. This put the emphasis back on the intentions of the owner. However, in *Pye (J.A.) (Oxford) Ltd* v *UK* (2008) 46 EHRR 45 it was held that UK law is compliant with the Human Rights Act anyway, a view confirmed in *Ofulue* v *Bossert* [2009] UKHL 16, and so it is clear that *Beaulane Properties* v *Palmer* is no longer good law.

Make your answer stand out

- Mention that the fundamental question here is about possession of land and that English law has always emphasised possession of land and not title.

- Read a detailed article on the Buckinghamshire case: Harpum (1990) *Buckingham County Council* v *Moran. CLJ* 23.

- Have a look at Tee (2000) Adverse Possession and the Intention to Possess. *Conveyancer* 113 and then read a different view in Harpum and Radley-Gardner (2001) Adverse Possession and the Intention to Possess: A Reply. *Conveyancer* 155.

📝 Question 5

'Adverse possession sometimes appears to constitute a primitive taking of land by theft.' (Gray and Gray (2005) *Land Law* (4th edn))

Examine this statement, illustrating your answer with decided cases and taking into account recent developments in the law relating to adverse possession.

Answer plan

→ Set out the issues raised in this question taking care to mention the importance of the changes made by the LRA 2002.

→ Set out different points of view on whether there should be a law of adverse possession.

→ Look at actual issues – different types of squatting.

Diagram plan

A printable version of this diagram plan is available from www.pearsoned.co.uk/lawexpressqa

Answer

1 This is a really good and
clear start: you are telling the
examiner at once that you
have thought about the issues
and have a plan about how
you will deal with them. Avoid
stumbling from one point to
another when it is clear that
you have no idea where you
are going!

There are four issues in this question:[1] one is whether the law on adverse possession is justified at all. If it is, then we need to consider whether the changes made by the LRA 2002, which have made it substantially more difficult to acquire title by this method, have made the law more or less fair and, linked to this, we need to consider the law where land is held by unregistered title. Finally, we need to consider the impact of the European Convention on Human Rights.

In ***J.A. Pye (Oxford) Ltd v Graham*** [2000] Ch 676 HC, Neuberger J, in giving judgment in favour of the squatters, said, 'As may be apparent from one or two passages in this judgment, this a conclusion which I arrive at with no enthusiasm. It seems to me that it is a result which does not accord with justice, and cannot be justified by practical considerations.'[2] This case involved a claim under the previous law where 12 years' adverse possession enabled the squatter to acquire title to the land from the paper owner.

[2] This is an excellent quote and easily recalled.

Claims by squatters are of various kinds.[3] ***Buckinghamshire CC v Moran*** [1989] 2 All ER 225 CA involved a claim to a small strip of land which had been annexed to a garden and the squatter was a wealthy Lloyd's broker who appeared in lists of the richest people in the UK[4] and in ***J.A. Pye (Oxford) Ltd v Graham*** 25 hectares of development land, worth 'untold millions with planning consent' was claimed by adverse possession. Cobb and Fox (2007) point out that 'In social and political discourse in this country, however, the term tends to be associated specifically with the *deliberate* [author's italics] occupation of empty residential buildings in metropolitan areas'.[5] An example was ***Ellis v Lambeth LBC*** (1999) 32 HLR 596 CA: a group of squatters successfully claimed a council house worth £200,000. This was not always so. As Auchmurty (2004) remarks, in the late nineteenth century adverse possession claims often involved 'disputes over the boundaries of railway land, which offered such a fruitful field for litigation that no railway company seems to have been exempt'.

Cobb and Fox (2007) point out that the Law Commission Report (2001) LC 271 recognised that unlawful occupation of property may

3 At once we have got away from a mechanical recital of the law and are addressing the issues in the question.

4 This kind of research detail makes your answer much more vivid. The law of adverse possession is full of interesting stories – research some for your exam.

5 This is a very important point to make: if most cases of squatting involved boundary disputes between neighbours would the topic arouse the same passion?

arise from acute housing needs, and the Commission expressed 'understandable sympathy' with squatters in cases where they took possession of empty properties when they were desperate for a home. However, Cobb and Fox argue that the Commission bypassed this issue by claiming that most cases of squatting involved 'the landowner with an eye to the main chance, who encroaches in his or her neighbour's land' (para. 2.70). In fact, Cobb and Fox argue that urban squatting does serve a social purpose and they quote statistics showing that there were 78,000 families living in temporary accommodation and properties lying empty that could potentially offer 600,000 new homes (ODPM 2002).[6] Thus, the argument of land theft is countered by the defences of necessity and social purpose and stewardship of the land. The Law Commission (para. 14.4) instead thought that cases involving acquisition of title to council housing by adverse possession represented a loss to the public purse and this was wrong. Dixon (2003, p. 151) agrees with Cobb and Fox in seeing a positive value in squatting as it encourages 'productive land use'. Cobb and Fox (2007) argue that 'Any stewardship duty should include a fundamental obligation to engage in an appropriate degree of supervision over empty land' and point to Lambeth Council's housing department not merely forgetting that it owned certain properties but actually losing them. Thus, in *Ellis v Lambeth LBC* the council did not notice that the squatter was in occupation for more than 14 years. By contrast, Neuberger J in *J.A. Pye (Oxford) Ltd v Graham*[7] considered that it was 'Draconian to the owner, and a windfall for the squatter, that, just because the owner has taken no steps to evict a squatter for 12 years, the owner should lose 25 hectares of land to the squatter with no compensation whatsoever'. The context was different as he was speaking of development land and not housing but the argument is the same.

In the end, the view which one takes on the merits of having a law allowing title to be acquired by adverse possession depends on the view which one takes on the purpose of land itself and the obligations of owners towards their land. What is clear is that the new regime introduced by the Land Registration Act (LRA) 2002 has made claiming title in this way much more difficult.[8] Under the previous law, which still applies where title to land is unregistered, it is where the

[6] This kind of question really does need you to mention some statistics. These ones are especially telling.

[7] It is always vital to have balance in an essay. You have given powerful arguments for saying that the law on adverse possession does serve a useful purpose and now you need the contrary view. Do not leave out an argument just because you do not agree with it. What the examiner wants in a question like this is a balanced presentation of opposing views with your own conclusion coming in at the end.

[8] Note the structure of this answer very carefully. We could have started with the point which we are making now about the details of the law and how it has changed with the LRA 2002. However, the danger of this is that we would have spent too much time on this and not enough on the policy issues which is what will gain the marks.

squatter has been in factual possession of the land for 12 years (s. 15(1) of the Limitation Act 1980) with the intention to exclude others. At that point, the paper owner's title is extinguished at once and the squatter has a new title. Thus, where the paper owner has taken no interest in the land and may not even know that it is his, as in *Ellis* v *Lambeth LBC*, he will lose title with no warning. In contrast, under the LRA, the squatter applies to be registered after 10 years but the paper owner then has 2 years in which to evict the squatter unless one of three situations applies, in which case the squatter is entitled to be registered after 10 years.

[9] You need to mention the ECHR: if the courts have regarded the law on adverse possession as ECHR compliant this is a strong argument that is worth keeping.

The final issue is whether the law on adverse possession is in breach of the ECHR.[9] The relevant part is Article 1 of the First Protocol 'No one shall be deprived of the peaceful enjoyment of his possessions except in the public interest and subject to the conditions provided for by law and the general principles of international law'. In *Pye (J.A.) (Oxford) Ltd* v *UK* (2008) the Grand Chamber of the ECtHR held that UK law does not infringe the ECHR and found that adverse possession was a justified control of use of land rather than a deprivation of possession and this was within the margin of appreciation. In *Ofulue* v *Bossert* [2008] EWCA Civ 7 the Court of Appeal held that this decision establishes that UK law complies with the ECHR. This decision was on the position where the Limitation Act 1980 applied and it is even more likely that the law in the LRA 2002 will be compliant with the ECHR with its safeguards for the paper owner.

✓ Make your answer stand out

- Read in full the articles cited in this essay – especially that by Cobb and Fox (2007) Living Outside the System? The (Im)morality of Urban Squatting after the Land Registration Act 2002. *Legal Studies*, 27: 236, which is exceptionally full and detailed.

- Look at the position in other jurisdictions – there is a helpful summary in Cooke (2003) *The New Law of Land Registration*, chapter 9.

- Read Radley-Gardner (2007) Good-bye to *Pye*. 5 *Web Journal of Current Legal Issues*, which gives a very clear account of the Pye saga and offers some reflections on the impact of the ECHR on the law of adverse possession. However, you should note that this article was written before the decision of the Court of Appeal in *Ofulue* v *Bossert*.

! Don't be tempted to . . .

- Just describe the law – this question is about the policy behind the law and if you do not recognise this in your answer you will probably fail on this question.
- Leave out, on the other hand, any mention of the actual legal position.
- Omit to stress the effect of the changes made by the LRA 2002 which make it more difficult to acquire title by adverse possession.
- Leave out a mention of the attitude of the ECHR.

www.pearsoned.co.uk/lawexpressqa

 Go online to access more revision support including additional essay and problem questions with diagram plans, You be the marker questions, and download all diagrams from the book.

11

A mixture of questions

How this topic may come up in exams

In land law, as in other areas of law, it is a mistake to assume that actual legal issues necessarily fit neatly into the categories where they appear in textbooks. Examiners recognise this and, accordingly, they set questions which cut across subject-divides. This also has the added benefit (or burden depending on whether you are a teacher or student) of ensuring that students do not confine themselves to only certain subject areas when revising, but need to revise the whole syllabus. There have already been questions in earlier chapters which have involved knowledge of more than one area but where one particular area was the main one. In this chapter, however, you will find a genuine mix.

Attack the question

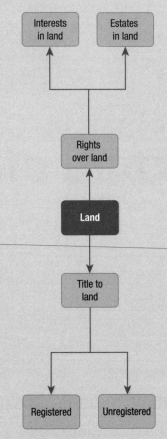

A printable version of this diagram is available from www.pearsoned.co.uk/lawexpressqa

Question 1

'The property legislation of 1925 was really a gigantic holding operation. If that was not obvious at the time then it is now.'

Critically comment on this view.

Answer plan

→ Identify the 1925 property statutes.

→ Consider the reduction in the number of legal estates.

→ Then go on to consider interests in land and distinguish between legal and equitable interests.

→ This takes us to third party rights in land and the distinction between registered and unregistered land.

→ Consider co-ownership and the problems where the legal estate was vested in tenants in common.

→ Mention briefly the problems where title to land is held in the name of one party but the other has contributed to the cost of acquisition.

→ Conclude with a mention of trusts for sale under the 1925 legislation and the changes made by TLATA.

Diagram plan

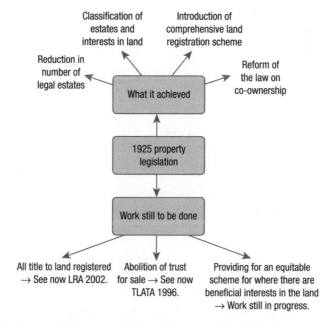

A printable version of this diagram plan is available from www.pearsoned.co.uk/lawexpressqa

Answer

The property legislation of 1925 contained the following six statutes:[1] the Law of Property Act (LPA), the Land Registration Act (LRA), the Settled Land Act (SLA), the Land Charges Act (LCA), the Trustee Act (TA) and the Administration of Estates Act (AEA). This essay will concentrate on the first four as the Trustee Act concerns trust law and the Administration of Estates Act deals with probate and other matters.

[2] It is important to achieve a balance in your answer: look at what the 1925 legislation did achieve and balance this against any perceived defects.

Although the question appears critical of the 1925 property legislation, it is often forgotten what it achieved.[2] First, section 1(1) of the LPA 1925 greatly simplified the law by introducing the idea of the estate owner who alone had the right to convey the legal estate. It reduced legal estates to two: an estate in fee simple absolute in possession (legal freehold estate) and a term of years absolute (legal leasehold estate). The holder of a legal estate in land which is in fee simple absolute in possession has the right to use the land for an infinite time and thus to convey that land to another. Before 1925 land might, for instance, be held under a life interest where the owner did not have the right to convey it as he only held it for his life.

[3] Having used the full 'fee simple absolute in possession' to start with you can then revert to the shorter fee simple.

Not only this but all land must have an owner in fee simple[3] and so all land must have an estate owner with the right to convey it. It is easy to forget what an advantage this is. All the other rights, such as life interests, can still exist but only in equity under a trust.

The scheme of section 1 of the LPA was that all other rights over land were classified as interests in land and so there was a division between estates, whether freehold or leasehold, which described the rights of the actual estate owner, and interests, which are rights which third parties have over another's land. Thus a right of way over another's land is an easement and is an interest in land.

[4] The use, where appropriate, of suitable examples can really bring your answer to life.

[5] If you have time you could of course mention the case law but the danger is that you would be getting away from the point.

There was, and still is, a further division between legal and equitable interests in land. Suppose Jack has a restrictive covenant over John's land which prevents John from building on his land.[4] John then sells his land to Richard. Is Richard bound by Jack's restrictive covenant? A restrictive covenant is an equitable interest in land and so Richard will only be bound if he is a purchaser in good faith of the land without notice of that covenant. How do we show that he is without notice? That will be a factual question and there is much case law on it.[5] Turning to the land that John has sold to Richard, suppose that Teresa has a right of way over it created by deed. These will be an easement and will be a legal interest in Richard's land. Legal interests bind all the world, including Richard.

It may be that Richard has bought the land and was unaware of either Jack's covenant or Teresa's easement. To prevent this from happening a lengthy investigation of title is needed. The obvious solution is to have a register on which interests are entered.[6] This was first proposed in 1739 but it was not until the Land Registration Act 1925 that a comprehensive scheme came into force. However, registration of title to land was not made compulsory in all areas until 1990 and even now there is a good deal of unregistered title.

Where title is unregistered there is a register of land charges, a kind of mini-land registration system set up by the Land Charges Act 1925, which was replaced without any changes of substance by the Land Charges Act 1972. If an interest is registrable as a land charge, as with registered land, a purchaser will take subject to it and if it is not registered it cannot bind a purchaser. If an interest is not registrable as a land charge then whether a purchaser is bound depends on whether it is legal or equitable and the same rules as stated above apply.

Meanwhile in 2002 the Land Registration Act 2002 was passed which replaced the 1925 Act and, whilst keeping the essential structure, changed many details such as a reduction in the number of overriding interests, which continue to bind purchasers of land even though not registered. One question is whether they should remain.[7]

Another area dealt with by the 1925 legislation was co-ownership of land. Before 1925 it was possible for title to land to be held by tenants in common who had undivided shares in land. This meant that many people could hold shares in the legal title to, for example, a small house, and, as the consent of all of them would be needed to a sale it could be practically impossible to sell. Here the LPA 1925 made a welcome change by simply providing by section 1(6) that 'A legal estate is not capable of subsisting or of being created in an undivided share in land'.[8] Now where there are co-owners of land the legal title must be held by joint tenants and there can be no more than four (s. 34(2) LPA 1925). There can still be tenancies in common, and indeed they are often found, but they can only exist in equity under a trust of land. Once again we see the policy of the 1925

[6] Here we are moving from estates and interests to another issue: registration, but note how they have been linked in this essay. Note that we have not said 'all interests' as overriding interests are not registered.

[7] If you have time you could say more on this.

[8] You cannot be expected to recall lengthy extracts from statutes verbatim but do try to recall the essentials such as this.

legislation in pushing back interests into equity, as with life interests, mentioned above. Where the title is held by joint tenants then survivorship applies and as joint tenants own no individual share, then they cannot leave any part of their joint tenancy by will, nor does it pass under the intestacy rules. Instead it passes to the surviving joint tenants.

[9] You need to mention this type of point: there have been enormous social changes since 1925 which could not have been foreseen.

What was not, and could not have been foreseen, was the great expansion in co-ownership[9] where, for example, one of the parties to a marriage or civil partnership may not be a legal owner of the property but has contributed to the purchase price of it. This has led to an enormous amount of case law (see *Jones* v *Kernott* [2011] UKSC 53) together with an emphasis on the rights of occupiers as overriding interests under land registration rules.[10] The framers of the 1925 legislation cannot be blamed for not foreseeing this!

[10] Note that in one sentence we have touched on two areas and so picked up marks: the law on co-ownership and overriding interests.

[11] You do need to say something on other areas in order to give this essay balance and a mention of trusts for sale is a good and clear example.

Finally, the Settled Land Act 1925 provided that where land was held on trust then it was held on a trust for sale.[11] Although by section 25 of the LPA 1925 there was an implied power to postpone sale it was the duty of the trustees to sell unless they unanimously agreed to postpone sale (*Re Mayo* [1943] Ch 302 HC). This made no sense in modern conditions. Suppose that Tim and Tom decide to buy a house to live in[12] but the legal title is in the name of Tom although Tim made substantial contributions to its cost. They bought the house to live in and not to sell but Tom has a duty to sell. It took until the Trusts of Land and Trustees Act (TLATA) 1996 for the law to change and now by section 4 of that Act trusts for sale are now trusts of land.

[12] Another simple example helps here.

[13] There is so much material for this question that there is time for only a short conclusion but you do need one.

Thus the statement in the question is partly correct:[13] the property legislation could have been more radical but there have been many social changes since it was passed that could not have been foreseen at the time.

✓ Make your answer stand out

- Do not go into too much detail on any one area – this question covers so much that you really have to make a selection and resist the temptation to write all that you know!
- There is some good material on the history of land law and the events leading up to the 1925 legislation in Simpson (1986) *A History of the Land Law* (2nd edn).

- Keep a theme running through your answer – i.e. from estates in land to interests in land to registered land to unregistered land etc.
- Keep the focus on the 1925 legislation – it is easy to stray into other areas.
- If you have time, mention that TLATA 1996 prevented the creation of new strict settlements. Why did it do this?

! Don't be tempted to . . .

- Give a summary of the 1925 legislation without commenting on it.
- Go into great detail on certain areas, e.g. write at length on overriding interests which is not justified in this type of question.
- Start the answer without having a very clear idea of what areas and themes you will be looking at. If you do not, you will find that you just wander from point to point and the essay will be very disjointed.

? Question 2

De Veloper Ltd is interested in purchasing a large piece of land extending to 250 acres with registered title. It intends, subject to planning permission, to build a mixture of residential units and light industrial buildings on it but before going ahead requires advice on the following matters which have come to light in the course of its preliminary enquiries:

(a) It has learned that Sid, a market gardener, has occupied an area of land of about 5 acres for about the last 8 years, which he has partially fenced off. At the moment De Veloper Ltd has no immediate use for the land and, as Sid is at least taking care of the land, is inclined to allow him to stay.

(b) Some of the houses which De Veloper Ltd wishes to build will be overlooking the sea with splendid views. However, there is a strip of land between the land on which De Veloper Ltd wishes to build and the sea, and this could itself be built on. If so, the view would be destroyed. Is there any way in which De Veloper Ltd can make sure that this view is preserved?

Answer plan

→ Note that the land has registered title and that our clients have not yet bought it.

→ Situation (a) – possible adverse possession claim if Sid is allowed to stay – solution – grant of lease/licence.

→ Situation (b) – consider if an easement is possible – if not look at the possibility of a restrictive covenant and how it can be made binding on subsequent owners.

→ Finish by a brief mention of the possibility of planning permission in (b).

Diagram plan

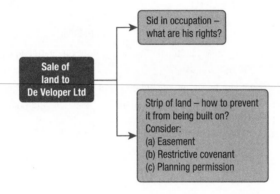

Sid in occupation – what are his rights?

Sale of land to De Veloper Ltd

Strip of land – how to prevent it from being built on? Consider:
(a) Easement
(b) Restrictive covenant
(c) Planning permission

A printable version of this diagram plan is available from www.pearsoned.co.uk/lawexpressqa

Answer

The first point to note is that title to the land which De Veloper Ltd is interested in buying is registered.[1] Moreover, the fact that it has not bought the land means that we need to advise the company on both the practical consequences of buying the land with any existing rights and also how, in view of those rights, it can best protect its position.

[1] As always, it is vital to check this first.

[2] Don't forget this basic point.

(a) The first point is that Sid is, at the moment, a trespasser,[2] and so can be ejected by the owner. De Veloper may do this when it acquires the land, although it would be better advised to require the present seller to do so. If the sale goes through and Sid is still on the land, the seller is in breach of his implied covenant to give vacant possession and so can be sued by De Veloper for damages or it can rescind the contract.[3]

[3] This is an important practical point often overlooked in answers to questions on adverse possession: if the seller sells and there is an adverse possessor on the land, then why not sue the seller?

[4] This is important: watch for whether the transferee is a purchaser (s. 29, LRA 2002 applies) or a donee, e.g. has acquired by inheritance (s. 28 applies).

[5] A good point of detail: if the land was not registered then of course the position would be different as De Veloper would be making an application for first registration.

[6] Note: only may be and not is in actual occupation. This picks up the point in the next paragraph that Sid may not be in occupation as he does not have control of the land.

[7] This shows a confident answer which will impress the examiner – as Sid's occupation is known to the buyer, the buyer will obviously be bound and so there is no point in setting out the rest of Sched. 3 Para. 2(b).

[8] You can find this information in the Land Registry Practice Guide 5: Adverse Possession (2010).

If De Veloper goes ahead and buys the land, it will be a purchaser[4] and this is a case where the title to the land is already registered.[5] Thus, under sections 29 and 30 of the Land Registration Act (LRA) 2002, it will be bound by interests which fall under Schedule 3 of the LRA. These include the interest of a person in actual occupation, which Sid may be.[6] However, De Veloper would not be bound if the interest is not within its actual knowledge at the time of the disposition but here it does know of it.[7]

We are told that De Veloper is inclined to allow Sid to stay. If it does so without taking steps to regularise the position, Sid may have a claim after 10 years to be registered as owner of that part of the land which he has possessed on the basis that he has been in actual possession of the land and that he has the intention to possess. In **Powell v McFarlane** (1977) 38 P & CR 452 Slade J held that the adverse possessor must show that he has dealt with the land as an occupying owner. This is demonstrated by exercising control over the land and, as Slade J pointed out, clear evidence of this is 'the locking or blocking of the only means of access'. We are told that Sid has partially fenced off the land. When he applies to be registered, the Land Registry will carry out a preliminary check to see that the claim is founded on reasonable grounds and it may be that it deems this not to be so.[8] Moreover, the lack of complete fencing may also mean that Sid is not a person in actual occupation for the purposes of Schedule 3 of the LRA 2002.

We are told that one reason why De Veloper is happy for Sid to remain is that it has no immediate use for the land which he is possessing. However, what counts is whether Sid had the intention to possess. In **J.A. Pye Ltd v Graham** [2002] 3 All ER 865 HL, Lord Browne-Wilkinson said that the view that the intentions of the owner of the land are relevant was 'heretical and wrong'.

The best course would be for De Veloper to grant Sid a lease or a licence as the grant of either would debar any claim by Sid based on adverse possession as his possession would then not be adverse to the owner. Thus, in **J.A. Pye Ltd v Graham** [2002] 3 All ER 865 it was accepted that the period when the claimant held under a licence did not count towards the period of adverse possession.

If De Veloper does not do any of these things, then after 10 years' adverse possession, Sid may apply to be registered as the freehold owner of the land he has possessed. If this application gets beyond the preliminary stage (see above) it is then served on De Veloper, which will have 65 working days to object by serving a counter-notice. Having done this, it has a further 2 years in order to take steps to evict Sid by, at the very least, commencing eviction proceedings.

(b) It appears that the land which De Veloper does not wish to be built on does not belong to it and so the only way would be to get the owner of this land to agree either not to build on it or, possibly, not to build at more than a certain height. De Veloper may consider acquiring an easement over this land but in fact a right to a view cannot be claimed as an easement because one of the characteristics of an easement is that it is capable of being the subject of a grant[9] (see **Re Ellenborough Park** [1955] 3 All ER 667 HC) and in **Aldred's Case** (1610)[9] Co Rep 57b HC, it was held that a view cannot be the subject of a grant as it cannot be precisely defined.

Instead it should be advised that it should seek the agreement of the owners to enter into a restrictive covenant which would give De Veloper an equitable interest in this land and could be protected by a notice under section 32 of the LRA 2002. Obviously, De Veloper will wish the covenant to be binding on successors in title to the original covenantor, and it was held in **Tulk v Moxhay** (1848) 1 H & Tw 105 HC that in equity a covenant can bind subsequent owners on certain conditions. This rule was refined in subsequent cases so that it only applied to negative covenants.[10] In **Haywood v Brunswick Permanent Benefit Building Society** (1881) 8 QBD 403 CA Brett LJ referred to covenants 'restricting the use of the land' and this is a good working definition of a negative covenant.[11] The benefit of this covenant could be expressly annexed to each plot sold by De Veloper so that each owner could sue for breach.[12]

If the covenant was breached, De Veloper would be able to seek an injunction to restrain this, but it should be pointed out that injunctions are equitable remedies and as such are granted at the discretion of the court. Thus, damages could be awarded

[9] You could go through the other characteristics of an easement as well but why? It is obvious that this right cannot be an easement so just make this point and move on.

[10] Although the actual covenant in *Tulk* v *Moxhay* was negative, the decision was not confined to positive covenants – this restriction came later, as we have explained.

[11] An average answer would simply refer to 'negative' covenants and leave it there. However, this answer goes one step further and looks more closely at what 'negative' means.

[12] Don't forget this point: if the burden of the covenant can be made to run then the benefit must be made to as well otherwise there will be no one who can take action for any breach.

[13] An excellent example of some lateral thinking which will impress the examiner. If our clients can get planning permission for their development then why can't their neighbours? Hence, this point.

instead to compensate for the loss of the view, which would not be so satisfactory.

A final thought is that if the owners of the adjoining land obtain planning permission[13] to build houses, this will not discharge the covenant and they will still be liable on it (***Re Martin's Application*** (1988) 57 P & CR 119 CA at 124.)

✓ Make your answer stand out

- This question has a strong practical element – so any evidence of ability to think as a land lawyer in practice will add to your marks!
- Go to the Land Registry website (www.landregistry.gov.uk) and look at the *Land Registry Practice Guide 5: Adverse Possession* (HM Land Registry (2010)) – it is extremely clear and helpful, especially where the question has a practical slant, as here.
- Could any of the reasons mentioned in Schedule 6, Paragraph 5 enable Sid to be registered at once? Possibility of estoppel? Unlikely but perhaps worth a mention.
- Mention exactly how the benefit of covenants can be annexed to the land.

! Don't be tempted to . . .

- Overlook that title to the land is registered.
- Overlook the significance of De Veloper being purchasers and whether Sid's rights are binding on them.
- Just deal with the adverse possession point. Instead, think of how the owners can solve their problem by granting a lease or a licence.
- Stop at the point where you have said that there cannot be an easement, in the question concerning a right to a view: again, take it further.

❓ Question 3

Hanbury Ltd is considering buying a freehold factory building with about 10 acres of land and which has unregistered title. It wishes to develop the land with high-density housing, but the following matters have come to light:

(a) Bert has written to Hanbury Ltd enclosing a written agreement signed by him and the present owner, John, under which John gave Bert the exclusive right to store materials on about half an acre of land. Hanbury wishes to use this land as a car park.

(b) There is a seven-year lease on a small area of neighbouring land which Hanbury Ltd would like to acquire. This is presently used for agricultural purposes but Hanbury Ltd wishes to use it for temporary storage whilst development is completed.

Advise Hanbury Ltd on the legal implications of these matters.

Answer plan

→ Situation (a) – explain that it could be an easement but cannot have an easement of exclusive use. Then move on to consider if it could be a lease or a licence.

→ Having looked at the possibilities, then consider how the agreement was made and if it could be legal or equitable.

→ Then decide if it binds John – note that title is unregistered and make sure that your answer takes account of this.

→ Situation (b) – landlord's consent to an assignment.

Diagram plan

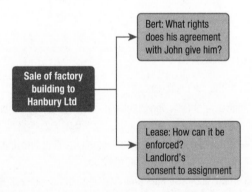

A printable version of this diagram plan is available from www.pearsoned.co.uk/lawexpressqa

Answer

[1] A wonderful start! You have immediately latched on to the essential point and this will immediately impress the examiner.

(a) This agreement does not state what type of interest in the land it is intended to create.[1] It may have been intended to create an easement of storage but the problem is that on the facts Bert has the exclusive right to store materials on the land. In

Copeland v *Greenhalf* [1952] All ER 809 HC the claimant owned land on which the defendant had stored and repaired vehicles for 50 years. He claimed an easement by prescription. It was held that this was a claim to beneficial use of the land and so could not be an easement. Upjohn J described it as, 'virtually a claim to possession of the servient tenement'. In *Moncrieff* v *Jamieson* [2007] UKHL 42[2] Lord Scott in the House of Lords proposed a different test of whether the servient owner 'retains possession and, subject to the reasonable exercise of the right in question, control of the servient land'. Even on this basis Bert does not have an easement as it seems that Bert did not have any right to possession at all.

The next possibility is that Bert may have a lease. The three indications[3] of a lease were stated by Lord Templeman in *Street* v *Mountford* [1985] AC 809 HL as an intention to grant exclusive possession,[4] for a fixed term, in consideration of periodical payments (rent). In *Bruton* v *London and Quadrant Housing Trust Ltd* [2000] 1 AC 406 HL, Lord Hoffman indicated that the first two are essential but referred to 'usually' the payment of rent. There is no indication here of any rent, although it would be surprising if John had allowed Bert to use the land for nothing. There is no mention of a fixed term but it may well be that Bert does have exclusive possession.

If there is no lease, the final possibility is that Bert has a licence which will be contractual if he pays for the use of the land. Contractual licences do not create a proprietary interest in land[5] and so, in general, they are not binding on third parties. An example is *King* v *David Allen* [1916] 2 AC 54 HL, where a licence to place advertisements on the wall of a cinema did not bind a third party. Thus any licence would not bind Hanbury Ltd.

If Bert has an easement or a lease, it will need to be created correctly in order to be an interest in land capable of binding Hanbury Ltd. A written agreement is clearly not a deed and so it cannot be a legal easement or lease. However, it may be an equitable easement or lease under the principle in *Walsh* v *Lonsdale* (1882) 21 Ch D 9 CA.[6] Section 2 of the Law of Property (Miscellaneous Provisions) Act 1989 provides that any contract for the sale or disposition of an interest in land, which

[2] This is the type of extra detail which really boosts your marks. The average student will simply mention an old case such as *Copeland* v *Greenhalf* and not be aware of recent developments.

[3] A vital word: these are not absolute rules and, in particular, if there is no requirement to pay rent this will not necessarily mean that there is no lease.

[4] Note that intention is relevant at this stage although, as mentioned in chapter 6, the intentions of the parties to actually create a lease or a licence are not relevant.

[5] If you just say 'a contractual licence will not bind a purchaser' you have said something which is correct but you have not said enough. Why will it not bind a purchaser? Explain and now you have earned all the marks for this point!

[6] A very important point to remember in general: the principle in *Walsh* v *Lonsdale* does not only apply to the creation of equitable leases but also to equitable easements – and to equitable profits and mortgages also.

includes an equitable lease, must be in writing, signed by the parties and contain all the terms. Although we know that the agreement is in writing, we do not know if it was signed by both parties, and we do not know if it contains all the terms,[7] and so we cannot be certain if it satisfies these requirements. If not, then Hanbury Ltd will not be bound.[8]

If the agreement does satisfy section 2 of the Law of Property (Miscellaneous Provisions) Act 1989, then, as title to the land is unregistered, an equitable easement will need to be registered as a Class D (iii) Land Charge and equitable leases such as estate contracts must be registered as Class C (iv) Land Charges otherwise by section 4(6) of the Land Charges Act 1972 they will be void[9] against a purchaser such as Hanbury Ltd.

If the right is not protected in this way Bert may still be able to claim that he has an overriding interest under Schedule 1 of the LRA 2002, which applies on first registration.[10] This is because Hanbury Ltd will have to apply to be registered as the owner as the sale to Hanbury will trigger registration (s. 27(2)(a), LRA 2002), and on first registration certain rights are overriding interests. Schedule 1, Paragraph 2 provides that an interest of a person in actual occupation overrides and so the question is whether Bert is in actual occupation. He has the exclusive right to store materials on the land which implies some degree of permanence and continuity which Lord Oliver in *Abbey National BS v Cann* [1991] AC 56 HL held was an essential requirement of occupation. It is difficult to go beyond this on the limited facts given[11] but if Bert is in actual occupation Hanbury Ltd will be bound by his right, whether it is an easement or a lease. If he is not in occupation then, always assuming that the right was not protected on the Land Charges register, it will not be bound.

(b) The reference to Hanbury Ltd acquiring the lease presumably means that it wishes to have the lease assigned to it, and this will require the consent of the landlord. Section 19(1) of the Landlord and Tenant Act 1927 provides that in such a case the landlord cannot withhold consent unreasonably. In *International Drilling Fluids Ltd v Louisville Investments Ltd*[12] [1986] All ER 321 CA it was held that the landlord is entitled to be protected from having the premises used or occupied in an

[7] This point often arises as in an exam question there will not be time to set out all the terms of the agreement. So remember that it is likely that you will not be able to come to a definite conclusion on this point.

[8] Remember: even if the right or interest could be a valid easement or lease it will not be valid if it is not correctly created.

[9] Note that as we were not certain which category this right fell into it is important to mention both possibilities.

[10] Where title is not registered and so the transfer will trigger a first registration then do remember that it is Schedule 1 which applies. The wording is not the same as Schedule 3 which applies on a subsequent registration – look at them and compare them!

[11] There comes a point in an answer where further speculation will not get you any more marks and we have reached this point now! Try to recognise when this is so.

[12] This is where you will start to score above average marks: do not just quote the statute but also the cases which interpret it.

undesirable way by an undesirable assignee but consent to an assignment cannot be refused on grounds which have nothing to do with the relationship of landlord and tenant. So, a personal dislike would not be enough. In **Kened Ltd and Den Norske Bank Plc v Connie Investments Ltd** [1997] 1 EGLR CA, Millett LJ said that the essential question is, 'Has it been shown that no reasonable landlord would have withheld consent?' However, where the landlord reasonably believes that a proposed assignment would lead to a breach of covenant in the lease consent may be refused (**Ashworth Frazer Ltd v Gloucester City Council** [2001] UKHL 59 HL). In this case Hanbury Ltd wishes to use the premises as temporary storage but the present use is agricultural. The lease would need to be checked to see what the permitted use is and, if the proposed use is indeed in breach of the lease, the landlord can refuse consent. However section 1(3) of the Landlord and Tenant Act 1988 provides that if the tenant asks for consent in writing, the landlord must give or refuse consent in writing and must do this in a reasonable time and that under section 1(6) it is for the landlord to prove that a refusal of consent was reasonable and that that consent was given or withheld in a reasonable time. Nevertheless, it looks as though consent could be refused. Perhaps Hanbury Ltd should simply offer to purchase the land?

✓ Make your answer stand out

- Mention the Law Commission Report (2011) *Making Land Work: Easements, Covenants and Profits à Prendre* (LC 327) recommends in its draft clause 24 that use of land 'should not prevented from being of a kind which may be the subject of an easement by reason only of the fact that it prevents the person in possession of the land from making any reasonable use of it'.

- Briefly mention the debate on whether a contractual licence can ever be a proprietary interest – mention, e.g. *Errington* v *Errington* [1952] 1 All ER 149.

- Read Samuels (2002) The Tenant Seeks Consent for Assignment: Is the Refusal of the Landlord Reasonable? *Conveyancer* 307, who reviews the circumstances in which a landlord can refuse consent to an assignment. There are some clear principles which you could integrate into your answer.

! Don't be tempted to . . .

- Decide that the right claimed by Bert is an easement or a lease and neglect any other possibilities. This question is about thinking across the subject.
- Fail to follow through the crucial point: we cannot be certain if this is an easement, lease or licence. This means that at all stages you need to look at the implications of it being any of these.
- Miss the point that title to land is not registered.
- Miss the point that when the land is sold then there will be a first registration – this point can often occur in land law exams and means that, in particular, the law on overriding interests is different than if title was already registered.

www.pearsoned.co.uk/lawexpressqa

Go online to access more revision support including additional essay and problem questions with diagram plans, You be the marker questions, and download all diagrams from the book.

Bibliography

Andrews, G. (2002) Undue Influence – Where's the Disadvantage? *Conveyancer* 456.

Auchmurty, R.S. (2004) Not Just a Good Children's Story: A Tribute to Adverse Possession. *Conveyancer* 293.

Bandali, S.M. (1977) Injustice and Problems of Joint Tenancy. 41 *Conveyancer* (NS) 243.

Bogusz B. (2011) Defining the Scope of Actual Occupation under the LRA 2002: Some Recent Judicial Clarification. *Conveyancer* 268.

Bridge, S. (2009) Prescriptive Easements: Capacity to Grant. *CLJ*, 68(1): 40.

Bright, S. (2000) Leases, Exclusive Possession and Estates. *LQR*, 116: 7.

Bright, S. (2012) The Uncertainty of Certainty in Leases. *LQR*, 128: 337.

Burn, E. and Cartwright, J. (2011) *Cheshire and Burn's Modern Law of Real Property* (18th edn). Oxford: Oxford University Press.

Cobb, N.A. and Fox, L. (2007) Living Outside the System? The (Im)morality of Urban Squatting after the Land Registration Act 2002. *Legal Studies*, 27: 236.

Cooke, E. (1994) Adverse Possession – Some Problems of Title in Registered Land. *Legal Studies*, 14: 1.

Cooke, E. (2003) *The New Law of Land Registration*. Oxford: Hart Publishing.

Cooke, E. (2009) To Restate or Not to Restate? Old Wine, New Wineskins, Old Covenants, New Ideas. *Conveyancer* 448.

Cork Committee (1982) *Insolvency Law and Practice*. Cmnd. 8558.

Cowan, D. and Hunter, C. (2012) 'Yeah but, no but' – Pinnock and Powell in the Supreme Court. *MLR*, 75(1): 75–91.

Davis, C.J. (1998) The Principle of Benefit and Burden. *CLJ*, 57(3): 522.

Dawson, I. and Dunn, A. (1998) Negative Easements – A Crumb of Analysis. *Legal Studies*, 18: 510.

Dewar, J. (1986) Licences and Land Law: An Alternative View. *MLR* 741.

Dixon, M. (2003) The Reform of Property Law and the Land Registration Act 2002: A Risk Assessment. *Conveyancer* 136.

Dixon, M. (2007) The Never-ending Story: Co-ownership after *Stack* v *Dowden*. *Conveyancer*, 71: 456.

Dixon, M. (2009) Proprietary Estoppel: A Return to Principle. *Conveyancer* 260.

Dixon, M. (2012) *Land Law* (8th edn). Abingdon: Routledge.

BIBLIOGRAPHY

Douglas, G.F., Pearce, J. and Woodward, H. (2008) Cohabitation and Conveyancing Practice: Problems and Solutions. *Conveyancer* 365.

Etherton, T. (2008) Constructive Trusts: A New Model for Equity and Unjust Enrichment. *CLJ* 265.
Etherton, T. (2009) Constructive Trusts and Proprietary Estoppel: The Search for Clarity and Principle. *Conveyancer*, 73: 104.

Gardner, S. (1987) Equity, Estate Contracts and the Judicature Acts: *Walsh* v *Lonsdale* Revisited. *Oxford Journal of Legal Studies*, 7(1): 60.
Gardner, S. (1993) Rethinking Family Property. *LQR*, 109: 263.
Gardner, S. (2004) Quantum in *Gissing* v *Gissing* Constructive Trusts. *LQR*, 120: 541.
Garner, J. (1977) Severance of a Joint Tenancy. *Conveyancer* 77.
Gray, K. (2002) Land Law and Human Rights, in L. Tee (ed.) *Land Law, Issues, Debates, Policy*. Uffculme: Willan Publishing.
Gray, K. and Gray, S.F. (2005) *Land Law* (4th edn). Core Texts series. Oxford: Oxford University Press.
Gray, K. and Gray, S.F. (2005) *Elements of Land Law* (4th edn). Oxford: Oxford University Press.
Gray, K. and Gray, S.F. (2009) *Elements of Land Law* (5th edn). Oxford: Oxford University Press.
Greer, S. (2009) *Horsham Properties Group Ltd* v *Clark*: Possession – Mortgagee's Right or Discretionary Remedy? *Conveyancer* 516–24.

Haley, M. (2008) Easements, Exclusionary Use and Exclusive Principles: The Right to Park. *Conveyancer* 244.
Harding, M. (2009) Defending *Stack* v *Dowden*. *Conveyancer*, 73: 309.
Harpum, C. (1990) *Buckingham County Council* v *Moran*. *CLJ* 23.
Harpum, C. and Radley-Gardner, O. (2001) Adverse Possession and the Intention to Possess: A Reply. *Conveyancer* 155.
Hill-Smith, A. (2007) Rights of Parking and the Ouster Principle after *Batchelor* v *Marlow*. *Conveyancer* 223–34.
Hopkins, N. (1996) The Trusts of Land and the Appointment of Trustees Act 1996. *Conveyancer* 267.
Houghton, J. and Livesey, L. (2001) Mortgage Conditions: Old Law for a New Century?, in E. Cooke (ed.) *Modern Studies in Property Law*, Vol. 1. Oxford: Hart Publishing.
Howell, J. (2002) Subterranean Land Law: Rights below the Surface of Land. *Northern Ireland Legal Quarterly*, 53: 268.
Hudson, A. (1984) Is Divesting Abandonment Possible at Common Law? *LQR*, 100: 110.

Junior, G. (2008) Warning – Parking Problems Ahead (*Montcrieff* v *Jamieson* Applied). *SLT*, 1: 1–2.

Kerridge, R. and Brierley, A.H.R. (2007) Adverse Possession, Human Rights and Land Registration: And They All Lived Happily Ever After. *Conveyancer* 552.

Land Registry Practice Guide 5: Adverse Possession (HM Land Registry, 2010). www.landregistry.gov.uk/professional/guides/practice-guide-5#guide-mark-0

Law Commission (1987) Report, *Property Law – Third Report On Land Registration*, No. 158. www.bailii.org/ew/other/EWLC/1987/158.pdf

Law Commission (1989) *Transfer of Land, Trusts of Land*, No. 181. www.bailii.org/ew/other/EWLC/1989/181.pdf

Law Commission (1991) Report, *Transfer of Land – Land Mortgages*, Report, No. 204. www.bailii.org/ew/other/EWLC/1991/204.pdf

Law Commission (1996) *Landlord and Tenant: Responsibility for State and Condition of Property*, No. 238. http://lawcommission.justice.gov.uk/docs/lc238_landlord_and_tenant_responsibility_for_stake_and_condition_of_property.pdf

Law Commission (1998) Consultation Paper, *Land Registration for the Twenty-first Century*, No. 254. http://lawcommission.justice.gov.uk/docs/lc254_land_registration_for_21st_century_consultative.pdf

Law Commission (2001) Report, *Land Registration for the 21st Century: A Conveyancing Revolution*, No. 271. http://lawcommission.justice.gov.uk/docs/lc271_land_registration_for_the_twenty-first_century.pdf

Law Commission (2002) *Sharing Homes, A Discussion Paper*, No. 278. http://lawcommission.justice.gov.uk/docs/lc278%281%29_sharing_homes_discussion_paper.pdf

Law Commission (2004) *Termination of Tenancies for Tenant Default*, No. 174. http://lawcommission.justice.gov.uk/docs/cp174_Termination_of_Tenancies_Consultation.pdf

Law Commission (2007) Report, *Cohabitation: The Financial Consequences of Relationship Breakdown*, No. 307. http://lawcommission.justice.gov.uk/docs/lc307_Cohabitation.pdf

Law Commission (2008) Consultation Paper, *Easements, Covenants and Profits à Prendre.* No. 186. http://lawcommission.justice.gov.uk/docs/cp186_Easements_Covenants_and_Profits_a_Prendre_Consultation.pdf

Law Commission (2011) Report, *Making Land Work: Easements, Covenants and Profits à Prendre* (LC 327). http://lawcommission.justice.gov.uk/docs/lc327_easements_report.pdf

Lee, J. (2012) 'And the Waters Began to Subside': Imputing Intention under *Jones* v *Kernott*. *Conveyancer*, 5: 421.

Lower, M. (2010) The *Bruton* Tenancy. *Conveyancer*, 1: 38.

Luther, P. (2004) Fixtures and Chattels: A Question of More or Less. *Oxford Journal of Legal Studies*, 24: 597.

MacMillan, C. (2000) A Birthday Present for Lord Denning: The Contracts (Rights of Third Parties) Act 1999. *MLR*, 63(5): 721.

McFarlane, B. (2009) Apocalypse Averted: Proprietary Estoppel in the House of Lords. *LQR*, 125: 535.

Martin, J. (2009) *Hanbury & Martin: Modern Equity* (18th edn). London: Sweet & Maxwell.

Mee, J. (2012) *Jones* v *Kernott*: Inferring and Imputing in Essex. *Conveyancer*, 2: 167.

ODPM (Office of the Deputy Prime Minister) (2002) *More than a Roof: A Report into Tackling Homelessness.* London: ODPM.

Omar, P. (2006) Security over Co-owned Property and the Creditor's Paramount Status in Recovery Proceedings. *Conveyancer* 157.

Pascoe, S. (2000) Section 15 and the Trusts of Land and Appointment of Trustees Act 1996 – A Change in the Law? *Conveyancer* 315.

Piska, N. (2008) Revisiting Resulting Trusts. *Conveyancer* 441.

Pritchard, A.M. (1987) Beneficial Joint Tenancies: A Riposte. *Conveyancer* 273.

Radley-Gardner, O. (2007) Good-bye to *Pye.* 5 *Web Journal of Current Legal Issues.*

Rotherham, C. (2004) The Property Rights of Unmarried Co-habitees: A Case for Reform. *Conveyancer* 268.

Samuels, A. (2002) The Tenant Seeks Consent for Assignment: Is the Refusal of the Landlord Reasonable? *Conveyancer* 307.

Scottish Law Commission (1998) *Real Burdens.* Discussion Paper, No. 106. www.scotland. gov.uk/News/Releases/1999/02/e055ed48-f8b3-46cc-ba3d-f08abe9d38a5#

Simpson, A.W.B. (1986) *A History of the Land Law* (2nd edn). Oxford: Oxford University Press.

Sloan, B. (2009) Estop Me If You Think You've Heard It. *CLJ*, 68(3): 518.

Stevens, R. (2004) The Contract (Rights of Third Parties) Act 1999. *LQR*, 120: 292.

Tee, L. (2000) Adverse Possession and the Intention to Possess. *Conveyancer* 113.

Thompson, M.P. (1987) Beneficial Joint Tenancies. *Conveyancer* 29.

Thompson, M.P. (2001) Do We Really Need Clogs? *Conveyancer* 502.

Thompson, M.P. (2003) Mortgages and Undue Influence, in E. Cooke (ed.) *Modern Studies in Property Law*, Vol. 2. Oxford: Hart Publishing.

Wade, H.W.R. (1962) Landlord, Tenant and Squatter. *LQR*, 78: 541.

Wallace, H. (1990) The Legacy of *Street* v *Mountford. Northern Ireland Legal Quarterly*, 41: 143.

Wilkinson, H. (1991) Farewell, Ladies Must We Leave You. *Conveyancer* 251.

Wood, J. (2009) *Horsham Properties Group Ltd* v *Clark*: A Year On. *Coventry Law Journal*, 14(2): 31–6.

Index

INDEX

INDEX

INDEX

INDEX